Hannah Arendt on Educational
Thinking and Practice in Dark Times

Also available from Bloomsbury

Hannah Arendt and the Politics of Friendship, Jon Nixon
An Intellectual History of School Leadership Practice and Research,
Helen M. Gunter

Hannah Arendt on Educational Thinking and Practice in Dark Times

Education for a World in Crisis

Edited by
Wayne Veck and Helen M. Gunter

BLOOMSBURY ACADEMIC
LONDON • NEW YORK • OXFORD • NEW DELHI • SYDNEY

BLOOMSBURY ACADEMIC
Bloomsbury Publishing Plc
50 Bedford Square, London, WC1B 3DP, UK
1385 Broadway, New York, NY 10018, USA
29 Earlsfort Terrace, Dublin 2, Ireland

BLOOMSBURY, BLOOMSBURY ACADEMIC and the Diana logo are
trademarks of Bloomsbury Publishing Plc

First published in Great Britain 2009 by the Continuum International Publishing Group Ltd
Reprinted by Bloomsbury Academic 2018

Copyright © Marilyn Dunn, 2009

Marilyn Dunn has asserted her right under the Copyright,
Designs and Patents Act, 1988, to be identified as Author of this work.

For legal purposes the Acknowledgements on p. vii constitute an
extension of this copyright page.

Cover design: Eleanor Rose
Cover image © Vince Cavataio/Getty Images

All rights reserved. No part of this publication may be reproduced or
transmitted in any form or by any means, electronic or mechanical,
including photocopying, recording, or any information storage or retrieval
system, without prior permission in writing from the publishers.

Bloomsbury Publishing Plc does not have any control over, or responsibility for,
any third-party websites referred to or in this book. All internet addresses given
in this book were correct at the time of going to press. The author and publisher
regret any inconvenience caused if addresses have changed or sites have
ceased to exist, but can accept no responsibility for any such changes.

A catalogue record for this book is available from the British Library.

Library of Congress Cataloging-in-Publication Data
Names: Klemme, Heiner, editor. | Kuehn, Manfred, editor.
Title: The Bloomsbury dictionary of eighteenth-century German philosophers /
edited by Heiner F. Klemme and Manfred Kuehn.
Other titles: Dictionary of eighteenth-century German philosophers
Description: New York: Bloomsbury Publishing Plc, 2016. | Originally
published under title: Dictionary of eighteenth-century German
philosophers: London: Continuum, 2010. |
Includes bibliographical references and index.
Identifiers: LCCN 2015040044 | ISBN 9781474255974 (pb) |
ISBN 9781474256001 (epub) | ISBN 9781474255981 (epdf)
Subjects: LCSH: Philosophers–Germany–Dictionaries. |
Philosophy, German–18th century–Dictionaries.
Classification: LCC B2615 .D53 2016 | DDC 193–dc23
LC record available at http://lccn.loc.gov/2015040044

ISBN: HB: 978-1-3500-6911-4
PB: 978-1-4729-8743-3
ePDF: 978-1-3500-6912-1
eBook: 978-1-3500-6918-3

Typeset by Deanta Global Publishing Services, Chennai, India

To find out more about our authors and books visit
www.bloomsbury.com and sign up for our newsletters.

Contents

Author Biographies	vi
A Note on Referencing Arendt's Publications	ix
Introduction: Hannah Arendt and the Promise of Education in Dark Times *Wayne Veck and Helen M. Gunter*	1

Part I The Promise of Education

1. Public Education: The Challenge of Educational Authority in a World without Authority *Roger Berkowitz* — 17
2. Thinking with Arendt: Education and Temporality *Faisal Baluch* — 32
3. Arendt and 'Worldliness': Education in and for a World of Difference *Jon Nixon* — 46

Part II Education and Crisis

4. Identity as Other and the Promise of the Narrative Imagination in Educational Theorizing: Arendt and Ricoeur *Jo-Anne Dillabough* — 63
5. Thinking Politically with Arendt: Depoliticized Privatism and Education Policy *Helen M. Gunter* — 79
6. Hannah Arendt, Education and the Refugee Crisis: Natality, Compensatory Education and Assimilation *Wayne Veck* — 93

Part III Education for Love of the World

7. Hannah Arendt and 'Holocaust Education': Rethinking the Political Educationally *Marie Morgan* — 109
8. Can you Learn Democracy in a Classroom? John Dewey and Hannah Arendt on the 'Paradox of Size' *Aaron Schutz* — 123
9. Thinking in Dark Times: Learning to Repair and Renew Our Common World *Eduardo Duarte* — 136

Conclusion: The Promise of Education Revisited *Helen M. Gunter and Wayne Veck*	151
References	167
Indices	180

Author Biographies

Roger Berkowitz is Founder and Academic Director of the Hannah Arendt Center for Politics and Humanities, and Professor of politics, philosophy and human rights at Bard College. His writing brings the humanities to bear on political and ethical problems to think about our world. Professor Berkowitz has authored, *The Gift of Science: Leibniz and the Modern Legal Tradition* and is co-editor of *Thinking in Dark Times: Hannah Arendt on Ethics and Politics*, *The Intellectual Origins of the Global Financial Crisis* and *Artifacts of Thinking: Reading Hannah Arendt's Denktagebuch*. He is the editor of *HA: The Journal of the Hannah Arendt Center*. His writing has appeared in *The New York Times*, *The American Interest*, *Bookforum*, *The Paris Review Online*, *Democracy: A Journal of Ideas* and many other publications.

Faisal Baluch is Assistant Professor of political science at The College of the Holy Cross. His work focuses on the history of political thought, with a particular emphasis on early modern and contemporary political thought. He has published on Machiavelli, Arendt and Heidegger. He is currently working on a book manuscript on Machiavelli's *Florentine Histories*.

Jo-Anne Dillabough is Reader in the Sociology of Youth and Global Cultures (Education), University of Cambridge. She has been a visiting scholar at universities in Australia, Argentina, Iceland, Norway and Sweden. Dr Dillabough was co-editor of *Education, Globalization and Social Change* (Oxford University Press), *Challenging Democracy* (Routledge) and *Troubling Gender*, and was co-editor of *Gender and Education* from 2012 to 2016. Other book publications including *Lost Youth in the Global City: Class, Culture and the Urban Imaginary* (with J. Kennelly, Routledge, 2010). Recent chapter and article publications include: 'Social Justice and Citizenship in Education: Engaging Space, the Narrative Imagination and Relationality' (Dillabough, 2016); and 'Youth Geographies of Urban Estrangement in the Canadian City: Risk Management, Race Relations and the "Sacrificial Stranger"' (with Yoon, 2018 in Children's Geographies). She has been reading and studying the work of Hannah Arendt for over 20 years.

Eduardo Duarte is a professor at Hofstra University, where he has been teaching courses in philosophy since 1996. Duarte is the author of *Being and Learning* (Sense Publishers: 2012), has published his scholarship in *Studies in Philosophy and Education, Educational Philosophy and Theory, Educational Studies, LAPIZ, Encounter, Educational Theory* and the *Journal of Philosophy of Education*, and is the editor of *Philosophy of Education 2015* (University of Illinois: 2016). Duarte's current philosophical research is focused on the ontology of rhythm, musicality of Being and the phenomenology of resonant subjectivity.

Helen M. Gunter is Professor of Educational Policy in The Manchester Institute of Education, University of Manchester, UK. She is a fellow of the Academy of Social Sciences, and recipient of the BELMAS Distinguished Service Award 2016. Her work focuses on the politics of education policy and knowledge production in the field of school leadership. Her most recent books are: *An Intellectual History of School Leadership Practice and Research* (in 2016 by Bloomsbury Press); *Consultants and Consultancy: the Case of Education* (co-authored with Colin Mills, 2017 by Springer); and *The Politics of Public Education* (by Policy Press, 2018).

Marie Morgan is Head of Department for Education Studies and Liberal Arts and co-convener for the Centre for Philosophy of Education at the University of Winchester. Underpinned by a philosophical understanding of education as human endeavour, her teaching and research interests include Holocaust education and higher education. Her most recent and ongoing works seek to develop an understanding of the 'educational' through rethinking the relation between philosophy, politics and education.

Jon Nixon is Honorary Professor, The Education University of Hong Kong, China, and Visiting Professor, Middlesex University, UK. He writes as an intellectual historian with a particular interest in educational thought and democratic theory. His recent publications include *Rosa Luxemburg and the Struggle for Democratic Renewal* (Pluto, 2018), *Hans-Georg Gadamer: The Hermeneutical Imagination* (Springer, 2017) and *Hannah Arendt and the Politics of Friendship* (Bloomsbury, 2015). He has also recently edited *Higher Education in Austerity Europe* (Bloomsbury, 2017), which includes contributions from leading educationists across Europe. He is currently working on a book provisionally entitled *Erich Auerbach and the Origins of Democratic Humanism*.

Aaron Schutz is a professor in the Department of Educational Policy and Community Studies at the University of Wisconsin-Milwaukee. His work focuses on theories of democratic education in schools and practices of collective action for social change in community settings. A book, *Empowerment: A Primer*, is forthcoming from Routledge. His other books are: *People Power: The Organizing Tradition of Saul Alinsky* (co-edited with Mike Miller, from Vanderbilt University Press); *Collective Action for Social Change: An Introduction to Community Organizing*; and *Social Class, Social Action and Education: The Failure of Progressive Democracy* (the latter two from Palgrave).

Wayne Veck is Reader in Education at the University of Winchester, and was Faculty Head of Research and Knowledge Exchange from 2015 to 2018. He has given key note addresses at the University of Bergamo, at the *Polish Disability Forum*'s conference, in Warsaw, and at Lillehammer University College. He has published in leading education journals, including the *Oxford Review of Education*, *British Journal of Sociology of Education*, *Cambridge Journal of Education* and the *International Journal of Inclusive Education*, for which he is on the editorial advisory board.

A Note on Referencing Arendt's Publications

In this book the authors have read and used a range of Arendt's published outputs, and in order to support the writing and reading process we have followed Bowring's (2011) approach of using abbreviations. We present the abbreviation in the date order of the publication being referenced.

S	Arendt, H. (1955) Statelessness. Lecture given at Berkeley on 22 April 1955. Hannah Arendt Papers. Manuscript Division, Library of Congress, Washington, DC. Available: http://www.hannaharendt.net/index.php/han/article/view/155/276
HC	Arendt, H. (1958) *The Human Condition*. Second Edition. Chicago: The University of Chicago Press.
DM	Arendt, H. (1959) Reflections on Little Rock. *Dissent Magazine* (Winter): 45–56.
EJ	Arendt, H. (1963) *Eichmann in Jerusalem*. London: Penguin Books.
OV	Arendt, H. (1970) *On Violence*. Orlando, FL: A Harvest Book Harcourt Inc.
CR	Arendt, H. (1972) *Crises of the Republic*. New York, NY: Harcourt Brace Jovanovich Inc.
RV	Arendt, H. (1974) *Rahel Varnhagen, The Life of a Jewish Woman*. New York, NY: Harcourt Brace Jovanovich.
LM1/2	Arendt, H. (1978) *The Life of the Mind*. New York, NY: Harcourt Inc.
JP	Arendt, H. (1978) *The Jew as Pariah*. New York, NY: Grove Press.
PAP	Arendt, H. (1990) Philosophy and Politics. *Social Research*, 57 (1): 73–104.
LK	Arendt, H. (1992) *Lectures on Kant's Political Philosophy*. Chicago, IL: The University of Chicago Press.

MD	Arendt, H. (1993) *Men in Dark Times*. San Diego: A Harvest Book, Harcourt Brace & Company.
EU	Arendt, H. (1994) *Essays in Understanding 1930-1954. Formation, Exile and Totalitarianism*. New York, NY: Schocken Books.
LA	Arendt, H. (1996) *Love and Saint Augustine*. Chicago, IL:University of Chicago Press.
CC	Arendt, H. (1999) The Concentration Camps, in Hamilton, I. (ed) *The Penguin Book of Twentieth-Century Essays*, 237–57. London: Penguin.
DKE	Arendt, H. (2000) 'Die Krise in der Erziehung'. *Zwischen Vergangenheit und Zukunft. Übungen im politischen Denken I. Texte 1954–1964*. ed. Ursula Ludz, Piper, 2nd edition.
RJ	Arendt, H. (2003) *Responsibility and Judgement*. New York, NY: Schocken Books.
PP	Arendt, H. (2005) *The Promise of Politics*. New York, NY: Schocken Books.
BF	Arendt, H. (2006) *Between Past and Future*. New York, NY: Penguin Books.
OR	Arendt, H. (2006) *On Revolution*. New York, NY: Penguin Books.
JW	Arendt, H. (2007) *The Jewish Writings*. New York, NY: Schocken Books.

Introduction:
Hannah Arendt and the Promise of Education in Dark Times

Wayne Veck and Helen M. Gunter

Introduction

In August 2018, Greta Thunberg, a fifteen-year-old Swedish student, refused to attend her school and instead stood outside the Swedish parliament in a solitary demonstration against human activities that cause climate change. Inspired by this stance, more than 20,000 children throughout Europe, along with the United States, Japan and Australia, have taken to the streets to protest against the human contribution to the environmental crisis (Carrington, 2018). As children lined the streets of thirty towns and cities across the UK, the spokesperson for UK's prime minister acknowledged the engagement of the young school strikers, but maintained, nevertheless, that 'it is important to emphasise that disruption increases teachers' workloads and wastes lesson time that teachers have carefully prepared for' (Drury, 2019). While in Australia, the New South Wales education minister, Rob Stokes, warned students and teachers against striking, asserting: 'These are on school days, school children on school days should be at school' (Tovey, 2019). Speaking at the UN climate change summit, Thunberg proclaimed: 'Since our leaders are behaving like children, we will have to take the responsibility they should have taken long ago' (Carrington, 2018: unpaged). Nothing, indeed, could speak more loudly of the shunning of adult responsibility to the young than the situation in which newcomers feel themselves left with no other recourse than to take up responsibility for safeguarding the earth.

Such inversions of responsible adult–child relations could hardly be more serious, given the fact that these children and their peers are living through a time variously named the 'age of environmental breakdown' (Laybourn-Langton, Rankin, and Baxter, 2019), the 'age of austerity' (Streeck and Schafer, 2013) and the 'age of surveillance capitalism' (Zuboff, 2019). In her renowned and provocative essay, 'The Crisis in Education', Arendt identified a diminishing of the promise of education to represent, and to guide the young to, the world, before going on to locate the source of this crisis entirely with adults 'who refuses to assume joint responsibility for the world' (BF: 189).

In the same essay, however, Arendt (BF: 174) observed that a 'crisis becomes a disaster only when we respond to it with preformed judgements, that is, with prejudices'. In this book, we present nine essays in which our co-authors have, in their distinct ways, precisely responded to the crisis, reality and potential exercise of adult responsibility in preparing the young to understand, to reflect on and to act within and for the world. Indeed, in each of the three sections that together make up this book, the authors advance new understanding of the meaning and the significance of the inversion of adult–child responsibility and the subsequent loss of authority in education and beyond. As we introduce the first section of the book, we illuminate the significance of educators responding to what Arendt (BF: 196) names 'the fact of natality', which is nothing less than the newness of the young and their potential to renew an old world. When we address the second section, we examine the importance of *understanding* and *judgement* in the kind of responsible education that simultaneously protects the young from and guides them to the world. Finally, in our introduction to the last of the book's three sections, we reflect on the nature and potential of *thinking* itself in direct relation to the responsibility of educators and educational researchers.

Addressing a Crisis of Education

We are hardly alone in turning to Arendt to understand the world we now live in. The quest for such understanding, along with the hope that Arendt's work might provide illumination, meant that in 2017, Arendt's seminal, *The Origins of Totalitarianism*, sold out on Amazon (Griswold, 2017), while academic and social media interest in Arendt abounds (Bernstein, 2018; Stonebridge 2019). This is rather remarkable, given both the complexity of Arendt's work and the fact such positive attention eluded her during her lifetime. Our especial focus is on education, and a range of important analysis continues to take place through Arendtian thinking (e.g. Biesta 2013; Nixon 2012; Norris 2011), and in the last twenty years, four major outputs have been published about Arendt and education.

The first landmark edited collection, *Hannah Arendt and Education: Renewing our common world* (Gordon 2001a) was published some eighteen years ago. The editor and co-authors of this book turned to Arendtian concepts to bring light to possibilities for education in democratic societies. We follow in this tradition, since we also want to think critically about what is happening in education and how our scholarship can provide convincing accounts and robust understandings of trends and events. In setting out to do this, we acknowledge that the origins of our edited collection are in a number of seminars that in 2016 produced five articles and an editorial in a special issue of the *Journal of Educational Administration and History*, entitled, 'Hannah Arendt 40 Years On: Thinking about Educational Administration' (Veck and Jessop 2016). The publication of the journal's special issue confirmed that a new examination of education by the Arendtian education scholarly community was necessary. Since Gordon's (2001a) productive debate, we have recognized the at once urgent and recurrent importance of Arendt's work at a time when societies are confronting dangerous political, economic and ecological crises, and when democracy itself is engulfed in crisis. Two books by Gunter have begun to explore this, with a particular focus on the relationship between public education and democracy: *Educational Leadership and Hannah Arendt* (Gunter 2014) and *The Politics of Public Education* (Gunter 2018). These books both deploy thinking with Arendt about and for public education, and investigate the methodological issues involved, along with the need for a research agenda that considers our responsibilities as education researchers. Our new edited collection provides a provocative opportunity to widen and develop the scope of enquiry, and to locate the debates about public education within with a range of issues from children in homes and classrooms to education researchers at their desks.

This contribution matters since we now live in times in which it is legitimate to speak not only of a crisis *in* education, but rather about the crisis *of* education. We confront, that is, a new type of crisis, one that encompasses the entire public realm, and this makes Arendt's insights more important now than ever for educators and for education. We currently deal, that is, not only with a crisis within public education that warrants a reform agenda but also, more crucially, with an existential crisis for the very idea of public education itself. And this is the case, not only because the privatization agenda has gathered pace around the world (Adamson et al. 2016; Gunter 2018) but also because the very promise of education is at risk in times where there is a growing unwillingness to accept the authority of anyone who claims to represent the world in its actuality.

Looming over this book there is, then, the rather discomforting question of how educators and educational researchers might find ways to prepare the young to take up their bearings in the world where adults may have all but lost their orientation. Arendt recognizes the tendency towards despair in times of political crisis:

> History knows many periods of dark times in which the public realm has been obscured and the world become so dubious that people have ceased to ask any more of politics than it show due consideration for their vital interests and personal liberty. Those who have lived in such times and been formed by them have probably always been inclined to despise the world and the public realm, to ignore them as far as possible. (MD: 11–12)

And yet, Arendt, as Bernstein (2018: 119) reminds us, persistently 'warned about giving in to despair and cynicism'. In fact, Arendt's very 'explanation of the meaning and dignity of politics was intended to be an act of retrieval and recovery – a reminder of a real possibility rooted in our natality' (Bernstein, 2018: 119). It is precisely natality, described by Arendt, as 'the birth of new men and the new beginning, the action they are capable of by virtue of being born' that is the 'miracle that saves the world, the realm of human affairs, from its normal, "natural" ruin'. It is natality – the newness of each child within an established world, the potential for a new beginning that is inherent in every action – that Arendt (BF: 174) identifies as the 'essence of education'. Indeed, it is by virtue of our natality that we are gifted a concrete reason not to equate the current state of world with its enduring reality and so to think anew, to attempt to understand and then to make original judgements about education and the issues that impact on it, such as political, economic and cultural disruption and uncertainty.

'Understanding', Arendt (EU: 307) insists, 'never produces unequivocal results'. And yet, by exercising understanding we may 'come to terms with and reconcile ourselves to reality, that is, try to be at home in the world' (EU: 308). But if understanding allows us to at least attempt 'to be at home in the world', it does so by creating the conditions in which we 'eventually can come to terms with what irrevocably happened' (EU: 322), and not by leapfrogging onto a firm ground upon which we can reside all too comfortably, our opinions deemed to have bypassed the challenges of a plurality of counter-perspectives. Arendt's point is that understanding is an *attempt* to find a home in the world. So, Arendt's (LK: 43) contention, that 'to think with an enlarged mentality means that one trains one's imagination to go visiting', needs to be accompanied by the awareness that without openness towards and trust in others, one would stay at home, smugly at ease with one's preformed or pre-established judgements.

It is for this reason that Bernstein (2018: 72) identifies Arendt's insistence that the very 'formulation of opinions requires a willingness to submit opinions to exposure and critique', as 'an important lesson to be learned from Arendt that has contemporary relevance'. This, Bernstein (2018: 72) goes on to observe, is because we witness 'a dangerous tendency today to refuse to listen to others who disagree with us'. When the acts and words of another person are dismissed from the start, when they are immediately situated within into a readily available framework, then what is missing is any trust in the potential of these words and acts to illuminate our shared and lived reality.

On the face of it, mistrust of other persons seems to find its expression in a judgement: it is they, the others, the 'Them', who stand in opposition to 'Us', that are judged suspicious and thus unworthy of trust. However, what is might be characterized as a judgement is better described as a non-judgement or prejudice. Hence Arendt (BF: 174) insists that all prejudices are 'preformed judgements'. Prejudices, in other words, are judgements untouched by the mental activities of thinking and imagination. So when Arendt points us to Plato's account of Socrates's capacity to bring people into a state of perplexity, as 'he purged people of their ... unexamined pre-judgments that would prevent them from thinking' (LM1: 173), she shows us that purging opinions involves grappling not only with the ways in which people can come to refuse to think about others but also with how they can refuse to trust them. To trust another person is to be open to them, to be willing to accept them and their words. To trust is to open oneself up to receive a reality that is other than the reality concocted within the space of one's own mind. It is only by way of this openness and trust that one might reach a judgement about the reality they have been exposed to. If we do not accept the other person, if we refuse to believe what they say even before they have uttered a word, we thereby supplant trusting acceptance with prejudices, and it is quite impossible for us to form a judgement about them.

Bernstein's (2018: 77) reading of Arendt's *The Origins of Totalitarianism* leads him to conclude: 'People who feel that they have been neglected and forgotten yearn for a narrative that will make sense of the anxiety and the misery they are experiencing.' This has serious implications for education and educational research. The attempt to secure a position that makes sense to me and to those I consider to be entirely the same as me means that I am utterly unable to enter into conversations that connect my sense of the world to what Arendt (EU, HC, BF) named a 'common sense'. It is this, common sense that reassures me that my perception of the world is shared by others. However, cut off from the world, relying entirely on my own perceptions of what might be true and what might matter, I am cut off from this common sense (EU). The loss of responsible educators, willing to guide the young to the world, means nothing less than the fact that children are too often unprepared for a sense of the world that is common. It is for this reason that Arendt (HC: 208) identifies, as the 'almost infallible signs of alienation from the world', a 'noticeable decrease in common sense in any given community and a noticeable increase in superstition and gullibility'. What Arendt shows us, then, is that alongside the loss of a common world, there is an accompanying loss of the distinction between what might be truths and what are, most certainly, lies. All this directs us to prepare the young for listening as well as for speech. Indeed, what Arendt demonstrates so strikingly is that if we cannot hear others, we cannot really begin to speak. Instead, our utterances spill out as just so many assertions. The task for educators is thus to prepare the young to seek out not whatever helps them make sense of their lives but a common sense. Preparing the young to love the world cannot, in short, be untangled from the task of preparing them to love the truth.

Sitting at a Table with Arendt: Our Approach

Arendt (EU: 44) opened an essay about Søren Kierkegaard by way of remarking that, during the course of his life, the Danish philosopher and theologian 'enjoyed not so much fame as notoriety'. The same observation may be made of Arendt herself. And nowhere is the truth of this observation borne out more starkly than in the response to Arendt's account of the trial of Adolf Eichmann in Jerusalem. Invited by the *New Yorker* magazine to cover the trial in 1961, Arendt's wrote five articles, appearing in February and March 1963, and a subsequent book, that gave rise to serious and persisting controversy. Arendt's account of Eichmann and his trial, especially the description of his 'banality', along with her accounts of the Jewish leaders and the Jewish councils – established by the Nazis to oversee the ghettos they had created – and her criticisms of the court proceedings, provoked profound anger. Indeed, Arendt, who had already endured anti-Semitism in her childhood, been classified as a 'stateless person' for eighteen years after fleeing Nazi Germany and endured detainment in Camp Gurs, in southern France, as an 'enemy-alien', now encountered a 'trial' that, at a personal level, 'amounted to nothing less than a second exile' (Sacks, 2013: 115).

When Arendt turned her critical attention to directly address education, the result was two essays that aroused perplexity and hostility that, while not on the scale of the Eichmann controversy, equally show little sign of abating. Indeed, such was the uproar evoked by Arendt's 'Reflections on Little Rock', published in *Dissent* in 1959, that the magazine's editors accompanied the essay with a qualifying note that separated them from its contents. In both this essay and 'The Crisis in Education', Arendt argued the school is not and must not be a site of politics. But where her essay on the crisis in education justified this conclusion on theoretical grounds, the essay on Little Rock expressed what Arendt saw as the imposition of political activity into the lives of African American children in the Southern states, as they entered schools that, after the landmark ruling of *Brown v. Board of Education of Topeka*, could no longer lawfully segregate children.

In both essays, Arendt's distinctions between what belongs in public and what needs to remain in the private realm, first expounded in *The Human Condition* (Bernstein, 2018), and informed by 'her memories of totalitarian politics, be it in their National Socialist or Communist variants, when political movements and party organizations would intrude into familial life and turn children against their parents' (Benhabib, 2010: 59), were brashly and insensitively applied to the America's Southern states. Here was an occasion in which Arendt was 'using lenses that actually blinkered rather than aided her vision of what was at stake' (Benhabib, 2010: 59). Significantly, in a letter to Ralph Ellison, responding to his complaint that she had 'absolutely no conception of what goes on in the minds of Negro parents when thy send their kids through those lines of hostile people', Arendt recognized that she had failed to understand neither the 'ideal of sacrifice' nor 'the element of stark violence' that motivated the African American parents and their children (Arendt and Ellison cited in Young-Bruehl, 1982: 316).

This raises important questions about how educators and educational researchers approach and draw on Arendtian thinking and concepts, lest they blinker rather than enlarge our vision of education and its possibilities. Here it is useful to consider that Arendt, by way of capturing the essence of the public realm, made use of the metaphor of 'a table [that] is located between those who sit around it' and which, thereby, simultaneously 'relates and separates' (HC: 52). It is in this spirit of gathering together around a table, in what Arendt (HC: 180) names 'sheer human togetherness', where 'people are *with* others and neither for nor against' each other, that the contributors to this book have turned to Arendt to examine educational matters worthy of our most serious and shared attention. We seek, then, not to apply Arendt's ideas as ready-made solutions to ongoing difficulties and dilemmas, but rather to enter into dialogue with her thinking so that, neither for nor against her, we can think anew about our educational concerns. It is this same spirit that we encourage readers of this book to engage with its ideas and discussions. The reader will find no definitive answers here, no ultimate or easy-to-implement answers to the current crisis engulfing education. What this book aims to provide, instead, are multiple opportunities for the reader to pull up a chair at Arendt's table, to think with her and with us as we attempt to understand the promise of education in dark times and, in this way, give breath to the possibility that this promise will endure. Indeed, it is as 'a political thinker of the uncomfortable and difficult' that Arendt 'has lessons for us today' (Stonebridge, 2019).

This book, divided into three distinct sections, elucidates the significance both of Arendt's educational insights and of education itself in the midst of current dark times. The first section of the book, entitled 'The Promise of Education', brings together new insights into the depth and complexity of Arendt's thinking about and for education and its promise. Thus it paves the way for the accounts that follow as they address the problems education faces and the prospects it might generate for addressing them. In the second section of the book, 'Education and Crisis', various social crises are examined in relation to education. Here, Arendtian understanding is drawn upon and exercised to illuminate the import and consequences of these crises. Arendt's thought guides the authors of the book's final section, 'Education for Love of the World', as they identify prospects for education in and despite of current and past dark times.

The Promise of Education through and beyond Crisis

The human capacity to act and, through our action, to begin a series of reactions means, for Arendt (HC), that human activity is inherently unpredictable. When we act, we potentially set into motion a sequence of responses that extend beyond both the stretch of our imaginations to envision and the scope of our power to control. The reason for this unpredictability is precisely the fact that our actions are witnessed by other actors, that is, by other persons and not by programmable machines. In a world where persons are able to think for themselves and to respond to actions in accordance with their own distinctiveness, the consequences of an action always rest, to some extent, in the hands of the spectators who witness, record and respond to the act. Living in the midst of such uncertainty, it is our ability to promise that saves us from the misery of a persistent and paralysing precarity (HC). Hence Arendt's (HC: 237) conclusion:

> Without being bound to the fulfilment of promises, we would never be able to keep our identities; we would be condemned to wander helplessly and without

direction in the darkness of each man's lonely heart, caught in its contradictions and equivocalities – a darkness which only the light shed over the public realm through the presence of others, who confirm the identity between the one who promises and the one who fulfils, can dispel.

In education, also, at that moment in which an educator extends their best wishes to a young person preparing to make an appearance in the world, they do so knowing that what they will encounter in the world and how they will be received in that world is not in our hands to determine. However, in the same way that our actions are accompanied by promises, so we send out the young into the world accompanied by the promise that they have been educated, that is, prepared to act with others and readied to think about and to judge the actions of others. Without this accompanying promise, we send out not educated young persons into the world, but passive entities, devoid of any comprehension that it is in their hands to proclaim their distinctiveness through speech and action and, in so doing, make a contribution to the very world they were guided to during their education.

The three chapters that together comprise the first section of the book demonstrate, in their differing ways, the promise of education. Each of the three chapters examines, through their distinct engagements with Arendt's writings and thought, how we might understand this promise and why this understanding is itself of educational consequence. It is a considerable strength of this section of the book that it demonstrates that the promise of education can be kept alive, even when dark times close in upon it to threaten its thwarting.

In the book's opening chapter, Roger Berkowitz draws on Arendt to illuminate the promise of education as a twofold transformation. First, the young are, through their 'preparation to enter the public world', transformed from 'private persons into public citizens'. Second, there is what Berkowitz, following Arendt, names 'the highest aim of education' that is realized wherever educators 'prepare students to change the world'. But the promise will remain unfilled, Berkowitz concludes, if educators do not 'take the responsibility for the authority of the world and teaching the world as it is, not as we wish it to be'. The promise of education is thus 'paradoxically both conservative and revolutionary'.

In his chapter, Faisal Baluch turns to Arendt to locate the promise of education firmly between what is established and what might yet become, noting that Arendt's 'thinking on education is motivated by her concern with temporality'. This leads Baluch to identify, as 'the prime service that Arendt's thought offers to those engaged in education', the understanding that the past, far from being 'a burden to be cast off', is instead 'the necessary condition for the emergence of the new'.

In the final chapter of Part One, Jon Nixon provides further insights into the transformative potential of education situated between the past and the future, while illustrating the import Arendt attached to education as 'a space devoted to thoughtfulness'. It is precisely because Arendt recognized that education is 'grounded in our shared capacity to think' that she was able to reveal its significance as 'a public good' that must be kept out of the hands of those all too willing to see it reduced to 'a commodity bought and sold for private gain'.

Understanding the Crisis in Education, Understanding Education in Times of Crisis

In the second section of this book on education in times of crisis, three authors examine distinct aspects of contemporary political and social crisis. In this way, they do something more than simply draw on Arendt's concepts and thinking to advance their understanding. More fundamentally, they work from and with Arendt's very understanding of understanding itself – its complexity, significance and potential.

Opening this section, Jo-Anne Dillabough, makes use of an Arendtian understanding of understanding to interrogate the idea of identity. In particular, Dillabough examines identity in relation to its 'constrained expression within the realm of citizenship', and to the rise of nationalism and populism throughout the world. Ultimately, this leads Dillabough to connect Arendt's understanding of recognition and plurality to ways of attending to the reality of other lives that are 'ethically meaningful'. Such attention, Dillabough's chapter suggests, might safeguard against the reduction of the other to 'the stranger, the exiled and the stateless', to 'that which we are not'.

Helen Gunter's chapter attends to a crisis in public education. Here Gunter follows Arendt's lead by connecting 'the colonization of public education by markets' to 'a wider upheaval and devastation to politics and the public realm'. What emerges is an account of how privatism has subsumed the public realm, 'not only in terms of "selling off" public assets but also in rendering what is political as a private matter'. To answer this twofold deprivation of the public, Gunter concludes, educational researchers must find ways of opening up spaces for dialogue where 'humans set out to present the self, to understand what others think', spaces where 'while we may disagree with one another, decisions are based on comprehending the realities of issues, evidence and opinions'.

Drawing this section of the book to close, Veck advances works through Arendtian concepts to understand the current refugee crisis in relation to education. In particular, Veck makes use of Arendt's understanding of natality to argue that merely compensatory approaches to the schooling of displaced children can 'do little to illuminate the role of education in protecting, responding to, and guiding the newness of these young people in ways that may prevent the current crisis of mass displacement from becoming a disaster'.

Renewing Educational Thinking for a World in Dark Times

Arendt (LM1), following the teaching of Socrates, attempts to ground responsibility in what she names the 'two-in-one', which is the internal dialogue between one and oneself, and that is actualized in thinking activity. In this way Arendt points us to how educators might invite young persons to transcend the narrowness of being *for* themselves and thus prepare them for being *with* themselves, both in action – through which one perpetually discovers oneself – and in thinking activity – through which one ceaselessly converses with oneself. In her account of non-thinking, Arendt writes:

> The more firmly men hold to the old code, the more eager will they be to assimilate themselves to the new one, which in practice means that the readiest to obey will be those who were the most respectable pillars of society, the least likely to indulge in thoughts, dangerous or otherwise, while those who to all appearances were the most unreliable elements of the old order will be the least tractable. (Arendt, LM1: 177)

Equally, if we attempt to reduce education to instruction, then we should hardly be surprised if the children most willing to confirm to methods and processes for improving their 'thinking' skills are perhaps those children who are 'the least likely to indulge in thoughts'. Moreover, those children who refuse to give up thinking, to supplant an open, internal conversation, with a series of pre-established mind games, might seem 'to all appearances' to 'be the least tractable'. Such defiant children may well, in fact, be disaffected by the attempts to alter or diminish their 'thinking' since, in them, the urge to think has not been extinguished.

Arendt's account of the consequences of both thinking and non-thinking are conveyed with particular lucidity in each of the chapters in the book's final section. In her chapter, Marie Morgan turns to Arendt to examine 'the educational nature of the political that not only informs us about the fractured post-Holocaust world … but also demonstrates the necessity to seek and gain a deeper understanding of the human condition, its vulnerabilities and potentialities'. What emerges from Morgan's own attempt to seek a 'deeper understanding' is a renewed sense of the prospects of education that emerge in and through the 'educational movement of the teacher of "Holocaust education"'. In this movement, the very freedom of the teacher to teach is conditioned by 'the responsibility that accompanies their role', that is, by 'a responsibility to and for themselves, the world and the vulnerable and impressionable minds and beings of others'.

Aaron Schutz engages with Arendt, in relation to Dewey, to consider 'the tensions involved in creating the kind of collaborative space' where 'both collective action and individual uniqueness' are valued equally. Schutz brings together Arendt's vision of the council system and her wider drive for democracy with Dewey's vision of 'collaborative democracy', to posit a conception of the polis in we might 'know the others in the space well enough to recognize the uniqueness of each person's contribution'. In so doing, Schutz illustrates both the complications inherent in tracing out connections between schooling and the political and the need to constantly think this relation anew.

In the closing chapter of this book, Eduardo Duarte traces the philosophical influences on Arendt's educational thought. In this way, he is able to demonstrate how Arendt's twin educational goal relating to the preservation of natality and thinking 'are carried forward precisely by teaching "the world as it is"'. This analysis illuminates both the necessity and the potential of an education that represents, and prepares the young to renew, the world in times when these newcomers 'are facing a contra-public ideology that threatens the co-flourishing of unity and plurality', times when before all else 'what the contemporary world is calling for is the formation thoughtful students'.

Thoughtful Educational Research in Dark Times

With just three weeks remaining before a referendum that asked UK voters to voice their support for either remaining within or exiting from the European Union, the country's former secretary of state for education, Michael Gove, was interviewed by Fasial Islam on Sky News. In response to a question about the concerns of esteemed economists about the consequences of leaving the European Union, Gove said: 'People in this country have had enough of experts' (Katz, 2017: unpaged). In a later interview, Gove claimed that his words had 'been taken out of context' and he had, in fact, countered Islam's words 'by saying people have had enough of experts from organizations with acronyms that have got things so wrong in the past' (Gove, 2017: unpaged). Either way, here is a prominent politician, who held major responsibility for determining the shape and future of education in the UK, juxtaposing what 'people' think with the conclusions of experts.

Gove's words bring to light a wider impatience with, and even denunciation of, experts and expertise that is central to debates about the renewal or even survival of democratic systems of government (MacLean, 2017). In response, important discussions are taking place about the status of experts as public servants (and not masters) in a democracy, and the responsibility of the citizenry to recognize that they cannot literally or authentically live without such expertise (Nichols, 2017). What such discussions illustrate is the expertise that is imperative for and about education. What emerges from the chapters in this book, through their examination of Arendt's accounts of natality and action, understanding and thinking, is a challenge to address anew, not only education but also educational research in times when trust in expertise is waning. We examine the implications of this provocation in our conclusion, where we suggest that the accumulated insights of this book point us directly to a conception of educational research as an essentially thoughtful activity.

A central contribution of the nine essays is how they demonstrate the importance of thoughtful research in times when the public realm itself is in danger. Arendt once wrote: 'The extent to which clichés have crept into our everyday language and discussions may well indicate the degree to which we … have deprived ourselves of the faculty of speech' (EU: 308). Equally, when education in classrooms is talked about in terms of effective delivery, when research is diminished to commissioned evaluations that seek to 'prove a point' or provide correlational data rather than independent enquiry, then clichés have successfully crept into our educational discourse. Arendt is clear, of course, that clichés pay an important social function. 'Clichés, stock phrases, adherence to conventional, standardized codes of expression and conduct', Arendt (LM1: 4) writes, 'have the socially recognized function of protecting us against reality, that is, against the claim on our thinking attention that all events and facts make by virtue of their existence.' However, unless we 'pay attention' in education and educational research (TB: 280), unless we extend our 'thinking attention' to the young and their potential (LM1: 4), there is the danger that we will, however unwittingly, contribute to the demise of the very public realm that education should guide the young towards. Hence the importance of Berkowitz (2010: 5) observation: 'Thinking, Arendt suggests, is the only reliable safety net against the increasingly totalitarian or even bureaucratic temptations to evil that threaten the modern world.'

It is precisely for this reason that we set out in writing this book by contending that thoughtful research has intellectual as well as practical implications. Throughout, we address the 'here-and-now-ness of research', and its place in and for a world in crisis, as we argue for thoughtful research and researchers. We now need research into and for an education that transcends the pressure to merely *deliver* results or findings; we need, instead, to embolden and work for thoughtful research that might deepen our understanding of the world, to elucidate potential for action, and to point out ways of protecting and realizing newness. Concluding her essay on the crisis in education, Arendt (BF) declared education to be the point at which love for the world meets love for those who are newcomers to it. It is the originality and significance of this book that its authors have responded to Arendt's call for responsibility and authority in education and educational research by way of advancing original thinking and analysis for public education and the world in dark times.

Part One

The Promise of Education

1

Public Education: The Challenge of Educational Authority in a World without Authority

Roger Berkowitz

Introduction

In his memoir *The Hunger of Memory: The education of Richard Rodriguez*, Richard Rodriguez imagines public education as a path from the privation of family life to the fullness of public citizenship. Rodriguez grew up in a Spanish-speaking household in Sacramento, California. He was acutely aware of the chasm between his Spanish-speaking private home world and the public world beyond. His parents were uneasy speaking English in public, but comfortable at home where Spanish flowed easily. English was the language of strangers, distant and dangerous; his native Spanish was the tongue of safety and security. School was terrifying, partly because it demanded a new language and, also, because it meant learning to navigate a foreign world.

Public school was also a revelation, an opening of transformative possibilities. At school, Rodriguez learned that he had 'the right – and the obligation – to speak the public language of *los gringos*' (Rodriguez, 1983: 19). For Rodriguez, education 'concerns my movement away from the company of family and into the city. This was my coming of age: I became a man by becoming a public man' (7). He argues that education is 'a long, unglamorous, even demeaning process – *a nurturing never natural to the person one was before one entered a classroom*' (68). It is in school that he first 'came to believe … [he] was an American citizen' (22). As a result of his introduction into the requirements of public life, Rodriguez learned what he believes is the 'the great lesson of school, that I had a public identity' (19).

Education, Rodriguez understands, is learning to be a public person. Part of this journey is linguistic, which is why Rodriguez reminds us that early schooling used to be called *grammar school*. In learning grammar, students learned the weave and web of navigating life in public. As Rodriguez argued in a talk given at the Hannah Arendt Center at Bard College:

> That's what we used to call those first few years of schooling: *grammar* school. We used to talk in America about public schools, but it turns out that a lot of public schools are not so *public* anymore, that a lot of students don't even have a sense of the public. They might have a sense of their tribe or their 'hood' but barely a sense of themselves among strangers. And we have told them that they have been to public schools, when in truth they haven't. (Rodriguez, 2013)

In arguing that education is about leading young people into a public world, *The Hunger of Memory* is a political book. Students must learn English not because of its superiority, but because it is the ticket of admission to the public world of citizenship. Even more than math and science, learning the public language guides young people into a public world, which enables them to transition from private to public life, from wardship to citizenship.

Rodriguez's argument that school prepares students to be citizens in a public world evokes Hannah Arendt's own thinking about education in her essay 'The Crisis in Education'. Arendt approaches the crisis in education as an opportunity to explore the essence of education. 'The essence of Education', Arendt argues, 'is natality, the fact that human beings are *born* into a world' (BF: 171). Education, from its Latin root *educo* (to lead forth), is the activity of leading young persons into the world, a world that already exists and into which they are inserted first by birth and second by education.

In Arendt's original German version of her essay, the word she uses for education is *Erziehung* (DKE). Formed from an intensification of the verb *ziehen*, to pull, education is imagined to be a pulling of the student into the public world. It is easy to think of education as simply teaching skills or knowledge; but in its root sense, education is an introduction into a shared way of life. For Arendt, as for Rodriguez, education must presume the existence of a public world that has some authority, a world to which the student must be led into. Education presumes that adults and teachers take responsibility for teaching young people how to grow up in the always-already-existing world. It is this preparation to enter the public world that enables the transformation of private persons into public citizens.

When Arendt speaks of 'the crisis of education', she means above all that educators refuse their responsibility to introduce students to the world as it is. The refusal of responsibility is a consequence of the loss of authority. And the loss of authority, she argues, means that 'the claims of the world and the requirements of order in it are being consciously or unconsciously repudiated; all responsibility for the world is being rejected, the responsibility for giving orders no less than for obeying them' (BF: 186–187). Having succumbed to a more general crisis of authority, teachers and parents today share a distrust of the world, a feeling that the world is comprised of prejudices and injustices that undermine its authority. They have, she writes, 'lost the answers on which we ordinarily rely without even realizing they were originally answers to questions' (BF: 171). Without confidence in those answers, we end up refusing to recognize the world as meaningful. When adults don't believe in our world, they find it is nearly impossible to lead young people into a meaningless world.

There is a Heideggerian echo in Arendt's understanding of education. Newcomers are thrown into an always-already-existing world where we have to 'find' ourselves. For Heidegger, being thrown into the world opens a question of one's essence (*Wesen*), the way one 'ex-ists' or stands-out in the world (Heidegger, 1993: 42).

For Arendt, however, the fact that the world into which children are introduced is 'a pre-existing world, constructed by the living and the dead', leads instead to two political questions (BF:174). First: How should a young person be taught and assimilated into the world as it already exists? This may be said to reflect Arendt's conservatism, that the world as it is must be preserved. And second: How can children begin to change the existing world into which they are born? Here Arendt expresses her revolutionary sympathies that the world is always subject to transformation by free and spontaneous newcomers. Together, these questions comprise what Arendt calls the 'double aspect' of education (BF: 184).

This essay argues that Arendt's understanding of education is simultaneously conservative and revolutionary. In Part One on the 'Double Aspect' of education, I explore this double aspect of education and show how Arendt reconciles conservation and revolution in the educational activity. In the second section on the 'crisis of authority', I argue that in the name of conserving the world against the onslaught of the young, Arendt insists that educators – in contrast to political actors – resist the crisis of authority, which is a disaster for education and threatens the ruin of the public world. Finally, the concluding section on the 'Revolutionary Child and the Private Realm' ties the revolutionary potential of education to its guarding of the private sphere of plurality. Throughout, I argue that Arendt shows that the revolutionary work of educating students comes not from educators, but from the students themselves. To prepare students to change the world, which is the highest aim of education, the educator must take the responsibility for the authority of the world and teaching the world as it is, not as we wish it to be. We educators must have faith in our students and leave the work of revolution to them.

Education's Double Aspect

In its 'double aspect', education is paradoxically both conservative and revolutionary. In its first aspect, education is conservative in the cultural sense of cultivating the past and honouring the traditions that give the existing public world gravitas and authority. The world is that which was there before the child was born and which will continue to exist after the child dies. It is the common world of things, stories and experiences in which all of us spend our lives.

All children are newcomers who are born into a world that is at first strange to them. The child confronts the world that they see as a strange and often unjust authority. The world as the locus of tradition, culture and authority, 'needs protection to keep it from being overrun and destroyed by the onslaught of the new that bursts upon it with each new generation' (BF: 182). Without education, the child is like a rebel whose newness threatens to upend the world that is, for the child, strange and oppressive. Thus, children must be taught to speak a common language, respect common values, see the same facts and hear the same stories. The world is a reality that young people must be taught to recognize as their own.

The reality of the existing world is grounded in a tradition, a culture. As Arendt identifies in her essay 'The Crisis in Culture', the word 'culture' comes from the Latin *colere*, which means 'to cultivate, to dwell, to take care, to tend and preserve – and it relates primarily to the intercourse of man with nature in the sense of cultivating and tending nature until it becomes fit for human habitation' (BF: 208). Mankind cultivates the world so fully that their artificial dwellings come to be his natural mode of being, literally and metaphorically speaking. Culture, in other words, names the humanly built world in which human beings live.

The cultured world is a world of art and architecture, but also of laws and states. Arendt adds that culture means 'the mode of intercourse of man with the things of the world'. and she explains that 'it is the polis, the realm of politics, which sets limits to the love of wisdom and of beauty' (BF: 210). A culture both gives rise to a polis and is limited by the polis, whose institutions set the limits for aesthetic and political judgements. The common element connecting art and politics, Arendt writes, 'is that they are both phenomena of the public world'. As such, both are mediated by 'a mind so trained and cultivated that it can be trusted to tend and take care of a world of appearances whose criterion is beauty' (BF: 215). Only educated persons, those trusted by the world because they are trained, are capable of political as well as aesthetic judgement.

To say that education must teach the young to reconcile themselves to the world is neither to say that the world is one of justice nor to say that it should not be changed. Rather, it is to accept that before one changes the world, one must understand and respect that world. The world we share is true neither in the sense that it is rational nor in being objectively verifiable. The common world is a fact of our lives only because it has come to be understood over time and through generations as the world we share. It is this shared and common world that educators teach the youth. The world we teach comprises the factual reality that surrounds us. Arendt calls this world the 'truth … we cannot change; metaphorically, it is the ground on which we stand and the sky that stretches above us' (BF: 259).

Undoubtedly the existing common world is imperfect and subject to criticism. The world is comprised of prejudgements which harden into prejudices, some of which are harmful. And while Arendt argues that educators must teach the world as it is, this does not mean that young people cannot rebel and seek to transform the world. Arendt calls the effort to change the world the activity of politics. (PP: 99). But she argues that in the political engagement to change the world, we must begin from shared premises of a common world. Only if they know and respect the world as it is, will those who wish to change it be able to persuade others. Revolutionary change cannot happen if there is not a shared world that can be changed. Education has the responsibility of cultivating and leading young persons into the common world.

In its second aspect, education is revolutionary insofar as education must prepare the student to change and even revolutionize the world. The young are 'newcomers' who are not yet mature citizens. The child 'shares the state of becoming with all living things; in respect to life and its development, the child is a human being in the process of becoming, just as a kitten is a cat in the process of becoming' (BF: 182). These young people are humans in development; they are in danger of being assimilated by the world, of having their newness and spontaneity overwhelmed by the power of what is and what has been. Education must, Arendt argues, afford the child 'special protection and care so that nothing destructive may happen to him from the world' (BF: 182). The teacher is charged with nurturing the independence and newness of each child, what 'we generally call the free development of characteristic qualities and talents ... the uniqueness that distinguishes every human being from every other' (BF: 185). Education thus provides a secure space for the child to thrive in his and her transformative uniqueness.

If education is to preserve the revolutionary capacity of young people, it must guard their newness. Man, as Augustine understood, is a beginner, and 'to be free and to begin' are intimately connected: 'Man is free because he is a beginning and was so created after the universe had already come into existence' (BF: 164–166). Children are miracles insofar as they can interrupt automatic processes and revolutionize the world with new beginnings. It is such children who 'because they have received the twofold gift of freedom and action can establish a reality of their own' (BF: 169). Educators must protect this faculty of beginning, of starting things anew, of bringing miracles to be within the context of an old world that is always superannuated and close to destruction from the standpoint of the next generation (BF: 189).

This double aspect of the relation between child and world means that education is both conservative and revolutionary. It is conservative because education conserves the common world against the rebelliousness of the new. But education is revolutionary insofar as it prepares the way for young people to become self-thinking citizens who will judge and act to make the world as they want it to be.

If teachers are to protect the revolutionary newness of each young student, teachers must not simply love the world, but as part of the world in which we live, must also love the *fact* – and it is a fact – that the world will change and be transformed by new ideas and new people. 'It is in the nature of the human condition', Arendt writes, 'that each new generation grows into an old world, so that to prepare a new generation for a new world can only mean that one wishes to strike from the newcomers' hands their own chance at the new' (BF: 174). Educators must love this transformative and revolutionary nature of children, and we must 'love our children enough' so that we do not strike from our children their birthright, to build a new world. Education is, in this aspect, revolutionary; it prepares students to strike out and create something altogether new.

The conservative and revolutionary aspects of education reflect two of Arendt's long-standing concerns: the important yet problematic place of authority in the modern world, and the need for privacy as a space for thinking and for the guarding of individual spontaneity and freedom. The following two sections deepen the understanding of Arendt's conservative and revolutionary approach to education. First, I argue that Arendt's conservative approach to education demands an artificial determination that educators assert a claim of authority that no longer exists. Second, I argue that the need for education to remain revolutionary lies behind Arendt's vibrant and highly controversial defence of education as part of the private realm. Each of these claims is highly controversial; and yet, they gird Arendt's argument that education demands reconciliation with both worldly authority and revolutionary change.

Education and the Crisis of Authority

The crisis of education, Arendt writes in the first sentence of her essay, is one aspect of the larger crisis, a 'general crisis that has overtaken the modern world' (BF: 170). The general crisis for which the educational crisis is a manifestation is the crisis of authority.

Arendt inquires after the crisis of authority in her essay 'What Is Authority?' She argues that authority has largely disappeared from the world; indeed, the essay should have been more wisely titled 'What was – and not what is – authority'. This is because 'authority has vanished from the modern world' (BF: 91). By authority, Arendt means tradition and religion, both of which establish customs and rituals that are like a 'chain fettering each successive generation to a predetermined aspect of the past' (BF: 94). The loss of authority 'is tantamount to the loss of the groundwork of the world' (BF: 95). Absent such an authoritative groundwork, all hierarchy appears to be unjust, and all rule comes to be arbitrary and backed by force. The problem Arendt raises in her essay on education is that teaching cannot happen absent a worldly authority that no longer exists; her solution is that education must proceed somewhat duplicitously by assuming an authority that cannot be.

The loss of authority is first and foremost a challenge for politics: 'This crisis, apparent since the inception of the century, is political in origin and nature' (BF: 91). Because authority yields obedience based on an authoritative hierarchy, it can produce order without violence. In fact, authority 'precludes the use of external means of coercion' (BF: 92). Authority exists when the one who commands is obeyed because of a hierarchy 'whose rightness and legitimacy' is recognized by all parties (BF: 93). Thus, only where there is authority can there be 'obedience in which men retain their freedom' (BF: 105). The political problem of the loss of authority is how to maintain freedom and obedience without resorting to violence.

Many attempts to address the problem of the loss of authority seek to resurrect an old authority in new forms; but Arendt rejects such a nostalgia for ruined traditions. The thread of tradition has been broken with the event of totalitarianism:

> Totalitarian domination as an established fact, which in its unprecedentedness cannot be comprehended through the usual categories of political thought, and whose 'crimes' cannot be judged by traditional moral standards or punished within the legal framework of our civilization, has broken the continuity of Occidental history. The break in our tradition is now an accomplished fact. It is neither the result of anyone's deliberate choice nor subject to further decision. (BF: 26)

While totalitarianism is enabled by the breaking of tradition, Arendt does not believe that the loss of authority necessarily leads to totalitarian rule.

The loss of authority should not 'entail, at least not necessarily, the loss of the human capacity for building, preserving, and caring for a world that can survive us and remain a place fit to live in for those who come after us' (BF: 95). There is, first, the possibility of the revolutionary creation of new authority, as she thinks happened in the United States at the time of the Revolution. And there is, second, the challenge unique to the modern world, of living without authority – without the 'trust in a sacred beginning and without the protection of traditional and therefore self-evident standards of behavior'. Such is the challenge of politics in a world without authority where we must somehow develop ways of living by mastering anew 'the elementary problems of human living-together' (BF: 141). This is what Arendt means by thinking and living without the banisters of religion, tradition and authority. It is on this positive valence and the opening of a possible rebirth of politics through revolutionary action that Arendt ends her inquiry into 'What Is Authority?'

There is, however, no positive upside to the loss of authority in education. She names 'the pre-political' areas as child-rearing and education as those areas of life 'where authority in the widest sense has always been accepted as a natural necessity'. Therefore, it is in education that she sees the 'most significant symptom of the crisis', of authority, and the significance is precisely because the crisis has spread to these pre-political realms. Every child is subject to the authority of the parents and the adults in their community; and yet 'even this prepolitical authority which ruled the relations between adults and children, teachers and pupils, is no longer secure' (BF: 91–92). It is in this sense that the loss of the traditional authority of the parent and teacher creates an impossible situation for education.

For Arendt, 'the problem of education in the modern world lies in the fact that by its very nature it cannot forgo either authority or tradition, and yet must proceed in a world that is neither structured by authority nor held together by tradition' (BF: 191). On the one hand, this double bind means that educators must embrace a non-existent authority. Without the authority 'held together by tradition', appeals to the past are always suspect. But to abandon that responsibility to teach what is means to leave children adrift, existing in a world they do not and cannot understand.

On the other hand, absent authority, 'there are no limits to the possibilities of nonsense and capricious notions that can be decked out as the last word in science' (BF: 191). When teachers and adults refuse the responsibility to teach what is, they open the door to quackery, conspiracy and ideology. Absent the claim of authority – even an authoritative presentation of the loss of authority – the world threatens to split into multiple worlds, and we 'grant each other the right to retreat into our own worlds of meaning, and demand only that each of us remain consistent within his own private terminology' (95). While each ideological movement may argue logically, multiple closed logical worlds easily coexist. Absent an authority that can say what is, we cannot agree upon and live in a common world.

It is possible to reconcile to the loss of authority in politics; the loss of authority in education, however, is a true crisis. Children must first be taught. They must not only be taught how to read, write and add. They must also be taught certain fundamental truths and the importance of truth. What is more, they need to be taught to reconcile with the world as it is in its plurality. (Berkowitz, 2016) No doubt, such education is prejudiced in favour of the world as it is. But within that existing world is the possibility of transformation. Only when children are first led into the world can they become the kinds of adult citizens who can change it.

Arendt's conclusion is that in education – as opposed to in politics – it is imperative that we somehow maintain authority in spite of its loss. All of us who help raise young people, parents as well as teachers, 'must take toward them an attitude radically different from the one we take toward one another' (BF: 191–92). She writes:

> We must decisively divorce the realm of education from the others, most of all from the realm of public, political life, in order to apply to it alone a concept of authority and an attitude toward the past which are appropriate to it but have no general validity and must not claim a general validity in the world of grown-ups. (BF: 192)

In spite of the break in tradition and despite the undeniable loss of authority, in the realm of child-rearing and education, we need to embrace a concept of authority that is simply not valid in the adult world of politics. In other words, for the sake of children who need to be educated into a world, we adults must maintain the semblance of authority that we cannot assert over and against other adults.

But what does Arendt mean by such an authority? It is not simply that teachers and educators have masters degrees. 'The authority of the educator and the qualifications of the teacher are not the same thing' (BF: 186). A teacher is qualified insofar as he or she is able to instruct young people regarding the world as it exists. But the teacher's authority is something else.

Authority comes a willingness to judge the past and present world as valuable. Authority is 'firmly grounded in the encompassing authority of the past as such' (BF: 191). In teaching history or math, the teacher builds upon the past as 'guiding examples' and stands on the shoulders of those who have come before. The teacher must embody an authority that 'rests on his assumption of responsibility for the world' over and against the child who he has the responsibility to educate (BF: 186). In assuming responsibility for the world, teachers acquire their authority from an active respect for the world. Even in the modern world where the authority of the past has lost its hold, we must continue to teach and interact with young people as if an authoritative world still existed. This is part of Arendt's conservatism.

Arendt's conservative approach is, she explains, to be understood 'in the sense of conservation' (BF: 188). Importantly, conservation applies only to education, not to politics. In politics, where grown-ups interact with other adults, everyone must treat each other as equal. This means that no one can presume to teach others what the world is. Each new generation has the right and the responsibility to set right a world that is always out of joint. Thus 'education can play no part in politics, because in politics we always have to deal with those who are already educated'. Any hint of education in politics suggests inequality, since the desire to educate adults – even the well-meaning effort to teach them what science demands – leads quickly to the desire to 'act as their guardian and prevent them from political activity'. There is always the suspicion that 'there is pretense of education, when the real purpose is coercion without the use of force'. It is for this reason that Arendt writes that 'education' has 'an evil sound in politics' (BF: 173–174).

In education, distinct from politics, the teacher does not approach the child as an equal. Unlike the teacher, the 'child is not yet acquainted with the world', and the child must, therefore, 'be gradually introduced to it'. The teacher 'stands in relation to the young as representatives of a world for which they must assume responsibility although they themselves did not make it, and even though they themselves may, secretly or openly, wish it were other than it is' (BF: 186). The teacher's responsibility is to lead the student into the world, to teach them the world as it is. It is to give the student as deep and as impartial an understanding of the world as possible so that the students themselves, when they become adults, can decide independently what to think about the world. For that reason, the teacher must hold his or her own opinions back and present himself or herself as an authority who teaches the world as it is.

It is possible to get a sense of what Arendt's conservative approach to education really means by looking at three sentences in the final two paragraphs of Part III of the English version of 'The Crisis in Education'.[1] Each sentence speaks of the conservative need that education 'preserve' something of the world as it is. As my colleague Thomas Wild has pointed out, in all three instances, the original German words translated by 'preserve' are different (Wild: 2018). First, Arendt writes that 'in politics this conservative attitude – which accepts the world as it is, striving only to preserve the status quo – can only lead to destruction' (BF: 189). The German word here translated 'to preserve' is '*erhalten*', which means, literally, 'to hold on to'. Conservatism, in politics, seeks to hold on to the status quo. Such a preservationist attitude 'can only lead to destruction', Arendt writes, because the world is always changing.

Second, Arendt writes that in a changing world, the agents of change are frequently young people for whom the existing world is 'out of joint'. 'To preserve the world against the mortality of its creators and inhabitants it must be constantly set right anew' (BF: 189). The German that she translates here with 'preserve' is '*im Sein zu halten*'. Education seeks to maintain that world, to hold it in being and prevent its being lost. To hold the world in being is to teach both what is and the possibility of its transformation. Teachers must therefore 'preserve' the newness of young people and keep this newness apart from the world so that tradition can persist.

---

[1] It is worth noting that Arendt originally wrote her essay in German in 1958 as a speech honouring Erwin Loewenson. The German edition '*Die Krise der Erziehung*' was published first as a special edition and then later in the German edition of *Between Past and Future, Zwischen Vergangenheit und Zukunft*. See Hannah Arendt: *Die Krise in der Erziehung*. In: *Zwischen Vergangenheit und Zukunft. Übungen im politischen Denken I. Texte 1954–1964.* Hrsg. Ursula Ludz, Piper, München 1994, 2. durchgesehene Aufl. 2000, ISBN 3-492-21421-5, S. 255–276. Arendt's English translation was first published in *Partisan Review* in 1958, and then added to the revised and enlarged edition of *Between Past and Future* in 1958. 'The Crisis in Education'. *Partisan Review* 25/4 (Fall 1958): 493–513. (Reprinted in *Between Past and Future*.)

Finally, teachers must 'preserve this newness and introduce it as a new thing into an old world, which, however revolutionary its actions may be, is always, from the standpoint of the next generation, superannuated and close to destruction'. Here, the word translated as 'preserve' is the German '*bewahren*', built from the word '*wahr*', which means true. *Bewahren* means to hold true and to protect.

Education is conservative and revolutionary because even as it protects and preserves the world, it also preserves and protects the newness of young people who, having been led into a common world that already exists, are able to act to constantly set it anew. 'Our hope', Arendt writes, 'always hangs on the new which every generation brings' (BF: 189). For the sake of the new, we old people who teach must take care not 'to try to control the new' and 'dictate how it will look'. As conservative, education must conserve, preserve, hold-in-being and protect not only the world, but also the revolutionary drive of the child. While the conservative sense of 'to preserve' indicated the necessity of safeguarding tradition *against* newness, the revolutionary sense indicates the need to safeguard newness against established, solidified traditions so that they might be reinvigorated by posterity.

Arendt's conservationist approach does not suggest that the world as it is must be maintained. On the contrary, to teach the world as it is means to introduce young people to a continuously changing world. Teaching, therefore, must also preserve the revolutionary aspect of the student. If children are to change the world, education needs to protect the child's uniqueness – their difference and eccentricities. It is at least in part to protect the possibility of political change that Arendt develops her defence of privacy.

The Revolutionary Child and the Private Realm

Arendt argues that privacy is especially important for children. It is only in privacy that children can grow freely in the dark. It is in the darkness of the private world where young people can imagine alternate and often impolite realities; it is in private where children can try out multiple identities; and it is in private where they have a place to hide, cry and grow into the unique individuals they are. Privacy secures a kind of depth, a darkness, that is the non-subjective place where 'who we are' is at home. It is a refuge of our exclusiveness and uniqueness as a person. Children need private space because children, if they're exposed to the public, will lose their ability to grow in their own way; they risk becoming shallow and conformist.

All living things, Arendt explains, need the darkness of privacy: 'Everything that lives, not vegetative life alone, emerges from darkness and, however strong its natural tendency to thrust itself into the light, it nevertheless needs the security of darkness to grow at all' (BF: 183). Children of famous people have a real problem because they think they're always being watched, and they don't develop the deep personal life that children need to mature into independent adults. If we are watched, surveilled and scrutinized too much as children, and even to some extent as adults, we are deprived of the necessary darkness needed for a rich mental life. The privacy of the family, with all of its problems – and there are multiple problems of sexism, racism and abuse that are often justified on the grounds of privacy – is needed to preserve a private realm separate from the glare of the public.

Arendt does not shy away from the dangerous and provocative implications of her defence of privacy. In 'Reflections on Little Rock' (RJ and DM), Arendt associates schooling with the private right of parents to educate their children as they want, even in ways the rest of us find wrong. The reason to defend the private sphere, Arendt argues, is that the private sphere protects plurality and uniqueness. She asks: Where will we defend unpopular privacy if not in the right of parents to choose how to raise their children? If we do not defend the rights of parents to raise their children in their personal and unique belief and value systems, what then does privacy mean? Meaningful privacy is always in contest with social and normal standards of mass society, standards of progress and conformity.

Privacy supports the depth of personal difference that will allow for meaningful differences to exist in an increasingly rational and conformist democratic society subject to the tyranny of the majority. Privacy, therefore, is the ultimate remedy for conformism.

> The danger of conformism in this country – a danger almost as old as the Republic – is that, because of the extraordinary heterogeneity of its population, social conformism tends to become an absolute and a substitute for national homogeneity. In any event, discrimination is as indispensable a social right as equality is a political right. The question is not how to abolish discrimination, but how to keep it confined within the social sphere, where it is legitimate, and prevent its' trespassing on the political and the personal sphere, where it is destructive. (DM: 51)

Privacy protects all persons from the dangers of conformism by offering the one space where individuals have the right to be different.

Arendt understands that in private we humans do shameful and at times antisocial things, hold unorthodox opinions and challenge the social and political consensus. It is in private that we express prejudices and learn to discriminate. In private, we acquire depth; and depth worries us. Depth is dangerous. It is in our depths that we all contemplate crimes, vicariously venture into vice and speak singularly and sinfully. And it is those sins, vices and crimes, as well as those intimate secrets, prejudices and weakness, that make us equally deep and interesting. Privacy protects the dark side of the inscrutability of human motivations.

In *On Revolution,* Arendt notes, 'the human heart is a place of darkness which, with certainty, no human eye can penetrate' (OR: 86). Maybe a god can see the nakedness of the human heart, but we do not. And for Arendt, it is a good thing that those ideas and thoughts in our hearts and heads remain secret. Privacy is an essential refuge for the dark and unconventional side of humanity. We may say the right things in public, but we also know that other thoughts come into our heads. We know those thoughts that pop into our heads – lusts, desires, vices. These are part of our selves. They need to be hidden, but they cannot be denied. If we limit our privacy, if we make ourselves reveal those secrets, we will repress the desires and needs of our heart and we will become less interesting; we will conform to social pressures; and we will be less human.

If privacy is so important for human plurality, the most important aspect of privacy is in child-rearing. In 'Reflections on Little Rock' (RJ and DM), Arendt assumes that how one raises one's children inclusive of where one sends them to school is a private matter. This is a controversial and possibly wrong assumption. It may be the case that in a multi-ethnic and multiracial democracy, public education serves an integrating function that is essential. Arendt even accepts this argument in her essay 'The Crisis in Education' (BF). As a 'land of immigrants', the 'enormously difficult melting together of the most diverse ethnic groups – never fully successful but continuously succeeding beyond expectations – can only be accomplished through the schooling, education, and Americanization of the immigrant's children' (BF: 172). Public schools in the United States serve multiple functions, one of which is to equalize differences; and for Arendt, while this drive for equality can lead to challenges, it also 'has great advantages' (177).

And yet, even as she recognizes that schools serve an essential public and socializing function, Arendt insists that education remains fundamentally private. She does so because of her conviction that privacy is essential for both plurality and politics. A private life is necessary for plurality and politics because privacy secures depth in and through which young people become independent and self-thinking persons: 'A life spent entirely in public in the presence of others becomes, as we would say, shallow' (HC: 71). It is in privacy where we have secrets. What do secrets do? They make me different from you. They make me worried about things that I know and no one else knows. They separate me from you. They create a darkness that my 'self' emerges out of; it is this depth that is crucial to who I am. It is this depth that makes each of us interesting and unique; it defines our humanity. Only when children are allowed to grow in private where they are free to experiment and offend can they mature into unique and independent adult citizens.

School is that institution that mediates between the private world of the home and the public world of the citizen. In school, the young person is gradually, over time, introduced into the common world. And yet, if we are to guard and preserve the revolutionary potential of young people, we must also protect their uniqueness.

The crisis of education emerges from the need to protect the authority of the world in a world without authority and the need for uniqueness in a world without privacy. We cannot deny the loss of authority, which is a fact of our time. But as free persons, we are faced with the judgement of whether to simply reconcile ourselves to the ruinous consequences of such a loss in the realm of child-rearing. The other option cannot be to embrace the fantasy of a resurrected authority. It is, rather, to choose to proceed in the educational realm on the basis of an authority that we fully know to be absent.

2

Thinking with Arendt: Education and Temporality

Faisal Baluch

Introduction

It seems fair to say that Arendt has a far greater number of admirers than detractors in the academy. Thus, even the criticisms of her thinking often come from this larger camp of admirers. One indication that this is indeed the case is the popularity of the phrase 'thinking with Arendt against Arendt' – a phrase not coincidentally coined by one of her admirers (Benhabib, 2003: 198). Apart from the controversy surrounding her *Eichmann in Jerusalem* (EJ), two topics have led to much 'thinking against' Arendt. First, feminist scholars have brought to bear Arendt's thinking on issues that she herself did not address, and indeed, dismissed (Honig, 1995). Second, Arendt's position on education, and in particular her intervention in the debate over desegregation, has led many of her admirers to correct her. Her position on both of these issues is informed by the many distinctions that lie at the heart of her analysis of politics and society. Contesting Arendt's position has thus meant contesting the rigidity of her distinctions – in particular, the distinction between the social and the political. While these contestations have brought to the fore some fruitful theorizing about politics, using the example of education, I show in this chapter that the 'thinking against Arendt' has not entirely done justice to her thought. My argument proceeds in three steps: I first consider the methodological implications of Benhabib's (2003) call for 'thinking with Arendt against Arendt' in light of Arendt's own method of reading. Informed by this method, I then offer an examination of Arendt's thinking on education. I argue that focusing on natality does not allow us to fully appreciate the force behind Arendt's thinking on education. Instead, I argue that her thinking on education is motivated by her concern with temporality, best expressed in the title of her work *Between Past and Future* (BF), which contains her most extended meditation on education. I finally argue that a divergence from her position on education, even if warranted by justified contestation of her distinctions, cannot but involve a divergent conception of the political. I thus show that neither her admirers nor her critics have paid sufficient heed to the fact that Arendt's very conception of politics is at stake in her thinking about education.

Pearl Diving with Arendt

Arendt was fond of quoting from the speech of the spirit Ariel in Shakespeare's *The Tempest*: 'Full fathom five thy father lies;/ Of his bones are coral made;/ Those are pearls that were his eyes:/ Nothing of him doth fade/ But doth suffer a sea-change/ Into something rich and strange.' These lines stand as an epigraph to a section of her essay on Walter Benjamin in which she discusses Benjamin's method, in particular, his use of quotations (MD: 193). Arendt resolves the metaphor as follows: the pearls are the quotations that Benjamin collected and used in his writings, the works from which the quotations are taken are the sediments and history the sea. The metaphor leaves open the question of what exactly history/the sea does to these sediments and what precisely the sea-change involves. In Shakespeare, the sea-change turns something that is dead into something new and valuable. The dead thing before it turned into pearls, while perhaps not valuable today, was of tremendous value before it ended up as a sediment– in *The Tempest*, the sea-change acts on the eyes of the king of Naples, Alonso – the father of the addressee of Ariel's speech, Ferdinand. Exhuming the entire sediment/the dead body from the bottom of the ocean will not, however, lead to the body coming back to life. Applying all of this to the case that Arendt is considering, we get the following: The texts that now form the sediments were once of tremendous value, but simply exhuming them from the ravages of history will not bring them back to life. Neither simple reversion to the past, nor emulation of it, is an option. Instead, the image suggests that only a part of what is in the sediment, the part that has undergone a sea-change, is worthy of being exhumed. Since full-scale retrieval is difficult – nigh impossible – the parts that are of value have to be torn out of the sediment and now viewed in an entirely new space. The desire to preserve thus manifests itself in a violent act that rips apart from the whole and brings into the present, but in a different form.

While all this is presented by Arendt as a meditation on Benjamin's method, Arendt quotes the same lines from Shakespeare in *The Life of the Mind* in the context of her own theorizing. She categorically refuses to term her reflections a meditation on her method, but allows that they may be read as conveying 'the basic assumptions of [her] investigation' (LM1/2: 212). Arendt too trades in the pearls that she terms 'thought fragments'. Wresting these thought fragments requires doing violence to the whole from which they are recovered. And after they are recovered, the sea-change they have undergone makes it such that they are no longer old, but in fact, new. In light of this, it seems fitting that some of her readers have sought to follow the method of 'thinking with Arendt against Arendt' (Benhabib, 2003). For like the thought fragments that animate Arendt and set her on her path, her readers have sought to chart their own courses.[1]

This tac taken by her interpreters, though seemingly justified, does not, however, do justice to the method suggested by Arendt's reflections on the assumptions behind her work. Pearl diving is only partly an enterprise that destroys, tears asunder and trades in the new. Arendt points out that there is a certain 'ambiguity of gesture' involved in the stance to history exemplified by Benjamin. Indeed, the gesture of pearl diving itself bespeaks the desire to preserve what is judged worthy of preservation. Arendt explicitly points to this aspect of pearl diving in her reflections on her own means of proceeding. She warns that 'if some of [her] listeners or readers should be tempted to try their luck at the technique of dismantling, let them be careful not to destroy the "rich and strange," the "coral" and the "pearls"' (LM1/2: 212). So even as we recognize that the loss of tradition and authority has meant that the past no longer speaks to us and what it has to offer must be violently wrested from its context, Arendt warns that the violence must be measured, lest it lead to the loss of what actually is in need of preservation. The ambiguity involved in the gesture comes from the fact that the movement is motivated by and calls for both the destructive and preservationist impulses. The difficulty involved in following Arendt's way of proceeding, and by extension interpreting her work, can be attributed to the challenge of balancing these two impulses. Focused on the destructive impulse and giving prominence to the new, readers who have thought 'against her' have sought to 'dismantle' in order to bring the new into the world. But in doing so, they have not paid sufficient heed to the latter – preservationist – impulse. Arendt's own thinking on education showcases how she combined the two impulses.

---

[1] An extended example of such a way of proceeding is offered by *Feminist Interpretation of Hannah Arendt*.

Education as the 'between'

The controversy surrounding Arendt's thoughts on education can be traced back to her essay 'Reflections on Little Rock' (DM), in which she put forward her views on school desegregation in the American South. The essay and the subsequent responses formed one of the many controversies of Arendt's life as a public intellectual. But Arendt, never shy of controversy, did not allow the furious response to her essay to detract from her thinking on education. Even after the controversy arose over her 'Reflections on Little Rock' (RJ), Arendt chose to include her extended discussion on education in a volume of her own essays.[2] This latter essay, 'The Crisis in Education' (BF), did not however put the controversy to rest, for in it Arendt elaborated the theoretical grounds of her position. The essay continues to generate discussion as is evidenced by the current volume. A clear examination of Arendt's thinking on education requires that we separate out the controversy over her position on a matter of public policy – namely, her position on school desegregation in the American South – and her theoretical position on the question of education. I concern myself primarily with the latter, and will reference the former only as necessary to elaborate on Arendt's theoretical position.

Arendt's essay, 'The Crisis in Education', was published in a volume titled *Between Past and Future: Six Exercises in Political Thought* (BF). The preface of the volume suggests that each part of the title is significant and worthy of our attention if we are to understand the aims and spirit of the considerations contained in the volume. The essays themselves, Arendt tells us, can be divided into the critical and experimental. The critical essays seek to remove the obfuscation of time that has covered over foundational concepts of politics. The experimental section considers issues current in the political realm at the time of Arendt's writing. Thus, the critical section is concerned with the past as it shapes us, primarily through words we still use to describe political phenomena, while the experimental deals with the shape of the future and how it impinges on us. Her essay on education fits into this latter category. Both types of essays – critical and experimental – in different ways ultimately deal with the 'between'

---

[2] Some of Arendt's interpreters have attempted to save her from herself by arguing that her exchange of letters with Ellison shows that she changed her view on the way desegregation was proceeding in the American South. This, however, does not seem to be the case, as evidenced by her essay 'The Crisis in Education' in which she upholds the distinctions that informed her view on how best to deal with the evils of segregation. That she did not change her position suggests that more than the topicality of the issue interested her – her position was informed by deeper theoretical concerns. Bohman makes a similar case. but on different grounds (Bohman, 1996: 57).

in the title: which is to say, the present. But about the present they offer neither prescriptions based on the study of the past nor prognostications about the future. They are *exercises* in political thought and must be read as such. Since they are exercises, the essays represent a kind of thinking which 'is different from such mental processes as deducing, inducing, and drawing conclusions whose logical rules of non-contradiction and inner consistency can be learned once and for all and then need only be applied' (BF: 14). Thus, as we turn to Arendt's essay on education we need to be cautious both about what we draw from it and how we judge it.

We can begin our examination by considering the question 'What drew Arendt to the issue of education?' The most immediate answer to the question is that Arendt, like many others, was moved by the famous photographs from the Little Rock Central High School in 1957 as African American students attempted to enrol in the school following the *Brown v. Board* Supreme Court decision. While this occasioned her essay 'Reflections on Little Rock', the essay 'The Crisis in Education' reveals that her thinking on education is in fact intimately tied to her theorizing about politics. Arendt herself encourages one of the main theoretical rationales that have been cited for her concern with education. Early in 'The Crisis in Education', she writes that 'the essence of education is natality, the fact that human beings are *born* into the world' (BF: 174). Since natality is an important category in Arendt's political theory, it is not surprising that she would concern herself with education. Yet Arendt wrote remarkably little directly about education and she infamously relegated the reproductive to the private realm.[3] If we consider the theme explored by the collection of essays in which 'The Crisis in Education' appears, we get beyond this obvious answer to why education concerned Arendt.

The new in education is of course represented by the newly arrived human beings who occupy the chairs in the classroom. The newly arrived who for now inherit the already existing world, which not only impinges on and orders their lives now but will continue to do so, are also going to shape the world of the future. The newly arrived, therefore, occupy the place indicated in the title of the collection. In this 'between' is precisely where the newly arrived are educated, and it is here that the educationist must thus define the posture that education takes vis-à-vis both the past and the future. 'The Crisis in Education' (BF) is precipitated by the failure in modern times to define this posture. The crisis is

---

[3] Given all this, Benhabib's remark that it is 'no accident' that a female theorist made natality a central concept of thought is quite surprising, for such an attribution seems rather foreign to the spirit of Arendt's work. (Benhabib, 2003: 135)

not the result of a modern lack of concern with natality or the new, but rather of the opposite – an ill-defined and increasingly troubled relationship with the past. The aspect of the human condition at stake here is temporality. To understand how our ability to deal with temporality has been compromised, we need to go back to Arendt's account of the Greeks.

While much has been made of Arendt's Grecophila, her stance towards the Greeks depends on whether she is dealing with the lived experience of the Greeks or the thought of the Greek philosophers. She viewed the 'fate of the political' as tied to the early problematic reconceptualization of politics found in the writings of Plato and Aristotle.[4] The reconceptualization begins with a denigration of the realm of human affairs most famously depicted in Plato's cave analogy. This denigration led first to the attempt to escape the realm of human affairs, and, as a second best, the effort to bring order to the realm of human affairs such that it becomes hospitable to the philosopher. This latter effort, in Arendt's telling, leads to conceiving of the political realm as the realm of making rather than doing (HC, 195). This in turn means that one introduces a maker and something acted upon. It is here then that expertise, and more importantly, authority are called upon. Yet it is also a Greek philosopher – Aristotle no less – who set the intellectual precedent for treating the political realm as the realm of equality. Despite making this move, in an effort to bring order to the messiness of human affairs and to protect the philosopher, it is also Aristotle who introduces authority into the political realm. This authority takes the form of the old ruling over the young. Thus, we go from a conception of the political realm as the realm of equality to importing into it a deeply inegalitarian vision of authority, one which relies on the educational relationship. Arendt views this move as more than a mere curiosity of intellectual history. The move continues to shape our world, for as Arendt writes 'on its grounds rulers have posed as educators' (BF: 119). Plato and Aristotle's introduction of authority into politics in the guise of the educational relationship led in Arendt's view to a fundamental reconceptualization of politics, allowing the introduction of inequality into a realm that ought to be characterized by equality. The reconceptualization in Arendt's view remains operative in modern times. The relationship between education and politics is thus not of local interest to Arendt's theory of politics; for her, the relationship is a critical part of the long story of how politics in the West came to take the shape that it did. What is at stake in the relationship between education and politics, then, is the very conception of politics.

---

[4] I borrow the phrase 'the fate of the political' from the title of Villa's book. (Villa, 1995)

Arendt's understanding of the relationship between education and politics is central to the work that in her words placed her in the ranks of the 'dismantlers' (LM1/2: 212). Since this dismantling work is what leads to her conception of politics, it stands to reason that a divergence from her view on education and politics would call for a conception of the political that differs from hers. 'Thinking with Arendt against Arendt' (Benhabib, 2003) thus requires much more than simply correcting her on particular issues; it may call for a conception of the political that is foreign to Arendt's works.

Arendt's dismantling work reveals the intellectual moment when authority found itself back into politics, covering over the political experience of the Greeks. This revelation is significant for it illuminates the political phenomena that characterized much of the twentieth century. Arendt was witness to the efforts of various regimes seeking to educate, and more often 're-educate', their people at a very high price (OT). But Arendt's narrative does not end with the deployment of the theoretical move of allowing the educational relationship into politics. It allows her to bring to light a new trend. Rather than an invasion of authority, the modern world, Arendt tells us, is characterized by a retreat of authority. Now given Arendt's critical account of the introduction of authority into the political realm when offering her reading of Plato and Aristotle, one would expect that the retreat of authority ought to be cause for celebration. But this does not turn out to be the case. Arendt seems to bemoan both the rise and fall of authority. This ambiguity in stance is not limited to her thinking about authority, and perhaps also explains how the same thinker can be diagnosed with Grecophila and also celebrated as the anti-foundational political thinker of our time. The ambiguity of her stance on authority is on full display in her thinking on education.

As authority has vacated the world, it leaves a void only briefly. An unpoliticized education is not what results when authority vacates the world. Arendt shows that, paradoxically, an educational realm vacated of authority leads to greater politicization. With the collapse of authority comes the collapse of the distinctions and protections afforded different realms. The educational realm then also becomes a site of political battles – events continue to bear out the accuracy of Arendt's analysis. Arendt's narrative begins with the intrusion of authority that properly belongs in the educational realm into the political realm and ends with the educational realm being invaded by the political realm. The politicization of education is thus tied to the collapse of authority in the educational realm. This crisis does not, however, only portend danger.

Crises, Arendt argues, offer us the opportunity to make a judgement. But she warns that any good that could have come from a crisis is lost when one simply responds with what she calls 'performed judgements' (BF: 174). Arendt equates performed judgements with prejudices, for such judgements are not the result of thinking, but rather of adherence to dogmas. Arendt makes no exceptions for dogmas even when their content is normatively desirable. In the prefatory note that she added to 'Reflections on Little Rock' upon its delayed release in *Dissent,* she warns against 'throwing around liberal clichés' (DM: 45). Given Arendt's position on school desegregation and insistence on a strict boundary between the public and private realms, the temptation to 'throw around liberal clichés' is particularly great – we must resist this temptation.

While officially sanctioned segregation in schools is no longer the law of the land in the United States, politics continues to feature prominently in debates about education. The relevance of Arendt's thought becomes evident early in 'The Crisis in Education'. She writes:

> Education can play no part in politics, because in politics we always have to deal with those who are already educated … since one cannot educate adults, the word 'education' has an evil sound in politics … but even the children one wishes to educate to be citizens of a utopian morrow are actually denied their own future role in the body politic, for, from the standpoint of the new ones, whatever new the adult world may propose is necessarily older than they themselves. (BF: 177)

While it is tempting to explain Arendt's misgivings as informed by the '(re) educational' efforts of the totalitarian regimes she lived through and witnessed in the twentieth century, the sentiment she holds is sufficiently prevalent in current discourse about education as to make national news in the United States. Those on the conservative side of the political spectrum find US colleges and universities politicized by radicals on the left, while liberals look on suspiciously as conservatives work to insert their views into academia (Saul, 2018). Despite their divergent political affinities, both sides accuse the other of politicizing education. Schools have not been spared in this struggle, as evidenced by the recurrent debate over textbook content in schools. The rhetoric on both sides claims to be inspired by the sentiment that educational institutions ought not to be the sites of political struggles. Events thus not only make Arendt's observations relevant, but suggest that her normative stance is not alien to present sensibilities. Arendt's categorical statement that 'education can play no part in politics', which has come under criticism even by her admirers, is thus seemingly shared at least in part by both sides in the contemporary debate over the politicization of education. Arendt therefore succeeds in the primary aim of her theorizing about politics – namely, capturing the phenomenon underlying politics. Since Arendt insists on the separation of education and politics and her stance is seemingly shared across the political spectrum, it behoves us to consider her argument for the separation carefully. Before doing so, we do, however, need to pre-empt a few objections.

While it may be true that liberals accuse conservatives of politicizing education, and conservatives accuse liberals of doing the same, it does not follow that either of the two sides hold Arendt's opinion. We ought at least to bring to the fore one other possibility. Might it be the case that the banding about of the term 'politicizing' is more a reflection of how politics is viewed, rather than of a stance on the relationship between politics and education? In other words, to accuse one's opponent of politicizing something is perhaps to question one's opponent's scruples and suggest that they are merely feigning regard for the matter that they are subjecting to politicization (Euben, 2001). Conceding this does not, however, diminish the relevance of Arendt's statement, since it is precisely this instrumentalization that she opposes. A second possible objection to the relevance of Arendt's strict separation of politics and education could also be made. The fact that colleges and universities, and indeed schools, have become the site of political battles could be viewed as empirical evidence that the rigid separation that Arendt wishes to uphold is not tenable. And depending on one's ideological commitments, one could see the various campus activism movements, the efforts by conservative organizations and donors, and the mobilization of school-age children for gun control as suggesting the normative undesirability of Arendt's position on the matter. Here one must be on guard against falling foul of Hume's guillotine. The empirical reality of the entrance of politics into the educational realm does not compromise Arendt's position, for it does not bear on the normative desirability of the situation.

The criticism that Arendt has received on her thinking on politics is not on her view that politics not be modelled on the educational relationship between adults and children, but on the corollary that politics needs to be kept out of education. Arendt's reservations can perhaps best be understood by taking an example. To liberal sensibilities, the recent marches in the United States by grade-school children in support of gun control laws are a welcome sight (Mazzei, 2018). The children, viewed as purveyors of the shape of things to come, are potent political actors for they themselves are increasingly affected by gun violence and by virtue of their age and place in society are likely to reach the consciences of lawmakers more effectively than adults. The protests also serve as good training in citizenship for children who will soon form part of the voting public. But viewed through Arendtian lenses, one would read the events very differently.

The appearance of grade-school children into the public realm demanding a change of laws would for Arendt be first and foremost a sign that adults have vacated the world and no longer take responsibility for it. Even those who support the protests would not be in grave disagreement with her on this, for they too would concede that the appearance of children in the public realm does in fact represent the failure of adults to effectively address the issue. Adults are responsible for the political world, most obviously since they form part of the voting public and thus can ultimately impact these laws, something that most grade-school children cannot do on their own. The appearance of children is thus either a sign of apathy about the issue on the part of adults or their failure to be heard. Second, for Arendt, to have children out in the streets to campaign for laws is to turn them into pawns in a realm where they do not belong. For the political realm is the realm of equality, but children and adults are not equal in the political realm. To see the logic of Arendt's position as reconstructed here, consider how someone with liberal sensibilities would view the presence of children at pro-gun demonstrations that were timed to coincide with the gun control demonstrations. Children at pro-gun demonstrations would indeed be seen as pawns in the pro-gun lobby's campaign, yet their presence may be celebrated at gun control rallies. Arendt does not admit this stance. By her lights, the children would be pawns no matter the content of the political struggle. Arendt thus holds a consistent position on the place of children in the political realm. She is of course not naïve enough to think that the boundaries are fixed. She acknowledges that 'where the line between childhood and adulthood falls in each instance cannot be determined by a general rule; it changes often, in respect to age, from country to country, from one civilization to another, and also from individual to individual' (BF: 195).

While Arendt's distinctions and policing of boundaries of politics may seem to reduce the autonomy of children, the contrary turns out to be the case. Arendt's refusal to countenance the deployment of children in political causes reveals a far greater concern on her part for ensuring their autonomy, than is shown by her detractors. For through her stance, she resists any attempt to use children as means, even for good ends. Thus, efforts by interpreters to adjudicate between acceptable and unacceptable roles for children in politics fail to recognize what is really at stake in Arendt's position. Arendt's refusal to countenance a political role for children is a necessary result of her conception of politics.[5] To allow children to be made pawns in a political cause is to contravene one of Arendt's principle stances on politics, namely, to allow the means–ends calculus to enter the political realm. Thus, if one grants that grade-school children, to the extent that they do not form part of the franchised population, are not equals in the political realm, something that does not seem difficult to grant, one cannot be completely clear of the charge of using them as means when allowing them to enter the political fray. Opening the possibility of such use leads in turn to a fundamentally different conception of politics – one that allows means–ends calculations and thus differs profoundly from the conception of the political found in Arendt's texts.

Descendus dans la rue is not the only form that politicization in education takes. The more common occurrences that raise the spectre of politicization for both liberals and conservatives in the United States are changes to syllabi and the resulting choice of texts, and what has come to be called 'campus climate'. Here again Arendt's position is not immediately clear. In 'The Crisis in Education' she writes: 'It seems to me that conservatism, in the sense of conservation, is of the essence of the educational activity' (BF: 193). But this raises the question of how the political theorist who wrote of 'thinking without a banister' could be opposed to changes and revisions that seek to embrace the new and different and offer a reckoning with the past that corrects for its errors. To understand this, we need to query both the phrase 'thinking without a banister' and Arendt's self-professed educational conservatism.

The original force of the phrase 'thinking without a banister' is neither celebratory nor normatively prescriptive (Hill, 1979). That we must think without a banister is the conclusion that Arendt reaches after diagnosing the modern human condition. It is a necessity in our times, and one that is a heavy burden. While it may allow us to think the new and untold, it makes thinking difficult. In the preface to the collection that contains the essay on education, she writes: 'Remembrance, which is only one, *though one of the most important*, modes of thought, is helpless outside a pre-established framework of reference, and the human mind is only on the rarest occasion capable of retaining something which is altogether unconnected' (BF: 6, my emphasis). The burden of thinking without a banister is a heavy one even for adults, and thus should not be taken lightly. It does not, by Arendt's lights, belong properly on the shoulders of children. She

---

[5] It is therefore questionable whether a political struggle that 'opens up a space for politics that powerful opponents would foreclose' would not in the end run afoul of Arendt's strictures against the use of means–ends calculus in politics (Honig, 1995: 280).

bemoans the fact that authority which has vacated the rest of the world has also vacated the educational realm where it rightfully belongs. The educational realm for Arendt of necessity needs to be the realm of remembrance and authority. How she might differ in this then from those on the left of the political spectrum is evident, but Arendt cannot also be numbered among the ranks of present day conservatives, for she warns that conservatism in education must not be allowed to leak into the political realm. Just as a lack of authority and remembrance in the educational realm makes the birth of the new difficult, such conservatism in the political realm is pernicious to the new. Arendt recognizes what is often lost in many of today's debates – that concern needs to be simultaneously shown for the old and the new, but also that 'these two responsibilities do not by any means coincide; they may indeed come into conflict with each other' (BF: 186). Pointing out this tension is the principal service that Arendt provides us in navigating the 'between' occupied by education. Rather than occupying this 'between', there is a temptation to either focus on the new or the old without adequately paying heed to the fact that natality requires an already existing old world, and the already existing world cannot survive and sustain without the new.

What Arendt's position means outside the classroom should be evident from what has been said in the preceding paragraphs. But more needs to be said about what precisely this means inside the classroom. In Arendt's telling, the possibility of the new entering the world is further endangered when schools become the site where children are 'instructed in the art of living' (BF: 195). What Arendt means by this goes beyond the fact that education even up the college level has increasingly become vocational training. The 'art of living' need not just take the form of minting fresh economically productive individuals who have been suitably apprenticed for a trade (the trade in today's world may well require intellectual rather than physical skill, but that changes little). When education takes the form of a conscious effort to matriculate citizens of a particular hue – even if it is one to our taste – then too one is engaged in 'instruct[ing] in the art of living'. And to offer such instruction in the art of living is to use children as a means to a predefined end, and thereby rob them of the opportunity to shape the world. As to what can be done inside the classroom to ensure that children are not robbed of this opportunity, Arendt only offers a hint. In the closing lines of the first volume of *The Life of the Mind*, Arendt approvingly quotes the following from Auden: 'Some books are undeservedly forgotten, none are undeservedly remembered' (LM1/2: 213). Education for Arendt then calls for ensuring that students are exposed to the books that continue to be remembered. And in this, more than a simple defence of the old is at stake. While modern times call for thinking without a banister, the ability to do so once out in the world requires that those who are new to the world be introduced to the old. Since remembrance is a central mode of thought, in the effort to introduce the new to the old, the very ability to think is at stake. In Arendt's reckoning, when one is ensuring that students are exposed to the old, one is not defending the old but the new, for without introducing the old to the new it is the possibility of the new entering the world that is endangered. This, it appears, is the essence of Arendt's conservatism in education – the new need the old to bring the new into the world.

Conclusion

I close with a second rich metaphor that Arendt returns to in more than one of her texts. This image, taken from a parable written by Kafka, is of a man who is on a road confronted by two antagonists. One pushes him forward and the other pushes him backward. Thus, the one pushing him forward helps him in his fight with the one that pushes him backward, and vice versa. The hope – Kafka calls it a dream – is that the man may be able to step off the road and become an umpire over the two antagonists. Arendt offers a brilliant reading of the parable. She reads the two antagonists as the past and the future both pushing on the protagonist who occupies the present. But her reading dismisses the dreamt of resolution to the conflict. For she contends that without the protagonist, the struggle would not take place at all, and even if the conflict were to take place the two forces would have destroyed themselves, 'since as forces they clearly are equally powerful' (LM1/2: 203). In place of Kafka's dream, Arendt proposes her own resolution. She argues that since the two forces are acting from opposing directions, the resulting movement would be diagonal to the road on which the protagonist faces the two forces. If the protagonist occupies the present, and the two forces represent the past and the future, the diagonal represents the result of the pressures of the past and the future on the present. This diagonal is how Arendt conceives of the new coming into the world. The metaphor encapsulates in a pithy manner Arendt's thinking on education. The new is born of a confluence of the past and future. To dismiss Kafka's dream of stepping outside the struggle is to reaffirm that we cannot escape the pressures of either the past or the future. To insist that without the protagonist the two forces would destroy each other is to give equal valence to the past and future. And finally, to follow the diagonal is to journey on a new course which does not take us inexorably into the future but is conditioned by the past. The force of the future cannot, in fact, produce the new without the push of the past. This is the prime service that Arendt's thought offers to those engaged in education – the past mustn't be thought of as a burden to be cast off, but as the necessary condition for the emergence of the new. Education thus must show as much concern for the old, as it does for the new.

3

Arendt and 'Worldliness': Education in and for a World of Difference

Jon Nixon

Introduction

We are living within a very different geopolitical context and historical era than that in which Arendt became a public thinker and intellectual. But in acknowledging the differences between the conditions prevailing in the first quarter of the twenty-first century (our time) and those of the mid-twentieth century (her time), we should not overlook the significant continuities. These continuities are, for example, evident in the increasing dominance of market-led consumerism that – in her early encounter with 'the new world' – provided her with deep forebodings regarding the implications of 'the American dream': forebodings that Sheldon S. Wolin (2010) was later to identify as 'the specter of inverted totalitarianism'. But they are also evident in the resurgence of a new wave of political populism that now dominates much of our public discourse, erodes public trust in the institutions of civil society and creates a context in which demagoguery has re-emerged as a mode of mainstream political leadership.

In this chapter, I consider the claims of populism – as manifest in the contemporary political mainstream – prior to presenting Arendt's insistence on the plurality of the human condition as a rebuttal to those claims. What we have in common, argued Arendt, is also what potentially divides us: our capacity to define ourselves and our place in the world through actions the outcomes of which are always uncertain and unpredictable. We can only avoid the divisive and potentially tragic consequences of the uncertainty and unpredictability of the human condition by acting, not as self-interested individuals nor as an undifferentiated mass, but *together* as free and equal citizens. Such action, she maintained, is the source of all genuine power and forms the basis of all democratic politics.

It is, however, crucially dependent upon the human potential for what – following Kant – she termed 'enlargement of mind': the potential to understand the world from different viewpoints and perspectives and to form judgements on the basis of that enhanced understanding. Education is the point at which we acknowledge that potential within ourselves and one another, and begin to take responsibility for its realization in our own lives and that of others. We are living in a world of difference, and will need to learn – and teach future generations to learn – to live together in such a world. Arendt has, I believe, much to teach us regarding the nature and purpose of this educational endeavour within our own particular dark times.

Dark Times

The political theorist Jan-Werner Müller (2017) has suggested that political populism involves two related claims. First, populists claim that 'the voice of the people' takes precedent over all other sources of legitimate political authority: the judiciary, parliament and local government. The complexity of democratic sovereignty is thereby collapsed into a notion of 'the sovereignty of the people' – a notion that licenses populists to decry any attempt by the courts to pursue their constitutional function, to demand that elected members adhere to a popular mandate rather than exercise their independent judgements and to inveigh against any sections of the free press that are critical of the supposed 'will of the people'. The aim of the populist, writes Müller, is:

> to pit an authentic expression of the *populus* as uninstitutionalized, nonproceduralized *corpus mysticum* against the actual results of an existing political system. In such circumstances, it is also plausible for them to say that the *vox populi* is one – and that checks and balances, divisions of power, and so on, cannot allow the singular, homogeneous people to emerge clearly. (62)

The separation of powers – the constitutional cornerstone of liberal democracy – is thereby put at risk.

Second, populists claim to know what constitutes 'the people'. This, argues Müller, is the populists' 'one big lie: that there is a singular people of which they are the only representatives' (114). Within populist political discourse 'the people' are variously defined as 'ordinary people', 'decent people' and even 'real people'. 'The people', in other words, are invariably defined against 'other people', who by implication are not 'ordinary', not 'decent' and not 'real'. At a campaign rally in his bid to gain the US presidency, Trump announced that 'the only important thing is the unification of the people – because the other people don't matter' (quoted in Müller, 2017: 22). It is these 'other people' who then become the targets – the scapegoats – of populist outrage: immigrants, refugees, religious minorities, recipients of state benefit, the unemployed … the list of potential scapegoats is endless. The point is to define 'the people' against some available 'other'. Pluralism – the cultural heartbeat of liberal democracy – is thereby not only put at risk but denied.

Anti-pluralism is the main charge levelled against political populism by the political theorist and policy analyst William A. Galston (2018). Having considered the dangers for liberal democracy of majoritarianism, he goes on to argue: 'More dangerous still is the populists' understanding of the "people" as homogeneous and unitary, which leans against the pluralism that characterizes all free societies in modernity' (4–5). The rejection of pluralist policies, he writes, 'challenges the liberal democratic order, which stands or falls with the recognition of individual rights, social diversity, and the need for reasonable compromise among competing interests' (44). In its rejection of pluralism, political populism is not only a threat to liberalism but also a threat to the basic tenets of democracy.

To these two claims a third should be added: namely, the claim to have a monopoly on the truth regardless of its factual accuracy. The truth is what political populism declares it to be, and whatever falls outside that declaration of truth is deemed to be untrustworthy. This is the means by which populism seeks to achieve cultural and ideological domination. Facts which clearly contradict the populist narrative are discounted, while those whose job it is to ascertain or report on those facts are disparaged and even vilified. At the same time, writes American literary critic Michiko Kakutani (2018):

> fake news and lies are pumped out in industrial volume … and sent flying across the world through social media accounts at lightning speed. Nationalism, tribalism, dislocation, fear of social change and the hatred of outsiders are on the rise again as people, locked in their partisan silos and filter bubbles, are losing a sense of shared reality and the ability to communicate across social and sectarian lines (11–12)

Nor, as she points out, is it just 'fake news': 'it's also fake science (manufactured by climate change deniers and anti-vaxxers, who oppose vaccination), fake history (promoted by Holocaust revisionists and white supremacists), fake Americans on Facebook (created by Russian trolls), and fake followers and "likes" on social media (generated by bots)' (12). The political strategy – deeply undemocratic and veering dangerously towards totalitarianism in its intent – is to assert power over truth.

Reaffirming the *polis*

Against these claims stands Arendt's insistence on the public sphere as a 'guarantee against the futility of individual life, the space protected against this and reserved for the relative permanence, if not immortality, of mortals'. (HC: 56) Within the public sphere – that for the Greeks was the *polis* and for the Romans the *res publica* – 'the people' constitute not a single voice, but a buzzing plurality for which critical thought and the exercise of free will are of paramount importance. She firmly rejected the notion of a 'general will'. Indeed, she argued that it was precisely this notion that had led to the tragic failure of the French Revolution. By dissolving individual free will into an undifferentiated generality, it denied its own libertarian precepts (OR: 50). For Arendt, the prime purpose of education was to enable each individual to develop the capabilities and dispositions necessary to enter the public sphere as independent minded citizens.

In affirming the plurality of the public sphere, Arendt was acknowledging both the individuality of the individual and the equal worth of each individual within that sphere. To acknowledge this plurality is to reject the claim that 'the people' can be reduced to a single voice ('the voice of the people') or a generalized will ('the will of the people') as evoked in populist rhetoric. It is also to reject the populist claim that all those who are not in tune with this single voice or generalized will are an entirely negative or deficit element within the body politic.

The *polis* as conceived by Arendt comprises neither a homogeneous mass in which all voices speak as one nor an exclusionary zone from which any voice deemed to be out of tune is automatically excluded. It is, rather, a civic space in which all individuals are deemed equal by virtue of their citizenship, and each is acknowledged to be different by virtue of her or his freedom of will: a space dependent upon the free interchange of opinion and reliant on the respect of all parties for a distinction to be drawn and maintained between truth and untruth in the expression of their opinions. When that distinction is lost – or deliberately blurred or flouted – the *polis* is put at incalculable risk.

To acknowledge the plurality of the public sphere is therefore to reject the claim that any one group has a monopoly on the truth. Truth is what we arrive at through a process of deliberation involving the ongoing testing and challenging of contrasting and sometimes conflicting judgements. Truth does not fall outside the world of human affairs, but is constituted within it as an ongoing process of agreement-making that is forever being reworked and re-fashioned. To seek to derail this process through the twisting or distortion of the truth for political gain is not only undemocratic but, in Arendt's terms, anti-political in that it renders inoperable the deliberative infrastructure upon which politics is founded.

Truth, argued Arendt in her analysis of the Pentagon Papers (leaked to the *New York Times* in 1971 and revealing the extent of the state cover-up of the death and casualty toll resulting from the Vietnam War), is one of the foundation stones of democratic politics. It is 'the chief stabilizing factor in the affairs of men', without which the *polis* is – as history shows – at risk of descending into totalitarianism:

> This is one of the lessons that could be learned from the totalitarian experiments and the totalitarian rulers' frightening confidence in the power of lying – in their ability, for instance, to rewrite history again and again to adapt the past to the 'political line' of the present moment or to eliminate data that did not fit their ideology. (CR: 7)

Untruth disempowers and ultimately disenfranchises the recipients of untruth; it discredits and ultimately corrupts the purveyors of untruth. Truth alone empowers.

Truth does not appear unbidden. The sifting of truth from untruth – from wishful thinking, wrong-headed belief, deliberate evasions, downright lies, etc. – presupposes the human capacity for what Arendt understood as thoughtfulness: a capacity which she saw as deeply dialogical (the 'two-in-one' of thinking, as she put it), as inclusive of divergent views and opinions (what she termed 'representative thinking'). and as fundamental to human flourishing (as elaborated in her notion of 'enlargement of mind') (LM1: 179–193; LM2: 257; BF: 241). To be thoughtful, argued Arendt, is to engage in the world of human affairs and thereby become worldly. To be unworldly is to be thoughtless and thereby disengaged from the world. Without the thinking person. the *polis* is unthinkable.

But not all ways of thinking route us through from the 'two-in-one' of solitary thought to the dialogical process of thinking whereby we are able to engage with the world. Throughout her life and work Arendt struggled to develop and practice a way of thinking that was, in her terms, 'worldly': a way of thinking that, while confronting the banality of thoughtlessness (and its all-too-easy collusion with evil), rejected the allurements (very real for a person of Arendt's intellectual disposition) of purely abstract thought. In order to understand the moral and ethical premium Arendt placed on thoughtfulness, it is necessary to understand how and why she distinguished it from the unworldliness of, on the one hand, *thoughtlessness* (as exemplified in the person of the Nazi operative Eichmann) and, on the other hand, *pure thought* (as expressed in the life and work of the Nazi apologist Heidegger).

Eichmann and Heidegger

Thinking was Arendt's lifelong occupation. She was committed to thinking through the topics that engaged her rather than to developing theories that could be stated as outcomes. Indeed, she saw the finality of any theory – or closed system of thought – as a potential danger to human freedom. She knew from her own experience that thinking is often conducted in solitude, that its consequences may be dangerous and that it is always deeply discursive – and she wasn't troubled by the seeming paradox that thinking can be at once discursive and at the same time solitary. She knew that to think is to think together. She was a thinker for whom thinking offered the promise of new beginnings.

In her final unfinished work, *The Life of the Mind*, she distinguished between – while at the same time highlighting the complementarity of – thinking as internal dialogue (the 'two-in-one' of thinking as she put it) and thinking in dialogue with others. In both cases, different viewpoints and standpoints are, in her terms, 'represented' in the thinking process, a process, which, she insisted, is grounded in common experience: 'not a prerogative of the few but an ever present faculty in everybody' (LM1: 191). Indeed, she developed a profound suspicion of any kind of thinking that risks trapping the thinker within what she saw as a closed, monological system.

This suspicion formed the basis of her 1946 assault on the 'terminological façade' and 'obvious verbal tricks and sophistries' that characterized Heidegger's magnum opus (EU: 176). *Being and Time* was, she claimed, marred by Heidegger's use of 'mythologising and muddled concepts like "folk" and "earth"' (EU: 181).

Later – in a handwritten journal entry dated July 1953 – she likened Heidegger to a fox attempting to lure potential victims into a trap which none of them can enter because the fox is itself trapped within it (Ludz, 2004: 304–5). Even when, years later in a 1969 radio broadcast, she sought to excuse Heidegger's Nazi past, she did so on the grounds that his residency in his own exclusive world of thought had made him a stranger to the wider world of human affairs. In defending Heidegger, she was forced to highlight what for her was a serious deficiency in his thinking: its self-absorbed unworldliness from which – like the fox in her earlier journal entry – he was unable to escape (Ludz, 2004: 160–2). For Arendt, thinking was of the world, worldly; and as such was nothing if not dialogical.

That is why the notion of 'thinking' played such an important part in Arendt's analysis of totalitarianism. Her 1951 *The Origins of Totalitarianism* (OT) characterized both Nazism and Stalinism as deeply dehumanizing in their denial of the human capacity for thinking. Later, in her highly controversial coverage of the Eichmann trial that culminated in her 1963 *Eichmann in Jerusalem* (EJ), she famously employed the phrase 'the banality of evil' to describe what she saw as Eichmann's unquestioning adherence to the norms of the Nazi regime. In concluding from the occasional lies and inconsistencies in his courtroom testimony that Eichmann was a liar, the prosecution had – she argued – missed the moral and legal challenge of the case: 'Their case rested on the assumption that the defendant, like all "normal persons", must have been aware of the criminal nature of his acts' – but, she added, Eichmann was normal only insofar as he was 'no exception within the Nazi regime'. The prosecution had, according to Arendt's analysis, failed to grasp the moral and political significance of Eichmann's 'abnormality': namely, his adherence to the norms of the regime he had served and therefore his lack of awareness of the 'the criminal nature of his acts' (EJ: 26).[1]

Later, in *The Life of the Mind*, Arendt returned to a consideration of the Eichmann trial (LM1: 3–6). Indeed, she used her earlier analysis of that trial as the springboard for what were to be her final reflections on the ethics of thinking. A world devoid of thinking, willing and judging would, she argued,

---

[1] Given what is now known of Eichmann's past in Germany and his life in Argentina where he lived when he escaped from Germany and boasted about his role in the Final Solution, Arendt's judgement on Eichmann himself may be seriously questioned. Christopher Browning, the distinguished historian of the Holocaust, has written: 'Arendt was fooled by Eichmann's strategy of self-representation in part because there were so many perpetrators of the kind he was pretending to be.' However, Browning also maintains that Arendt's concept of 'the banality of evil' remains an important insight (Browning, 2003: 3–4).

be a world characterized by 'thoughtlessness' and inhabited by automatons such as Eichmann who lacked freedom of will and any capacity for independent judgement. If Heidegger had represented the unworldliness of 'pure thought', then Eichmann represented the unworldliness of 'thoughtlessness'. Neither Eichmann in his 'thoughtlessness' nor Heidegger in his 'pure thought' connected with the plurality of the world as Arendt understood it.

The only notable characteristic she could detect in Eichmann 'was something entirely negative: it was not stupidity, but *thoughtlessness*'. He had displayed a complete 'absence of thinking', which, as she disturbingly pointed out, 'is so ordinary an experience in our everyday life, where we have hardly the time, let alone the inclination, to *stop* and think' (LM1: 4. Original emphases). In Arendt's view, his 'banality' left him no less culpable – and rendered the death sentence no less justifiable – but it shifted the basis of the argument against him: if he was a monster, then his monstrosity arose from an all too human propensity towards *thoughtlessness*.

That raised for Arendt a crucial question: 'Could the activity of thinking as such, the habit of examining whatever happens to come to pass or to attract attention, regardless of results and specific content, could this activity be among the conditions that make men abstain from evil-doing or even actually "condition" them against it?' (LM1: 5). The question arose in large part from her experience of totalitarianism, but also from her experience of political oppression under McCarthyism in 1950s United States and more generally from the ideological battle lines that defined the Cold War. She also viewed with increasing concern the unthinking consumerism and the assumption of ever-increasing affluence that fuelled 'the American Dream' prior to the stock market crash of 1973 and the oil crisis that followed later that year. Neither Hitler's Nazism nor Stalin's communism had, it would seem, exhausted the full potential of totalitarianism. So the question remained urgent and pressing even within the heartlands of the democratic superpower of which she was now a citizen.

The question raised by Arendt is no less pressing within our own particular dark times, and might be expressed in the following terms: Could the activity of thinking be among the conditions that actually condition us against the claims of political populism? Could thinking, by its very existence, challenge the claim that there is a single 'voice of the people', an all-encompassing 'will of the people'? Could it, by its very existence, represent those who are excluded from that all-encompassing generality: the dissenters, the new comers, the outsiders? Could it, by its very existence, question the untruths, half-truths and downright lies that are perpetrated in order to uphold those claims?

Arendt would seem to suggest that thinking, then as now, is up to the task – at least the words she wrote towards the end of her life would seem to suggest so:

> When everybody is swept away unthinkingly by what everybody else does and believes in, those who think are drawn out of hiding because their refusal to join in is conspicuous and thereby becomes a kind of action. In such emergencies, it turns out that the purging component of thinking (Socrates' midwifery, which brings out the implications of unexamined opinions and thereby destroys them – values, doctrines, theories, and even convictions) is political by implication. (LM1: 192)

In order to appreciate how – by drawing out the implications of unexamined opinions – thinking is 'political by implication', we have to understand the conceptual relation, as defined by Arendt, between thinking, action and judgement: a relation that is fundamental to her reworking of Kant's notion of the 'enlargement of mind' and informs her notion of 'representative thinking' and of the 'two-in-one' of thinking. It is to her last, great but unfinished work that we must again turn for an elaboration and clarification of these ideas.

'Enlargement of Mind'

The tripartite structure that Arendt had envisaged for *The Life of the Mind* (LM1/2) focused on thinking, willing and judging. In the event only the first two of those three conceptual building blocks were put in place, with the result that the work lacks not only a detailed discussion of the third element but also an overarching argument as to how the three concepts are related within the overall scheme – and, crucially, how these concepts are related to her notion of action. In posthumously editing the work, her close friend Mary McCarthy included as an appendix to the second volume excerpts from Arendt's lectures on Kant's political philosophy that had a particular bearing on 'judging'. Arendt's comments in these relatively brief extracts suggest that she considered judgement to be an indispensable element in enabling us to think politically.[2]

Arendt linked the human capacity for judgement to what – following Kant – she termed 'enlargement of the mind' (LM/2: 257). It is only by comparing our own judgements with other possible judgements that we develop our capacity for discrimination. Unlike thoughts, judgements are therefore *always* public. This distinction between thinking and judging is crucial: Whereas thinking involves

---

[2] These lectures have subsequently been published with a scholarly introduction by Ronald Beiner. (See LK.)

a necessary element of keeping oneself company, judging invariably presupposes the company of others; while thinking pulls towards 'the duality of the two-in-one' of solitary thought (LM1: 187), judging is firmly located in what Arendt had earlier termed 'sharing-the-world-with-others' (BF: 221). Judgements are in effect claims that are seeking assent, but may be challenged. For that reason, a judgement – even when couched in terms of an assertion – invariably involves an element of persuasion. 'To judge', as Dana Villa (1999: 98) puts it, 'is to engage in rational public dialogue, deliberating with others with whom I must finally come to an agreement and decision'.

Arendt had already covered some of this conceptual ground in a 1967 essay that she had written in response to the controversy following her coverage of the Eichmann trial.[3] In that essay – written in response to the controversy following the trial – she wrote: 'Political thought is representative. I form an opinion by considering a given issue from different viewpoints, by making present to my mind the standpoints of those who are absent; that is, I represent them.' She went on to argue that this process of representation 'does not blindly adopt the actual views of those who stand somewhere else'. Rather it 'is a question ... of being and thinking in my own identity where actually I am not'. Finally, she claimed that 'the more people's standpoints I have present in my mind while I am pondering a given issue, the better I can imagine how I would feel and think if I were in their place, the stronger will be my capacity for representative thinking and the more valid my final conclusions, my opinions' (BF: 241).

Imagination, claimed Arendt, is the faculty that allows us to feel and think as if we are in another's place. This faculty 'makes the others present and thus moves potentially in a space which is public, open to all sides; in other words, it adopts the position of Kant's world citizen' (LM/2: 257). As conceived by Arendt, imagination is diametrically opposed to both fancy and ideology. Both deny the public: in the case of fancy, by turning away from its externality; in the case of ideology, by violating its plurality. The imagination alone – drawing its inspiration from, and finding delight in, the plurality and specificity of the world – affirms the public through its willingness to reach out and accept its hospitality: 'To think with the enlarged mentality – that means you train your imagination to go visiting' (LM/2: 257).

In its interconnectedness and engagement, reading becomes paradigmatic of 'the enlargement of the mind'. For example, reading Kafka requires us to connect his life, work and context; to go beyond identification with a single character in

---

[3] Entitled 'Truth and Politics', the essay was published in *The New Yorker* and reprinted in the second 1968 edition of BF, pp. 227–64.

order to grasp the underlying structure of the work; and, crucially, to bring our own passion for truth to the act of reading (RLC: 94–109). We judge Kafka – as we would any modernist writer or artist – not only by the demands that his work makes on us as readers, but on our capacity as readers to meet those demands. Any judgement is, therefore, a judgement on the one who is judging as well as on that which is being judged: a judgement, that is, on the imaginative capacity – the capacity for 'enlargement' – of the judging mind.

The world, for Arendt, was an intersubjective reality that – in its objectivity – both divides us and unites us. What was of paramount importance to her was our own capacity to construct the world in such a way as to ensure that the centre holds; that the complementarities of division and unity hold firm. That was why the conceptual trinity of thinking, willing and judging was of paramount importance to her: thinking is rooted in the inwardness of our being in the world, willing asserts our selfhood within and to the world, and judgement reaches out to engage with the world as it presents itself to us externally and objectively. It is within the world – and only within the world – that we are capable of 'the enlargement of mind' that makes us fully and complicatedly human.

She was adamant that thought and action are distinct and that judgement is something different again. Nevertheless, these concepts are vitally connected. Her notions of 'representative thinking' and 'enlargement of mind', writes Dana Villa (1999: 88), 'point to the faculty of judgement as a kind of bridge between thought and action'. Only when thinking has done its work and judgements have been formed does action begin; but, conversely, '[o]nly when action has ceased and words such as courage, justice, and virtue become genuinely perplexing does thinking actually begin' (Villa, 2001: 19). It is by thinking that we form judgements, by forming judgements that we enter the public sphere and by entering the public sphere that we constitute a citizenry, a *polis*, and thereby open up the possibility of concerted action.

A World of Difference

In her 'Introduction *into* Politics' (originally envisaged as a short book parts of which formed the basis of a course she gave at the University of Chicago in 1963) Arendt wrote:

> If someone wants to see and experience the world as it 'really' is, he can do so only by understanding it as something that is shared by many people, lies

between them, separates and links them, showing itself differently to each and comprehensible only to the extent that many people talk *about* it and exchange their opinions and perspectives with one another, over against one another. (PP: 128, original emphasis)

Education was for Arendt the doorway into 'the world as it "really" is'. It is the space within which people begin to 'talk about [the world] and exchange their opinions and perspectives with one another, over against one another'. It is the in-between space where we are able to negotiate our way from the private space within which childhood is nurtured and protected, and the public space of adult responsibility and citizenship: a space in which to question and challenge, to imagine the world from different standpoints and perspectives, and to reflect upon ourselves as unique persons who share a common world.

Arendt made a distinction – if somewhat blurred in terms of age differentials – between the education of children and the education of young adults. Her two essays on the former – 'Reflections on Little Rock' (DM: 193–226) and 'The Crisis in Education' (BF: 173–196) – are premised on the assumption that children are as yet unformed, and that adults have a responsibility to guide them into the world of human affairs while protecting them from the full blast and turmoil of that world. This assumption lay behind her highly contested attack on the federal imposition of integrated schooling, as advanced in 'Reflections on Little Rock',[4] and her reflections, in 'The Crisis in Education', on 'the dangers of a constantly progressing decline of elementary standards throughout the entire school system'. (BF: 173) Arendt was acutely aware of the vulnerability of the child in an adult world, but aware also that 'the world too needs protection to keep it from being overrun and destroyed by the onslaught of the new that bursts upon it with each new generation' (BF: 186).

Her views on the education of young adults – and of the role of the university in that process – were markedly different. What few reports we have of her own teaching style within the university context suggest that she was centrally concerned with enabling her students to think for themselves, express their own opinions and argue and deliberate with one another. Jerome Kohn, now

---

[4] In response to 'Reflections on Little Rock', Ralph Ellison, the famous black writer, accused Arendt of failing to understand the plight of the Southern Blacks. Arendt subsequently wrote to him acknowledging her error (Young-Bruehl, 1982: 316). More recently Danielle S. Allen and Kathryn T. Gines have both written detailed critiques of the argument put forward in 'Reflections on Little Rock', pointing out Arendt's factual errors and highlighting what they see as her misguided opinions (Allen, 2004; Gines, 2014), while Richard J. Bernstein has acknowledged that Arendt 'failed to understand the disastrous consequences of hostile political, economic, and social discrimination of Blacks in America' (Bernstein, 2018: 50).

a distinguished Arendtian scholar and editor, studied under Arendt in the late 1960s. In an exchange of letters with Elisabeth Young-Bruehl, another erstwhile student of Arendt who went on to become her biographer, Kohn recalls the experience of being taught by Arendt during that period of student unrest and violent demonstrations against the war in Vietnam:

> For this theorist of action, teaching itself was an unrehearsed performance, especially in the give-and-take, what she called the 'free-for-all' of the seminar, where she asked her students real rather than rhetorical questions and responded, usually in entirely unexpected ways, to theirs … . In her seminar, every participant was a 'citizen', called upon to give her or his opinion, to insert him or herself into that miniature polis in order to make it, as she said, 'a little better'. (Young-Bruehl and Kohn, 2001: 254–5)

But education can only provide such a space if it remains uncluttered by what Arendt saw as barriers to thought. There were – and are – three such barriers.

The first is the assumption that the outcomes of thinking can be pre-specified – that we can think things through to a pre-specified (and therefore predetermined) end or goal. Against this assumption Arendt insisted – in her 1967 essay 'Truth and Politics' (BF) – that 'our thinking is truly discursive, running, as it were, from place to place, from one part of the world to another, through all kinds of conflicting views'. Thinking is heuristic and explorative, unpredictable in its outcomes, uncertain and indeterminate. It falls outside the frame of pedagogical approaches or assessment regimes premised on the notion of pre-specifiable goals, targets and outcomes. Insofar as we understand institutions of education as places within which we learn to think and – and, in so doing, enlarge our minds, then those approaches and regimes need to be realigned with practices of teaching, learning and assessment that place the emphasis on interpretive modes of thinking.

The second barrier relates to notions of academic categorization. Arendt understood the importance of disciplinary and methodological boundaries, but was aware that these could all too easily become barriers. In her own life and work, she insisted on the need to think outside – and between – the traditional academic categories: 'thinking without bannisters', as she called it. During an interview televized in 1964, she rounded on her interviewer who referred to her as a philosopher: 'I have said goodbye to philosophy once and for all. As you know, I studied philosophy, but that does not mean that I stayed with it' (EU: 2). Having distanced herself from philosophy, she never settled into an established discipline, but constantly crossed and re-crossed the boundaries between historical analysis, philosophical reflection and political theory.

Arendt's lifelong preoccupation with thinking highlights the need for approaches to teaching and learning that recognize difference and diversity, challenge and question and stimulate and provoke; for curriculum frameworks that are open and interconnective, flexible and responsive, and negotiable and provisional; and for educational purposes that focus on dispositions and qualities, on human flourishing and on the fulfilment of individual potential. Above all, Arendt reminds us that education is a public good: the more we participate in it the greater its potential contribution to the well-being of society as a whole and the vibrancy of the body politic. Against those who maintain that education is a commodity bought and sold for private gain, Arendt insists that it is grounded in our shared capacity to think – and that to think is to think together and in difference.

The collective problems we now face are increasingly global in scope and as such require collective solutions which in turn require the capacity and the will to think across our differences. As those differences become sharper and more intractable – particularly in the context of the rise of populism with its politically nationalist, economically protectionist and culturally xenophobic tendencies – it is worth bearing in mind Arendt's insistence that thinking is ordinary. It is the one faculty that binds us together while allowing us the freedom to become ourselves. In a deeply divided world, our capacity for thinking together – practical reasoning, *phronesis* – is the most valuable resource available.

Institutions of education are among the few remaining places within which that resource can be valued unconditionally. They are also – crucially – places in which we learn to think in such a way as to distinguish well-founded beliefs from wishful thinking, to distinguish less well-founded beliefs from more firmly founded beliefs and to understand why such distinctions matter. In our current context – no less than that in which Arendt insisted upon the ethical and political significance of thoughtfulness – thinking matters. For Arendt, thinking was always critical. The notion of critical thinking was, for her, a tautology. Because thinking is always critical; always dialogical; and always progressing through distinctions, exploring the intricacies of disagreements and sailing to its goal of consensus through the various side winds of *dissensus*. Only through the long, hard slog of thinking together in and through difference can truth be attained and preserved.

Conclusion

In dark times, thoughtfulness becomes an indispensable resource of resistance and hope. Without it, there can be no considered judgement and no concerted action based on deliberation and the weighing of alternatives. Education, argued Arendt, is a space devoted to thoughtfulness: a protected space for the young, and a more robust forum for those moving into adulthood. She would have warned against any suggestion that we are born thoughtful. Rather, we are thoughtful through our initiation into, and participation in, a supportive environment of learning that withstands the thoughtlessness of routinized behaviour and the blandishments of a thinking divorced from 'the world as it "really" is'. To be thoughtful is to be grown up, and to be grown up is to learn how to understand – and engage with – the world 'as something that is shared by many people' (PP: 128).

Part Two

Education and Crisis

4

Identity as Other and the Promise of the Narrative Imagination in Educational Theorizing: Arendt and Ricoeur

Jo-Anne Dillabough

Introduction

Identity, as a conceptual term, has been an abiding obsession in educational research, particularly across the last half of the twentieth century. However, as Hannah Arendt so aptly argued, and most particularly in *The Life of the Mind* (LM1/2), while the Latin origins of the concept of identity point to an immovable, internal, unchangeable and even biological entity across time – that is as 'sameness' or the state of being the same (see Gardner, 2010) – its very emergence as a language of governance and a common liberal reflection on the modern state was suggestive of a key idea, namely that one was free to define oneself, or at least to interrogate oneself as part of being a subject of modernity. In this way, identity provided a lexicon of description for the rise of the individual through modernity (see Simmel, 2003). Importantly, according to Arendt (OT, EJ), this notion of identity could never animate a subject of action. This was so, as Arendt (LM1) argued, because such a notion is time-limiting, dwells within the realm of the psychological and lacks uniqueness. It must therefore be put aside for the sake of the public realm and in the name of human courage because 'in politics, not life but the world is at stake' (BF: 155, see also Herzog, 2001, 2004; Honig, 1988).

Arendt, of course, was not the first to raise such matters about the problematics of identity and its paradoxical links to political action. Notions of personal identity have a history dating back to ancient Greece when notions of mortality and immortality were drawn upon to better understand the value of life as a philosophical entity that endures beyond bodily death (Fearon, 1999). Here, notions of identity as a biological entity were drawn upon to fuel philosophical discussions about wider questions of mortality, religion and faith. Later, a more pervasive discussion of issues relating to identity proliferated in the seventeenth century as the rise of modern science, including the study of psychiatry – alongside theories of modernity – became a predominant feature of the early twentieth century (see Foucault, 2002). The enduring elements of identity have also become highly influential in particular disciplines, including intellectual history, in part as a consequence of the rise of political movements and the burgeoning of identity politics across the political spectrum.

Despite this history, as Arendt (OT, HC, EJ, BF) tells us, the most insistent usages of the concept of identity paradoxically find their home in two pervasive forms: the first rests within political and authoritarian populism (OT, EJ, BF) and the second comprises currents of commercial populism such as self-help and self-improvement enterprises devoted to the study of the inner self (HC). Since Arendt's death in 1975, such ideas and enterprises have proliferated, finding a strong base in works of popular psychology (e.g. *Men are From Mars, Women are from Venus*), and accelerating disciplinary interest within fields such as education, sociology, psychology, anthropology and latterly neuroscience. Education, as a marginal field, often seen as peripheral to substantive knowledge-based disciplines, has been particularly susceptible to the circulation of identity-related discourses in the second half of the twentieth century (Grunenberg, 2002; Hall, 1996). Moreover, within education, though it circulated very widely across the post-war period, the notion of identity was often handled uncritically and without clear definition (see Fearon, 1999; Foucault, 2002; Honig, 1988, 2003; Skinner, 1969).

In this chapter, I argue that the exceptionally wide circulation of the term identity in education has, paradoxically and often inadvertently, led to a set of normative assumptions about its uses within educational policy and practice, many of which lead us back to Arendt's (HC, BF, EJ) midtwentieth-century concerns. These centred upon time-limiting, inauthentic and uniform expressions of the self, the state and the polity, leading to the paradigmatically dominant idea that identity may be read as a 'thing', a fixed entity capable of being programmed or enhanced within the sphere of education (e.g. working-class boys, girls and achievement, and boys and failure) or even eradicated if it reflected difference or otherness.[1] This has not always been the case. Before the

---

[1] Current forms of authoritarian populism and earlier incarnations of it during Second World War reflect such attempts at eradication.

mid-twentieth century and perhaps even earlier, the term was not reified as a programmable 'thing'. Rather, it was accorded a more fluid, less stable character (Mattingly, 2011).

Importantly too, in most educational research, we often find competing claims about identity in the form of, for example, a raced, gendered and classed identity, yet a more explicit definition is often masked or fails to examine the modalities of power by which they have been shaped. In consequence, the imaginative dimensions of selfhood remain elusive. The idea of identity often circulates as a strangely empty or vacuous term, shorn of a 'narrative imagination' or a poetics of selfhood. Instead it appears as trapped in forms of 'normative sameness' that find constrained expression within the realm of citizenship, announcing that there is always a stranger to the nation (see Dillabough and Yoon, 2018; Kearney and Taylor, 2005; Kearney, 2014). Such forms have become increasingly expressed and re-appropriated through the rise of reimagined nationalisms and rising populisms, particularly in Europe but also in the United States, Latin America and in Asia (e.g. Korea). One might identify this – using Arendt's political theorizing of the eradication of difference from the state and Ricoeur's phenomenology of narrative – at least in part as the power of late twentieth-century identity work – alongside accelerated forms of capital accumulation and ongoing dispossessions, displacements and expulsions. These forces, taken together, create the social conditions for populist imaginaries to flourish.

Here – alongside scholars who have drawn upon Arendt's work to theorize notions of the narrative imagination, historical responsibility and political life – I address a gap in the current theoretical literature on the wider uses of the term 'identity' as it relates in particular to the work of Hannah Arendt and Paul Ricoeur, but also to others following their work (see, for example, also, Benhabib, 2001; Caverero, 2000; Honig, 1988, 1993, 2003). My primary aim centres upon moving the discussion beyond the term 'identity' and recasting it within education as that which must necessarily carry a narrative and imaginative function. A key argument rests on the idea that identity – as a conceptual tool – is too heavily relied upon in education research, is often ill-defined and static, and is frequently misapprehended in terms of its origins and translations in education research. If we are to embrace Arendt's (HC) and Ricoeur's (2004) entwined notions of the narrative imagination as part of a social imaginary reflecting symbols, metaphors and dreams about oneself by revealing a storied life, then we may draw nearer to an educational theory of interpretation that invites a hermeneutic detour into the imaginative worlds of selfhood. As Kearney (1995) suggests, this imaginative notion of selfhood must necessarily express itself in relation to otherness, to put this more simply, the integration of social metaphors of experience, as they are interpreted and reinterpreted across time, are precisely some of the mediating dimensions of a reconfigured narrative imagination. These metaphors represent just one way we may begin to reimagine our lives through those who may, on first glance, seem distant from us. This recasting of identity through the processes of narrativization therefore allows for the capacity of the self to open itself up to new worlds and thereby reimagine it, only one of which constitutes the world of education.

To address these challenges, I seek to offer a short overview of some of the most significant features of an exploratory theoretical route that engages with what Arendt and Ricoeur each identified, albeit indirectly, as the 'enigma of semantic innovation' (Ricoeur, 1975: 5., English Translation) as it lives through metaphors and the temporal concept of the narrative imagination. This necessarily involves bridging the ideas of poetic narration as a language of selfhood, political action and an ethics of historical responsibility, with philosophical accounts of becoming as they are expressed through language (Caverero, 2000; Honig, 1988, 2003). At the same time, I also want to ask how notions of time and the other (and here we might think of the 'foreigner' and the stranger to the nation) come together to refigure such narratives (see Ricoeur 1995, 2004; Honig, 2003). This is particularly important as 'foreigners' are often treated as strangers to the nation and to normative conditions of citizenship. And so too are forms of cultural identity that do not conform to normative understandings of the citizen subject – for example, the heteronormative duality of the male–female subject, the 'immigrant' or the potential 'terrorist' who threatens British values. In following the work of Honig (1988, 1993, 2003), we should ask how the 'foreigner', as a cardinal site of both real and metaphorical difference, might force us to reconsider selfhood and citizenship, including our historical responsibility to such foreignness as a way towards new identifications and constellations of citizenship that might inform more critical understandings of education for citizenship. Honig (2003: ix) asks, 'should the foreigner be forced to be more like us?' Or should the 'foreigner' teach us that there was never an 'us' in the form of an essential identity or a normative citizenship? What lies behind this semantic innovation and how do new meanings of the self and the foreigner appear to be reconfiguring both past and future? As Ricoeur (2004) argues, 'life interprets itself' through a series of temporal mediations; to say 'self is not to say I' (Ricoeur, 2004: 5) and the self – as a hermeneutic entity – no longer becomes an inner experience isolated from another, but is, as Ricoeur has so aptly expressed, 'oneself as another' (Ricouer, 1995: 1). This is a self that has travelled beyond the illusory constraints of an 'identity', an 'I' or a 'moi', into a symbolic world of signs, symbols and metaphors that can only ever be associated with others or as a 'soi-meme come une autre'[2]; these others can only emerge and be represented in the plural as Arendt so aptly argued in *The Human Condition* (HC), as a 'soi' such that any real master of the self represents an illusory ideal. One is instead enlarged and thoroughly enriched through the temporal movements, metaphorical affiliations and social experiences of the hermeneutic detour.

The imaginative process of narrating one's storied account of life is a complex and challenging endeavour (Kearney, 2003). In addition to the imaginative act of narrating in the present, there is also a need to reimagine the past. This necessarily implicates a deployment of the historical imagination through emplotment. But as Kearney (2003), a keen follower of Paul Ricoeur, tells us, this historical imagination does not only re-appropriate the past as a straightforward act of reproduction. As Ricoeur himself puts it: 'The historical imagination has a duty to the otherness of the past by way of expressing a moment that is no-more' (cited in Kearney, 1995; 177; Kearney, 2017: Study 6). In this case, it is still the imaginary that resists the possibility – through resistance and translation – of otherness or the stranger from remaining hidden from view. These dual acts both of resistance and translation emerge when we move away from sameness or the 'same as' (identity), or even a toleration of the other towards otherness as a phenomenological narrative act, through meaningful imaginative dimensions of thoughtfulness and ethical concern for our own and others' differences; it is only at this juncture that the foreign other and the emergent tensions between sameness and difference can be brought closer to us to reduce human estrangement, resisting a retreat into the apolitical ideal of the inner self as identity. As Kearney (1996, 2017) tells us, this allows for an understanding of identity as something which can only be energized within the time of the narrative expression as it is mediated by, and reimagined through, the time of the world. Narrative time represents the expression of one's imagined storied life as it lives temporally and is animated through the time of one's social universe.

While Arendt (HC) does not address the question of identity directly because of her concern with its inertia and depoliticization, she focuses instead on the idea of the persona as it has been understood in Greek drama. Her argument asserts the necessity of the significance of historicity, responsibility and political action as part of the dramatic expression of narrative and as a way of challenging

---

[2] This is the French title of Ricoeur's book, *'Oneself as Another'*.

the essential features of identity that are often commodified and exploited by the state. This emphasis on responsibility suggests that we must challenge notions of identity when they emerge as a subordinate category and a tool of exploitation or a material but inert form of commodification, and confront the question of why such a classification exists as a trace of the imperial and colonial past or as an emblematic feature of a state-sanctioned identity that is fundamentally ahistorical and apolitical.

By contrast, what a hermeneutic detour of identity sets out to achieve is a portrait of a more ethically oriented account of the *self–other* relationship, structured by history, present circumstances and its capacity for a form of refiguration through the practices of narrativization themselves.

Temporality, Narrativization and Memory Work

In other works, drawing extensively upon the writings of Gardner (2010), I have concentrated on Arendt's usefulness in understanding young peoples' experiences of exile, estrangement and the political within education and the city (see Dillabough and Kennellly, 2010; Dillabough, Rochez and Balfour, 2019). While phenomenology has formed major parts of each of these works, I have only ever felt able to tacitly indicate the power of the narrative imagination in shaping the landscape of educational research, principally because of the complexity involved in outlining its characteristics. Here, I attempt to pursue this idea more substantively by concentrating on Arendt's concerns with two fundamental aspects of narrative as action: the narratability of the self as a symbolic and innovative form of becoming that is mediated by temporality, and the idea that narratives provide a fuller account of who we become in public space as against a 'what' or a 'thing' – often through those diminished and subordinated identities that are seen as outside the state and who represent the foreign, the stranger, as no one and therefore right-less (Felman, 2001; Grunenberg, 2002). Memory and metaphors represent two forms of this mediative function.

In the first instance, Arendt argues that the narrative imagination represents the social, symbolic and political elements of social life and that humans are in search of narrative by way of providing themselves with historical meaning systems to make sense of action in the present and future – thereby creating novel semantic and metaphorical understandings of otherness in the present. This idea is supported by Cavarero (2000), who identifies this practice as the narratability of the self. This form of narratability highlights the idea that all narratives are expressed and reconfigured as a temporal dimension of life as lived. It also represents a refiguring of the past – through images and metaphors – and in so doing a sense of newness within the world. This refiguration is what loosens identity's hold on an often essentialized sense of oneself and others.

A second Arendtian intervention relates to the idea of the narrative imagination as a political philosophy of *being* and *becoming through narration*. Here the imagination is important because a *philosophy and sociology of becoming* implies both a positive connection to the social world and, within the potentially negative realm of power relations, a place where identity cannot be claimed in the abstract, but is lived in the form of a contested, often regulated yet unfolding narrative. This feature of selfhood rests alongside the need for individuals and collectives to resolve ongoing conflicts – often operating as suffering, experiences of estrangement, questions about our legitimacy against those of others and the search for meaning – about why and how we have identified with particular images, signs and ideals of selfhood as they form part of the world. The narrative imagination is also relevant because the impasses invoked by many contesting positions on identity become, as Chanter (2001) suggests, more and more concerning as academics theorizing identity wage territorial war on each other about which category of identity is more or less significant at a time when understanding how we become someone can embrace the dual processes of reconfiguration and renewal – both historical and imagined. This territorial war is important to challenge in order to assert both responsibility beyond such classifications and the necessity of affiliating with others (some who we may not know or ever know) in deeply worrying political moments. Such moments may, for example, be characterized as spaces held hostage to rising and revitalized extreme populist practices, which include forms of tolerated violence and sectarian division not witnessed since before the rise of the modern state (e.g. Syria and Yemen). Highly restricted notions of identity are also accompanied by rising xenophobia within political and educational contexts where insecurity and risk about the other, the 'foreigner' and the stranger represent part of normative political discourse. In recognizing that subordinated identifications (e.g. the refugee) can be a substantive target of abuse in times of mass violence and growing populism, Arendt's concerns over state-sanctioned selves – inert selves unmediated by difference – point to the symbolic power of such hegemonic ideals built into the lexicon and symbolic universe of its very language. Here, for example, we might witness the erasure of political histories of genocide linked to identities that a totalitarian state may sanction, or the eradication of advances made by marginalized subjects who have sought intergenerational justice through an energized state apparatus purely through a belief in essential notions of citizenship. As the late Stuart Hall (1996: 4–5) writes:

> Above all, and directly contrary to the form in which they are constantly invoked, identities are constructed through, not outside, difference. This entails the radically disturbing recognition that it is only through the relation to the Other, the relation to what it is not, to precisely what it lacks, to what has been called its *constitutive outside* that the 'positive' meaning of any term – and thus its 'identity' – can be constructed [...] Throughout their careers, identities can function as points of identification and attachment only because of their capacity to exclude, to leave out, to render 'outside', abjected. Every identity has at its 'margin', an excess, something more. The unity, the internal homogeneity, which the term identity treats as foundational is not a natural, but a constructed form of closure, every identity naming as its necessary, even if silenced and unspoken other, that which it 'lacks'. Laclau (1990) argues powerfully and persuasively that 'the constitution of a social identity is an act of power'. (Original emphasis)

Hall's (1996) now seminal reflections on the limits and excesses of identity point to the need for more ethical understandings of narrativization, which embrace both processes of the fictional and the refigurative other; an unknown, often elusive, stranger to our own reproductive dimensions of identity. As Kristeva (1991), following Arendt and W.H. Auden, intimated in the title of her book *We are Strangers to Ourselves*, this kind of narrativization stands against what Arendt (HC) identified as a non-political condition where one is not recognizable to the world and expelled from it (see also Sassen, 2014), particularly when it is grounded in territorially bounded and nationalist notions of identity. As Arendt (cited in Young-Bruehl, 2004) writes: 'As long as mankind is nationally and territorially organized in states, a stateless person is not simply expelled from one country, native or adopted, but from all countries … which means he is actually expelled from humanity' (p. 285). While history, humanity and the imaginative elements of the narrative can never be the same, there is always a convergence between what is possible to understand as part of historical discourse – that distant other – and a refiguring of it within a human narrative through imaginative practices. Here we witness the capacity of the historical consciousness to 'stand in for the past' (see Kearney, 2003) and recall it in ways that highlight powerful refigurative narratives of empathy, temporal interdependence and what Arendt refers to as visiting the other (HC). In this way, there is no audible, tangible or explicit maker of the narrative because there can be no master of the narrative – rather it is kind of truth-telling exercise which is imaginative. This does not represent a denial of either a real or an unreal past, truthfulness or pure fiction. Rather, historical consciousness can only translate into historical responsibility when we are capable of imagining in unique ways how our own thinking and interdependence can be translated into a new and unanticipated perspective on a historical event, forcing us to energize the power of history and society, to visit other worlds and the future in new ways through surplus and overflowing meaning. This means we need to retrace the past and re-inscribe it into lived time. As Kearney (1995) tells us, this necessitates a reading of the past that is necessarily political in that we recognize all people have a right to a recognition of their past 'reminding us of our debt to those who have lived, suffered and died […] the gas ovens did exist, Nagasaki and Cambodia were bombed, show trials and gulags were inflicted on countless innocent people' (177).

This debt to the past is not insignificant in eradicating atrocities into the future. For example, in *Eichmann in Jerusalem* (EJ), Arendt reflects on the part played by the role of totalitarian and identitarian thinking in the making of essential national identities – naming Hitler's bureaucrats – as they sought to marginalize, decimate and diminish otherness during the Holocaust through a loss of belonging and selfhood: 'The refugees' condition can certainly be recounted only negatively. Their loss is absolute: 'We lost our home … We lost our occupation … We lost our language … We left our relatives … and our best friends have been killed in concentration camps' (LM1: 55–7). The only place such losses can dwell is in a zone of nowhere, a camp of living corpses, and in a state of abjection; their only visibility can be found in the memory of those who no longer exist. And in *The Origins of Totalitarianism* (OT) Arendt again describes the de-politicization of dark times as the loss of egalitarian frameworks for understanding selfhood because of the historical erasure of the speaking human subject. As Herzog (2004) reminds us, Arendt compares the political and right-less condition of stateless peoples with that of ancient slaves dwelling in the city who, despite their substantive subordination and dehumanization, were still affiliated to a relational community of belonging. Herzog (2004) goes on to argue that Arendt's work on the human experience of exile demonstrated that the development of the 'right-less' condition of stateless people, meaning the loss of political narrativization and its associated forms of recognition, came together as a consequence of two entwined processes: the rejection of a Jewish identification (a vilified essentialized identity made abject through ideology rather than narrativization) and many other 'strangers' to the German state, and the desire for the expansion of imperial powers through the eugenic creation of superior identities and associated hierarchical ordering schemes. The enormity of this condition of rightlessness, she tells us, lies in 'the deprivation of a place in the world' (EJ: 297) and the elimination of a poetics of imagination. Those individuals identified as 'stateless', as living in a zone of nowhere, are not given the right to express their own intergenerational narratives of selfhood and/or suffering.

What then are the implications of such a concern over the concept of identity within educational research, particularly when such narratives make reference to the past and desires for a future? The specific character of a historical reference to the past is that it functions to inscribe the temporality of a narrative within the context of a wider political universe, in which we must act, with education being a significant site of action. This historical reference to the past obliges us to see that an identity cannot be founded upon an individual operating outside of other political and historically defined narratives because to do so would lead to its depoliticization (e.g. education as administrative and bureaucratic, for example, research audits such as the Research Excellence Framework in the UK, testing and ranking), the replacement of the public world with an entirely governed and private self, and its rejection of language and symbols as part of such a universe. Rather, in narrating selfhood, the potentialities of narrativization challenge the immutability of both privately and bureaucratically defined notions of identity which are often time-limiting or forced upon a collective as part of state discourse (see Honig, 1988). However, if narrative, as a mobile action, can be equated with social freedom (not identity), it can move past individual motives to consider others whom we may have never, met but with whom we coexist within the polity and the world of education. This is why the self (not identity) as a 'soi' must appear as part of a world of appearances beyond motives through the will to act (Gardner 2010).

On the one hand, this reading of a narrative through time involves an act of translation such that one recognizes traces of a past narrative in operation in the present. An 'imaginative mediation operative' (Kearney, 1995: 178) is therefore inscribed into the 'polyvalent' character of the historical trace as a 'sign effect' and then moves towards a re-inscription into the body of the narrative through translation. This mediating function of the imagination, Kearney (1995) tells us, provides a pathway for recognizing a trace of the past and a mediated re-enactment of history, but it is this mediating function that also simultaneously allows us to see narrative anew. We may also sometimes recognize its mark on the body of persons and people as embodied forms of power. This recognition of the role of history and memory within a storied narrativization as a mark of power means that we can also witness and refigure otherness not only as a critique of 'normative sameness' (Kearney and Taylor, 2005) – seen as part of the legacy of imperial power formations – but as a way towards historical responsibility. We would, as Gardner (2010) and Samuel (1996) argue, be reminded, for example, that the British Empire invented the concept of the concentration camp, deploying it first during the Anglo-Boer war, that the Armenian genocide was indeed a genocide or that millions of Syrians are permanently displaced from a place they refer to as home. Here the poetics of a refigured otherness and recognized human injury necessarily provide the capacity for our historical responsibility to respect these historical narratives. Consequently, Kearney (1995) tells us that the imagination imposes itself upon a storied life as a necessary and unassailable interlocutor which provides a reimagining of this past as an ethical duty to the alterity of history. As Ricoeur (2004) and Arendt (HC, BF) each therefore suggest, this task can only be accomplished by way of expressing, through narrative and action, a moment that has come to pass. In this way, only the narrative imagination is able to resist difference from being subordinated into oblivion or masked by the identity management strategies of the state. It is through this transfer from normative sameness and subordinated selves to an account of another, with both critical empathy and imagined newness as our guide, that this 'stranger' or 'foreigner' to citizenship and legitimacy can move closer to us (see Ricoeur, 2004; Kearney, 1995, 1996, 2003). It is this very proximity and recognition – this recognition of our own estrangement from historical otherness – that the desire for democratic inclusion finds its most substantive and meaningful expression.

On the other hand, such actions also suggest that identity is not necessarily time or motive-bound or emblematic of the indistinctive 'homos' named by the Greeks, and later appropriated as identity. Rather, for Arendt (PP), the narrative imagination is grounded in a personae, as originally announced in classical times. Arendt (PP: 12–13) writes that

> persona, at any event originally referred to the actor's mask that covered his individual personal face and indicated to the spectator the role and the part of the actor. But in this mask, which was designed and determined by the play, there existed a broad opening at the place of the mouth [where] the undisguised voice of the actor could sound. It was from this sounding that the word persona was derived, the mask is the noun. […] Persona was somebody who possessed civil rights, in sharp distinction from the word homo, denoting someone who was

nothing but a member of the human species … without any specific qualification or distinctions, so that homo, like the Greek anthropos, was frequently used contemptuously to designate people not protected from the law … . They were identical to each other in the lack of distinctiveness.

As this latter argument suggests, narrating ourselves into the world presents an indefinable quality because the narratable self must necessarily reflect an otherness that cannot be 'seduced by the great temptation for recognition which, in no matter what form, can only recognize us as such and such, that is, as something we are fundamentally not' (PP:14).

The Implications of Arendt and Ricoeur for Education

Perhaps the first port of call when considering the role that Arendt (HC) and scholars such as Ricoeur (2004) might play in reconfiguring conceptualizations of identity in education are their accounts of the human condition as it lives through time and in public space through the concepts of metaphor, symbol and dramatic representation as a narrative and theatrical form. Within public space, Arendt acknowledges that humans are not static, time-bound or placeless, but instead represent a 'plurality of spectators' mediated by the overflowing, surplus effects of temporality, sociality and spatiality. Selfhood, the thinking and socially embedded self, therefore positions itself in a sometimes agonistic relation towards, or as a challenge to, a hegemonic vision of political selfhood (the 'we'), with similarly positioned others (semblance) in the state and education. Here Arendt opens out the analysis of public space to the concrete workings of an agonistic pluralism, drawing upon the tools of the historical imagination and historical responsibility, something that education sorely needs in the midst of conflict, growing authoritarianism and routinized and extreme forms of bureaucracy and as a responsibility to the world. This responsibility, and in particular historical responsibility, is significant as we witness the rise of regimes (both autocratic and far-right populist states) that seek to eradicate narration and the recognition of alterity as a moral obligation of education for citizenship. Importantly, too, Arendt places thinking – as an educational action – at the centre of narrativization because it resists wider political concerns about collective guilt and inertia, and non-action about who we ought to become as actors responsible for the past as well as the future (Herzog, 2004). Arendt castigates, for example, Eichmann, during the Holocaust, for non-action, alongside the routinized, highly nationalist, fascist and stagnant German education system of the time – both as a consequence of ideology and nation-building exercises – and argues that we need to take distance from bureaucratic laws and policies that confine narrative expressions to a dominant identity and non-thinking mindsets. Instead we must respond to the debt we owe to the past. For thinking ultimately implicates one in a plurality that cannot, and should not, be destroyed by punitive policies, narrow conceptions of citizenship or the wide acceptance of fixed ideals of identity that are often tied to rational education programmes or to forms of surveillance and monitoring that lead to the policing of difference as a narrative of fear and insecurity, serving as a putative model of the non-citizen subject (see Sassen, 2014). These include, for example, programmes such as Prevent, which over-determine the young Muslim male as the radical other in need of monitoring and surveillance (Yeung, 2019). In the following section, and as a final step in bridging the political aspects of educational theory to phenomenology, I move forward to detail the role of Arendt's and Ricoeur's thinking on history and memory in transcending the concept of identity.

Transcending Identity: Reviving the Self–Other Relationship through Memory and History

As Weir (1997) suggests, we bear the social and political obligation as part of human existence to engage in 'identity work'. We must, she suggests, 'struggle to resolve conflicts through an openness to difference' (188). However, in Arendtian terms, we cannot do this until we recognize that we are operating as embedded political subjects always and forever in the face of difference not only as a human endeavour deserving of recognition but also as a site for the carriage of history and memory. It is this obligation to memory and the struggle to resolve the conflicts it presents that forces us to reconcile our own practices of identification as ultimately social and necessarily ethical and political – and it is our human responses that ought to bring us closer to the 'other', the 'foreigner' and the stranger as something which we can recognize in ourselves (Kristeva, 1991).

As Paul Ricoeur (2004) and Hannah Arendt (PP) tells us, temporality, history and particularly memory are key foundations of the narrative imagination – that is, the stories that we construct of our lives and others and the sense we make of them through relational contexts. Importantly, memory is not a linear construction – as mainstream history aspires to be – and nor is identity. Moreover, memory work should not be constrained to seek to validate its claims by reference to evidence. Memory, as Gardner (2010) tells us, is rather an amalgamation of the factual, the half-forgotten and sometimes the entirely fictive. It may therefore present accounts that can be conceived as inaccurate but true (see Gardner, 2010). It is this very characteristic of narrative that also points to its social mediation with space, time and the social world as it lives in memory – as the political agent both actively constructing himself or herself within public space, at the same time as being constrained within the narrative as a representation of time. To explain this mediation means we must strive to reconstruct the relational contexts in which any kind of memorable 'identity' has unfolded. Aristotle's distinction between mneme (memory that comes unwittingly to mind – habits of mind – borne forward by) and anamnesis (that which separates us from animals with memory, that is, the active searching for something that happened in the past) seems particularly apposite here. Here actors with memory make decisions not to forget that which is beyond their own history. Yet remembering always also involves forgetting as well as the repetition of atrocity. The Vichy syndrome is only one such example but there are many others – we might, for example, remember what it was like to have been a young women during the Holocaust, but not the Armenian Massacres, Stalin's purges or the many dead ANC revolutionaries who were not commemorated after the end of Apartheid (see Dillabough and Dillabough-Lefebvre, 2018). Remembering is therefore a modality of power as well as of memory, and may take a variety of forms over time, and it is an educator's duty to confront these forms both as historical forces and as counter-narratives to authoritarian or nationalist conceptions of citizenship.

Additionally, we need to ask where we might situate the past and the unique role of history and memory in shaping narrative selfhood as part of the diverse plurality of actors within the field of education. Who would we be or who are we to become as realizable political actors without both the past and memory as we narrate ourselves into possible futures? We would be incapable of even imagining a hopeful educational future, as the most persuadable and ambitious heart would lose the capacity – as Arendt tells us – for drawing upon the past as a conceptual language for more responsible futures. Importantly then, our memories of the past operate with a sense of continuity and intergenerational justice (Sutoris, 2019); the relational model for memory is of our own recollection of our life as an interconnected 'bio-theoretikis' (see Caverero, 2000; Dillabough, 2016). This interconnectedness through memory provides new ways of imagining citizenship as a less bordered and more meaningful political concept through education. So the question of 'who' we think we are – as necessarily plural beings – is critical to our ability to engage ethically with others as an educational intervention. Perhaps this is where philosophy might meet history and sociology in challenging bureaucratic forms of education, Ardent's notion of administrative massacre and its identitarian and symbolically violent tropes in productive and generative ways. Kristeva (2001) writes:

> Who is a self that is hidden, but hidden more from the person than the multitude, or rather from the temporality of the memory of others. (25)

It is here – the disclosure of the self to the other – that we find meaning for there can be no action without a 'who'. As Cavarero (2000: xiii) writes: 'Indeed to presume [] that unique beings can become intelligible only through the critical category of the subject is part of a philosophical legacy which seeks to efface the unique, the particular.' She argues that uniqueness, the absolutely particular existence, has a meaning that is revealed through the narration of that person's life story, precisely insofar as the person is not already subjected to philosophical definition or to the circular paradox of subjection. Calhoun (2001) echoes this sentiment when he suggests that

> our whole approach to issues of large scale identity or difference has been informed by naturalist assumptions usually left tacit. To take categories of nation and people as the given of discourse (or merely regulated by it), without complicating them either by critical history or inattention to internal contradictions and possibly divergent futures, is a prime example of what Horkeimer and Adorno challenged as altogether affirmative discourse, that which affirms the present as all there could be (273).

Reading Social Recognition as Political Pedagogy

My own concerns about the absence of historical responsibility presented through the narrative imagination within education research, I believe, resonates with Hannah Arendt's emphasis on an engagement with 'acts of recognition', her belief in the idea of a 'plurality of public space', alongside Ricoeur's (2004) preoccupation with the unique 'interesse' and reconfiguration of selfhood that arises between the 'self' and 'other'. Arendt does not ask whether the category 'identity' should remain intact as a thing outside of narrative; rather she forces us to examine how it is that the category identity – as a particularly dominating force associated with the rise of the modern state – ever came into existence, how we recognize and misrecognize each other, the need to see authenticity as ethically meaningful and what might be the temporal significance of these practices, and the associated potential for rising conflict, violence and ultimately, where possible, peace-building. It is this struggle to recognize and engage with the authenticity of others that becomes ethically meaningful rather than identifying the stranger, the exiled and the stateless as constituting that which we are not:

> A characteristic of human action is that it always begins something anew. [...] Such change would be impossible if we could not mentally remove ourselves from where we are physically and imagine that things might as well be different from what they actually are. [...] They owe their existence to the same source: the imagination. [...] Without the mental freedom to deny or affirm existence, to say yes or no – not just to statements or propositions [] to express agreement or disagreement [...] no action would be possible and action, of course, is the stuff of politics. (CR: 5)

Similarly, as Benhabib (2003) suggests, we are both author and object of the tales we tell of ourselves. If our life stories can only be told by others, then 'identity' is only a noun without action. If we relish telling our own life story, at the expense of others, and from our isolated perspectives, then we have failed to narrate ourselves into worlds of difference and solidarity, and we have failed to reach beyond individual narcissism. Education ought not to be about narcissism and complicity. However, as long as it is bureaucratized in the name of endless and perilous competition, and human monitoring at the expense of the narrative imagination, then we are at risk of remaining in the world alone. As Alexander (2015) and Simon (2000) tell us, the most powerful and meaningful dimensions of education are interventions that move us beyond ourselves precisely for the sake of others, and in the name of others, including those we will perhaps never meet or ever know. Here, education becomes a medium for addressing Arendt's greatest concern – that is, to privilege action over the actor. As Honig (1988) argues, if identity is anything at all it is the outcome of the constellation of an active and moving life story and therefore the product of action. Education is in need of that storied self – in all its multiplicities and contestations – if it is to survive as a vibrant political space where 'theatres of justice' (see Felman, 2001) can rest at the centre of democratic education rather than standing as divided sites of proliferating advantage and disadvantage achieved in the name of identity but at the expense of a plural polis in search of meaning and action.

5

Thinking Politically with Arendt: Depoliticized Privatism and Education Policy

Helen M. Gunter

Introduction

Arendt is very clear that in a post-Holocaust world, the social sciences and social scientists may remain 'trapped by their own ideas' (EU: 11), and so be unable to confront dangerous trends in politics. In this chapter, I would like to use Arendt's thinking in order to understand contemporary education policy rather than accept and implement categories about human beings. The provocation into thinking otherwise is generally seen by her readership as revelatory, whereas Canovan (1995) argues Arendt had a 'habit of following trains of thought' (138), and so when seeking to understand an issue she 'sets off, then, to think "without a banister" to hold on to, reflecting freely upon events' (6). Such an approach gives confidence to challenge the ordinariness in which the disposability of humans happens and is enabled in Arendtian terms by the crystallization of totalitarian conditions. The break in tradition through the Holocaust means that we can no longer hold onto 'givens' and 'assumptions' as fixed and true. In other words, there is a need to dispense with the methodological security of a social science handrail, and instead we need to take risks with how we think about what is unfolding in plain sight. As Judt (2009) notes, 'Arendt was at her best in short bursts, when she was commenting, appraising, critiquing, or merely thinking out loud on some issue of contemporary significance' (84), and so I intend following this approach.

The issue I examine is the segregation of children as proactive education policy by the UK government for the provision of schools in England, and in particular I focus on the various ways in which biological determinism and eugenics impacts policy strategy and tactics. I begin by examining Arendt's characterization of 'The Crisis in Education' (BF), and I take this as a starting point for arguing that what is currently unfolding is actually a catastrophe that is being enabled through governing by depoliticized privatism. I illustrate this by focusing on the endurance of intelligence testing and grammar schools in England, where I identify the dangers emerging regarding the idea and practices of politics, and how Arendtian scholarship provides a novel way of thinking anew.

Crisis in Education?

For Arendt 'The Crisis in Education' was the failure of adults to assume authority and exercise responsibilities on behalf of and in relation to children – either as teachers (BF) or as citizens (RJ). Arendt argued that far too often children are required to sort out adult problems – whether this was going to a particular school in regard to the desegregation reforms (RJ), or the learning process once in school in regard to the role of children in the design and experience of progressive learning (BF). Arendt encapsulates her position:

> And education, too, is where we decide whether we love our children enough not to expel them from our world and leave them to their own devices, not to strike from their hands their chance of undertaking something new, something unforeseen by us, but to prepare them in advance for the task of renewing a common world. (BF: 193)

Unpacking this statement through deploying Arendtian thinking in *The Human Condition* (HC) regarding 'action', 'natality' and 'plurality' enables understandings about the purposes of education to be developed further.

Arendt argues that action is distinct from labour and work (HC). What she means is that labour is about securing the necessities of life (e.g. food) that are consumed immediately, and work is about crafting outcomes (e.g. an artefact) that can outlast the mortality of the producer. While labour and work are vital, it is action through talking and doing in relationship with others that enables the human to be in the world and to understand the world, and through 'natality' and 'plurality' have the 'chance' to be in the public realm. For Arendt, natality matters because when we are born, the entry of a new life into the world means that there is the capacity to spontaneously undertake 'something new, something unforeseen by us' (BF: 193). Interplayed with this is Arendt's idea of plurality, or how we all share the condition of humanity but we are all unique, where the fact of plurality means there is an infinite variety of people who share 'the task of renewing a common world' (BF: 193).

Arendt published her main essay on education in 1954 (BF), and if she was alive today, she would no doubt be provoked into writing again. Her argument at the time was that teachers did not assume sufficient authority and responsibility for education, whereby action is underpinned by plurality and natality. While Arendt argued that the 'crisis' was that teachers abdicated their authority, the current 'crisis' is premised on teachers having *too much* authority over teaching and learning (see Gewirtz, 2002; Ravitch, 2010). Notably right-wing and libertarian researchers and commentators argue in very influential ways that the provision of education to enable a 'common world' (BF: 193) to be renewed actually denies parents and children from their entitlement to exercise choice (see Friedman, 2002). Here 'crisis' is treated differently to Arendt's analysis, as it is now being used as a political tool to justify major reforms that are actually doing damage to teachers and so to children's chances. The impact of these arguments on policy ideas, strategies and enactments means that the 'common world' is different to what Arendt envisaged, and is in effect a 'school-place-shopping mall', with vendors offering education products, where parents and children as consumers experience commodified forms of plurality and natality through notions of 'aspiration', 'diversity' and 'needs'.

Based on independent primary research (e.g. Gunter, 2011, 2012, 2014, 2016, 2018; Gunter and Mills, 2017) I argue that these reforms mean, in Arendtian terms, that children continue to be the object of adult plans regarding major interventions into the purposes and structures of schooling. There is a 'catastrophe' unfolding in public services education where schools and teachers are being taken away from families and children, and where the Arendtian 'common world' is being reduced to notions of security and popularized nationalism. Even those who are deemed to be advantaged by having the private resources necessary to purchase a 'good school place' are in effect losing out as they are living and studying within a segregated system that prevents them from learning across economic, gender, class and race borders. There are accounts of the changes in other national and globalizing contests (e.g. Au and Ferrare 2015; Ravitch 2014; Seppänen et al., 2015; Verger et al., 2016), and here I outline what is happening in England.

UK government education policy in England is premised on the construction of crisis-induced solution imperatives, designed to fracture 'in concert' action as professionals and within communities (OV). From the 1970s onwards, there has been a policy strategy focused on denying and removing provision of education for all, and in particular through attacks on the establishment of and outcomes from the 'common school' within a community at primary (aged five to eleven) and secondary (aged eleven-sixteen) levels. While major reforms from the 1940s onwards have focused on providing universal, local and inclusive provision for all 'in common' with each other, there is no settlement. and gains remain fragile. Successive UK governments from Thatcher onwards (took office in 1979) have enacted policies that are in effect a restoration project regarding the necessity and normality of the 'uncommon school': first, payment for schooling from 'private providers' remains elitist at 7 per cent of the population and is informing the idea and reality of vouchers so that those without the necessary income to pay full fees can engage in faux choice processes (see Feintuck and Stevens, 2013); second, biological deterministic binary is used to produce 'boy' and 'girl' only schools in ways that are resistant to research evidence (see Rivers and Barnett, 2011); third, parental faith is used to categorize children with 37 per cent of primary and 19 per cent of secondary schools determined by faith (the number is increasing), where the curriculum, pedagogy, workforce composition and admissions are variously structured in regard to private beliefs (Long and Bolton, 2017); fourth, intelligence selection is based on an examination at the age of eleven (called eleven-plus) where children are divided into 'grammar' schools (currently 164 are left in thirty-six local authorities in England) with an academic education, and 'secondary modern' schools with a vocational education (Gunter, 2017); and fifth, children are 'home schooled' where parents make private provision to educate their children either by themselves and/or tutors (Ball, 2017; Batty, 2018). While school places cannot legally be offered on the basis of race and class, the operation of 'choice' impacts on school mix, where there are clear class and racial divides in regard to achievement (Gillborn et al., 2017; Gov.uk, 2017).

Reforms have led to changes in the supply and demand process for school places, where the supply has shifted from a focus on public provision to that of marketized segmentation, and demand from access to the local school to notions of choice and preferences. In England, there are now between seventy and ninety different types of schools (Courtney, 2015) where parents are offered a 'choice' in regard to fees or no fees, religious or secular, intelligence testing or mixed ability, or accessing school products or not. Parents with resources can make a choice (e.g. to pay fees in the private sector, or to home school or to pay for private tutoring ready for the eleven-plus examination), but those who depend on the public system are enabled to exercise a preference in regard to their first-choice school with back-ups if they are not allocated a place (but also depending on parental resources in relation to housing costs near popular schools, and/or travel costs to reach schools).

Integral to these changes is the redesign and re-culturation of the teacher into assimilated 'parvenu' (RV) who deliver performance data that is deemed to prove the vitality and legitimacy of segregation. This change is historically embedded. From the 1970s onwards, the 'crisis' in school 'common' provision has been constructed through attacks on the teaching profession. Major reforms from the 1940s onwards have secured a graduate, trained and accredited profession, with national transparent terms and conditions of service, and with a focus on developing the curriculum, pedagogy and assessment separate from parental and elite resources. However, successive UK governments have underpinned reforms with negative claims regarding the teaching profession as first, self-serving, resistant to change and unaccountable; second, disrespecting the demands of parents regarding the curriculum, assessment and pedagogy; third, lacking in the efficiency and effectiveness of business delivery and outcomes; fourth, protecting status based on forms of esoteric 'professional' knowledge, even though everyone knows 'what works' and so there is no need for special training and accreditation; and fifth, failing children, parents and employers because standards are not world class, and in a globalizing economy, children are lacking in basic skills.

The reforms have led to changes in the composition and identities of the profession, with a shift from the educational professional who exercises judgement in regard to purposes and practices to that of the workforce delivery operative who is controlled by national regulation and branded school employer. The composition, identity and practices of the profession has been 'reprofessionalized' through the adoption of delivery-by-template; allowing the appointment of non-accredited people to teach and assess children; the purchase of learning packages where outcomes are to be supplied to the consumer; and the measurement of performance through test data, performance evaluation and contractual renewal (or termination). A range of corporatized developments are taking place in order to enable this workforce to work within schools as businesses: first, the focus is on corporate leadership including the practices necessary for the running of a business in a highly competitive supply and demand market, and so education is a product to be traded rather than a developmental learning process; and second, the shortfall in people applying for teaching posts has been dealt with through schools being enabled to appoint who they wish to teach, and through schemes such as *Teach First* where people who aspire to and are destined to take up careers in the city or high-flying professions do teaching before they move on.

In summary, the language used is about the new freedoms invested in 'choice', but primary research shows that schools actually choose children (and parents) through access criteria (income, religion, and sex), and schools employ people to teach who fit with and enhance the school brand. Parents use their family and networked resources (financial, educational and cultural) in order to pass on their advantages and to gain further in the market, and so diversity is a fabricated veil that covers and protects the endurance of elite control (see Gunter et al., 2017). The devastation to the public services school landscape is evident in a range of evidence: first, the introduction of markets to teacher training is not producing sufficient applicants (Richardson, 2017), and the corporatization of school leadership is legitimizing the disposability of trained teachers from schools if they are deemed not to fit the brand vision (Courtney and Gunter, 2015); second, new schools can be opened and they can close, leaving parents and children without a choice, and where those parents who are savvy in how they operate can manage risks and know how to use their resources to gain and retain a good school place for their child (Gunter, 2018); third, the supply of schools is increasingly controlled by private interests (faith, philanthropy and business) who are concerned to design and manage the curriculum and pedagogy in order to protect and further those interests (Gunter, 2011).

This is more than a crisis in education, but is a calamity for the human condition. Based on the earlier quotation from Arendt's summation of how we need to think and do differently about education (BF:193), I presume to scope a new version that encapsulates the consumer in the education market place:

> And education, too, is where I decide that I love my children enough not to expel them from the education I want for them, not to strike from their hands their chance of undertaking an education that will prepare them for the world that I want for them, and so prepare them in advance for the task of renewing our private world.

This generates some clear implications for action, where there may well be busy activity in the home and the school, but the reforms outlined actually deny action and is in effect generating a form of 'consumer authorized inaction' where the teacher, the student and the parent are rendered producers of the right type of data necessary for the school to operate in the market place. This has consequences for plurality, where the espoused diversity of choice is in effect a form of 'rhetorical plurality' where parents engage in fabricated choice opportunities that mimic elites, but cannot enter or compete in their world. In addition, it seems that action is limited by a form of 'regulated natality' where only certain children are deemed worthy of doing new things, and where segregation limits aspirations and achievements (Gunter, 2018).

If Arendt was alive today, she would be writing less about teachers failing to exercise authority and would be more concerned about the colonization of public education by markets where authority is located with especial entrepreneurs from faith groups, businesses and charities. In this sense, she may well update her statement in the following suggested way:

> And education, too, is where we decide whether we love all children enough to provide publicly funded 'in common' schools and teachers, not to strike from their hands their chance of undertaking something new, something unforeseen by us, but to prepare them in advance for the task of renewing a common world.

Unpacking this reworking of Arendt's thinking about education and the human condition helps with the identification and problematization of the unfolding tragedy in homes and local communities. Importantly, there is a need to locate thinking about education with thinking politically about and for education, and it is to this that I now turn.

Crisis in Thinking Politically?

The catastrophe unfolding in public services education is located in a wider upheaval and devastation to politics and the public realm. The UK, like other Western-style democracies, has adopted governing by depoliticization (Gunter, 2018) where the dominant strategy is privatism. Following Burnham (2001), what is unfolding is '*the process of placing at one remove the political character of decision-making*' (128, original emphasis). This relocation to 'out of the public eye' decision arenas enables privatism to dominate, not only in terms of 'selling off' public assets but also in rendering what is political as a private matter. Table 1 outlines the key features:

Table 1 Depoliticized Privatism

Depoliticization	Privatism
Government	Privy
Social	Privatization
Discursive	Private

Following Wood and Flinders (2014: 165), I am adopting the three approaches to depoliticization and interconnecting it with privatism:

Government depoliticization: Issues are transferred through delegation from the politician to arms-length bodies that have a codified remit with technical accountability. In education, we have witnessed the National College for School Leadership for national training of professionals as corporate leaders, and the provision of schools includes the Baker Dearing Trust, the Studio Schools Trust and the Future Leaders Trust. What was once public (e.g. debates in parliament, on the minister's desk for decision-making) is now a privy matter to be led and managed by people in external organizations who promote their interests, and where the use of contracts means that decision-making is about technical delivery rather than questions of equity.

Societal depoliticization: Issues are transferred from the public to the private domain or the privatization of the individual (and within personal networks such as family). So access to a school is based on parental choice and application, where private income is used to support entry into a school catchment or zone, to enable additional tutoring and/or to use private faith. Issues that were once on a public agenda (e.g. a local government committee regarding planning for school places) are now ones for private decision-making in regard to personal resources, claims and plans, with a 'shift towards individualized responses to collective social challenges' (Wood and Flinders, 2014: 165).

Discursive depoliticization: Issues are transferred from the privatized individual to the private in the sense of not existing, except as 'as elements of fate' where 'things just happen' (Wood and Flinders, 2014: 165). Issues of school exclusion rates (and what this means for equity) are no longer important in regard to entitlement to an education, but only matter if this impacts in ways that are recognized. For example, parents challenged St Olave's grammar school for preventing sixteen children from moving to the final year of A level study (qualifications necessary for university entry) on the basis that they did not obtain high enough grades in the AS level examinations. It seems that the school was protecting its pass rates and league table position, and only 'backed down' when protests equally threatened its reputation (Weale, 2017). This case also brought other stories of 'off-rolling' (or removing children in order to protect performance branding, Savage, 2017) from different areas of England where this practice had been prevalent, but all of a sudden was recognized as a 'political' matter through parental protest (Marsh et al., 2017). An issue is only a problem if there is a 'happening' and is not worthy of deliberation and decision-making unless that event is brought to public attention.

As Starr (1988) argues, privatization is complex package of interventions into service provision based on letting public services run down through to allowing and financing private providers, and selling off and transferring public assets, where education is one service in England where the public are learning to be and do private. But privatism is more than this; it is about the 'private' in privatization or how the public has had to learn very quickly to insure against risks that previously were pooled and protected with fellow humans through the state and taxation (Peters, 2017), and so following Chandler and Reid (2016), the public have had to learn to adapt and be resilient. The subjectivity of humans is being controlled in ways that are dangerous for the individual as well as wider humanity, where new freedoms are actually insidious controls through 'populism' (see Geiselberger, 2017).

A useful example to illustrate these trends from UK education policy in England is a product of 'pearl diving' in the Arendtian sense (MD), where I take inspiration from her argument that our thinking can be enabled not by excavating the past, but 'to pry loose the rich and the strange' as 'thought fragments' (MD: 205) that can be surfaced for investigation. I intend diving into contemporary policy history and bringing to the surface the proactive segregation of children through intelligence testing as a 'new crystallized forms and shapes that remain immune to the elements' (MD: 206). While primary schools (five to eleven years of age) have traditionally been accepted as 'in-common', secondary education from the age of eleven has only been 'comprehensive' from the 1950s onwards, where a combination of local and national policy interventions brought about the end of the eleven-plus intelligence test in most of the country. So instead of children being divided into an academic curriculum in the grammar school or a vocational and domestic curriculum in the secondary modern school, all children would go to the same school. This change was located in a range of evidence: first, success in the eleven-plus was linked to the socioeconomic status of the family (children of working-class families were and are more likely to 'fail') and sex (more boys failed than girls but in order to ensure parity in the school composition the pass level was differentially adjusted to allow boys to 'pass' and girls to 'fail') (see Jackson and Marsden, 1962); second, the eleven-plus itself is based on flawed notions of intelligence, biological determinism and fraudulent data (Chitty, 2007; Rose et al., 1984); and third, grammar schools did not always produce the academic outcomes that were expected for the children who attended them, and secondary modern schools had to change the curriculum in order to meet the academic needs of their students (Jackson and Marsden, 1962; Taylor, 1963).

The introduction of the comprehensive secondary school has been successful (see Benn and Chitty, 1997), but ongoing resistance means that the eleven-plus remains in some parts of England, and with plans by recent Conservative governments (2015–2017, 2017 onwards) to expand this type of provision. In taking office in 2016, Theresa May initiated a policy move to repeal legislation preventing new grammar schools from opening; however, following the loss of her majority in the House of Commons in 2017 it seemed that this strategy was put on hold, with the focus now on the expansion of existing grammar schools (Busby, 2018). The original arguments that challenge eleven-plus segregation remain in play, but in addition are biographical claims as well as primary independent research evidence that demonstrate the impact of segregation on the education and outcomes for all children in areas that retain the eleven-plus. As Sibieta (2016) states: 'There is robust evidence that attending a grammar school is good for the attainment and later earnings of those who get in. But there is equally good evidence that those in selective areas who don't pass the eleven plus do worse than they would have done in a comprehensive system' (18). Importantly opposition to the protection, development and expansion of the eleven-plus cuts across traditional political divides, where claims to have improved the test have been refuted (Gunter, 2017).

What this case illuminates are the workings of depoliticized privatism par excellence. While the direct involvement of the prime minister in the revitalization of the grammar schools suggests government repoliticization, in effect, it is essentially a populist move to render education a private matter. Her leadership of this issue is located in the biographies of those who have benefited, where at Prime Ministers Question Time in the House of Commons, she reminded the Leader of the Opposition:

> We want to ensure that children have the ability to go where their talents take them. I gently remind the right hon. Gentleman that he went to a grammar school and I went to a grammar school, and it is what got us to where we are today. (May, 2016, unpaged)

While substantial and significant research findings challenge the eleven-plus, it seems that policy is actually resistant to such evidence (Gorard, 2018), where major investment is planned based on one person making claims for the self and 'people like me'. Populist claims are framed as inclusive (all parents and children can potentially benefit), but it is actually exclusionary where the education of children who fail the eleven-plus is left to the fate of discursive 'fateful' recognition.

How might this be read through Arendtian scholarship? At face value, it could be that the traditional conflation of politics with systems of rule (institutions, political parties and elected representatives) is a problem that could be solved by depoliticization. Indeed, Arendt did worry about sovereignty:

> The most obvious salvation from the dangers of plurality is mon-archy, or one-man-rule, in its many varieties, from outright tyranny of one against all to benevolent despotism and to those forms of democracy in which the many form a collective body so that the people 'is many in one' and constitute themselves as a 'monarch'. (HC: 220–221)

Consequently, a convincing argument could be made that Arendt would be in favour of depoliticization, but only through the politicization of the public realm. For Arendt, politics is not the property of a human or the especial job of a professional politician in a public institution, but rather 'politics arises *between men*, and so is quite *outside* of man' (PP: 95, original emphasis). While humans think and imagine ideas and arguments in private, it is the taking of action through entering the public realm that matters because 'politics arises in what lies *between men* and is established as relationships' (PP: 95, original emphasis). This approach to politics is rooted in plurality and natality, and it means that storytelling-exchanges are based on the formation of standpoints, where humans set out to present the self, to understand what others think, and while we may disagree with one another, decisions are based on comprehending the realities of issues, evidence and opinions.

UK government's active support for grammar schools in England is based on a standpoint from a person who holds the highest executive office, that is presented as populist and is in effect a wonderful example of what Arendt (CR) identified as 'lying in politics'. Such planned deception glosses fabricated arguments and evidence, and may well ignore or even expose the fragility of facts that can never be absolute truths for and about a social matter. The renewal of the grammar school is consistent with depoliticized privatism in the commodification of school types, where at least 70 per cent of children are excluded.

Thinking with Arendt in regard to current education policy through a focus on the grammar school question generates understandings about why Arendtian depoliticized politicization is absent. Importantly, while much primary research is focused on governmental depoliticization through the relocation of public issues to the privy work of elite interests, enabled by templates and contracted deliverers, there is a need to examine the complexities emerging through the militancy underpinning the ongoing the advocacy and realization of school supply and demand processes. Contrary to claims, a place at a grammar school cannot be chosen by a parent, as the school chooses the child through the use of a test (and potentially biology and faith), but the fabrication of this choice opportunity remains and connects into wider notions of freedom located in the 'possessive individual' (Macpherson, 2011). The human can self-determine who they are and what they achieve unencumbered by others within civil society or through public institutions, and so certain parents can make peripheral but effective choices through paying for private tutoring for the eleven-plus. When combined with eugenics then the right to choose in effect conflates human with civil rights, because 'my' child has inherited talent that must be recognized, liberated and educated separately from those who have been born differently. Modernization of these ideas is taking place through the appropriation of neuroscience as a form of socio-technological determination of the human, where the answers to the human condition lie *a priori* in the brain (Rose and Abi-Rached, 2013).

Biological determinism is seductive because it categorizes children before they are born (through sex, class, race and religion), where entitlement to a suitable education means that elite interests dominate through the great public schools (that are private), and those who cannot access due to lack of economic, social and cultural capitals are able to be socially mobile by gaining access to a form of distinction through the grammar schools. The endurance of eugenics and the popularity of social mobility is founded on the lies that deny the educability of all children and is in Chitty's (2007) terms an established fear of mass education. The causal connection between poverty and intelligence remains a vibrant claim, where Toby Young (2015) has identified 'teenage pregnancy, criminality, drug abuse, ill-health' as 'poisonous heirlooms' that are passed on from one generation to the next (15). While his claims have been refuted (see Feinstein, 2017), he continues to argue for 'progressive eugenics' for 'parents with low incomes with below-average IQs' (Young, 2015: 14), and these ideas are resilient within policy design and rationales (Chitty, 2007).

While all children can be educated and can benefit from education, as the success and potential of comprehensive education in England (see Fielding and Moss, 2011) and elsewhere (e.g. Finland, Sahlberg, 2015) show, it is the impact of the fear by elites that other people's children may do better than one's own that is fuelling depoliticized privatism (see Gunter et al., 2017). Arendt's conceptualization of politics is challenging to such a position, particularly because her thinking exposes the limitations of right-wing agentic notions involved in freedom to choose (e.g. Friedman, 2002). Importantly she argued that 'freedom exists only in the unique intermediary space of politics' (PP: 95), and so autonomy is not about owning freedom independently of other humans or possessing moral qualities that set one human or group of humans as superior to others. As Biesta (2010) argues, 'instead of thinking that it is morality that makes politics possible, Arendt suggests that it is political existence that makes morality possible' (568). In other words, we have to seek to understand in order to agree, and so what Arendt's thinking does is at least two things: First, it demonstrates how autonomy is created within and for the public realm, and through depoliticized privatism this conceptualization is under attack, where 'the resilient subject is one that has been taught, and accepted, the lessons concerning the danger of autonomy and the need to be "capacity-built" in order to make the "right choices" in development of sustained responses to threats and dangers posed by its environment' (Chandler and Reid, 2016: 1). Second, Arendt's ideas create the conditions in which there is an alternative to the false liberation narrative embedded in the privatism necessary for education to 'work better'. The failure to consider this possibility brings my analysis to a very dangerous moment, particularly how the ordinariness and acceptance of the claims for what Dorling (2011) calls 'apartheid schooling' (55) is not only deeply shocking but also challenges the maturity of the political culture necessary to sustain democratic ideas and practices.

The consequences of governing by depoliticization through privatism is that the idea and reality of politics is being degraded to the extent that established institutions, public office holders (politicians and officials), and the political cultures and practices necessary to sustain them, are under attack from forms of 'anti-politics' (Stoker, 2017). Notably the consumer trumps the citizen, experts are denounced in favour of assertion and sound bites, and democracy is characterized as an expensive and cumbersome waste because the corporate model and actor instinctively knows what matters and how to do deals. As Stoker (2017) argues, there is too much 'fast thinking in politics', and what Arendt does is to provide a rationale and process for slowing down.

The case could be made that the claims about the scrabble for a good school place is chaotic and of concern, but is hardly a catastrophe. However, the trends that are evident within depoliticized privatism signal the potential for a complete breakdown of civil society that Arendt identified through her analysis of totalitarianism (see Gunter, 2014, 2018). Arendt (OT) identified that the conditions for totalitarianism are with us all the time, but it is the crystallization of those conditions where the danger lies. The reform of education as illuminated by the grammar school case is premised on the disposability of children, families and teachers, or how the majority are rejected and rendered unworthy of being educated in the same way as those 'proved' to be talented and precious. A fictitious world of all children being expertly measured and allocated the right school place to meet their needs is narrated and enabled through investment of words and deeds, and legitimized through normative claims about what is right and proper. Importantly, Arendt identified propaganda as a form of 'traditionally accepted mysteries' (OT: 351), where the eugenics underpinning the segregation of children in England is not named as eugenics, but 'what convinces masses are not facts, and not even invented facts, but only the consistency of the system of which they are presumably a part' (351). In other words, the categorization, the sorting of people into hierarchies and the acceptance that 'I am' better or worse than 'you' is so normalized through the structuring and shaping of biology, class, gender, age, sexuality and race that the claims about parental choice makes sense. There is literally no alternative. Indeed, terror works by making thinking otherwise and taking action in the public realm absurd. What Arendt (EJ) identified as the banality of thoughtlessness is evident in how those who design and manage school admissions tend to focus on making the system work effectively and efficiently as distinct from considering core purposes and universal access.

Arendt (OT) reminds readers that the crystallization of totalitarian conditions into totalitarianism is not inevitable. Researchers in the social sciences do recognize that within education there are alternatives to depoliticized privatism, with evidence of contestation that suggests possibilities for depoliticized politicization (Gunter, 2018). What is helpful about Arendtian scholarship made evident in her essays and talks is that as researchers, we are encouraged 'to remake the world rather than to remake the human' (Chander and Reid, 2016: 168). Consequently, our job as social science researchers is not to look for the rationality in the segregation and disposability of children within education, but to challenge the attack on humanity, and how this requires us to think and take action politically.

6

Hannah Arendt, Education and the Refugee Crisis: Natality, Compensatory Education and Assimilation

Wayne Veck

Introduction

The final sentence of Arendt's 1943 essay, *We Refugees*, reads: 'The comity of European peoples went to pieces when, and because, it allowed its weakest member to be excluded and persecuted' (JW: 247). Over seventy-five years on, we face another crisis of forced migration on a massive scale. What, if anything, is the role of education and educators in ensuring that the people of Europe and beyond do not once again allow their shared, higher ideals to fall to pieces? How, in short, are educators to respond to the refugee crisis? How we answer these questions turns precisely on our understanding of what it means to be an educator and a refugee, along with what it means to live in the midst of a crisis.

In 1954, Arendt wrote another essay about a crisis; this time she attended to 'the crisis in education' and, in particular, within American schooling. A crisis, Arendt notes in this essay, need not become a disaster. Indeed, latent in every crisis is 'the opportunity, provided by the very fact of crisis … to explore and inquire into whatever has been laid bare of the essence of the matter' (BF: 174). The essence of the refugee crisis is mass displacement. It is the fact that we now live in a world where sixty-eight-and-a-half million people have been forced to leave the place they were born to confront a new reality of either internal or external displacement and where some ten million stateless people live without a nationality and thus with no access to education, healthcare or employment (UNHCR, 2018).

Divided into two sections, this chapter examines the education of displaced children as an activity that aims at the realization of their newness within the world. In the first section of the chapter, the difficultly of responding to the newness of displaced children is set within the context of Arendt's (OT) recognition of the condition of statelessness as the deprivation not of certain rights, but of the very possibility of having rights. The second section of the chapter examines Arendt's account of the assimilation of German Jews as they sort refuge from the Nazis. In contradistinction to such assimilation, and the loneliness it creates within individuals, there is the thinking process, the mental activity that, as Arendt (LM1) understood, involves a 'withdrawal' from the world. Contained within Arendt's insights into this process there are profound implications for the type of schooling that allows displaced children the time and space they need to be with themselves in a thinking dialogue that might enroot them in the world. It is the task of the second section of this chapter to cast light on these implications and, in so doing, illuminate ways of including displaced children in schools that bypass 'official proclamations of hospitality and goodwill' (JW: 270–71).

Natality and the Education of Displaced Children

The significance of the exclusion of displaced children in relation to schooling has been emphasized by the organization *Save the Children* (2016a), which reports that 50 per cent of the world's primary school-aged refugee children and 75 per cent of secondary school-aged refugee children are absent from education[1]. Much has been written about the disrupted education experiences of displaced children (Avery, 2017; Macdonald, 2017), and of the difficulties they encounter when learning a second language (Bajaj and Suresh, 2018; Rumsey et al., 2018). More still has been said about the experience of trauma and mental health difficulties experienced by displaced children (See: Avery, 2017; Bajaj and Suresh, 2018; Block et al., 2014; Due, Riggs and Augoustinos, 2016; Gormez et al., 2017; Macdonald, 2017; Richardson with MacEwen and Naylor, 2018; Rumsey et al., 2018). To counter such difficulties 'targeted interventions' have been proposed (Block et al., 2014: 1339) along with 'specialist support and care' (Macdonald, 2017: 1183), and 'effective approaches to teaching' (Due, Riggs and Augoustinos, 2016: 1). It is the central connection of this chapter that while such accounts direct attention to significant aspects of the experience of

---

[1] Tanya Steele (cited in Save the Children, 2016b), Interim CEO of *Save the Children*, notes that this exclusion is persistent, pointing out that 'millions of children and young people will miss out on some – if not all – of their education'.

displaced children, they cannot and do not amount to an *educational* response to the refugee crisis.

Each of these responses emerge from the same compensatory view of the schooling, and this means that while they can throw some light on some crucial issues faced by displaced children, they offer little to the elucidation of how education might protect, respond to and guide the newness of these young people and thereby help prevent the current crisis of mass displacement from becoming a disaster. If, as Arendt (BF: 174) observes, every 'crisis forces us back to the questions themselves', then this crisis of mass displacement requires educators to return anew to the question of what demands our most serious attention in education. Arendt is adamant that 'the essence of education is natality, the fact that human beings are *born* into the world' (original emphasis, BF: 174). What prompts this return to the question of education's essence in relation to the refugee crisis is the fact that uprooted and displaced young people are newcomers, not in one but in two senses. These children are new to the world and new to the condition of displacement. In other words, for displaced children, the world is simultaneously too much and too little with them: the same world that has impressed upon them its terrors and brutalities has now turned its back on them, indifferent to their plight and potential. This twofold newness raises significant questions of education and of the responsibility of educators. Perhaps there is no question more pressing among them than that of how adults are to understand and respond to newness of displaced young people.

Arendt insists that education brings together the vibrancy of the human world with 'the human condition of natality', since 'the new beginning inherent in birth can make itself felt in the world only because the newcomer possesses the capacity of beginning something anew, that is, of acting' (HC: 9). The capacity to begin, does not, however, necessarily result in the actualization of newness in speech and action in the world. Between the capacity to speak and the life of speech, where words inform, alter and inspire viewpoints, there is the spectator, the person who listens and then produces an account of what they have heard. Between the potential to act and the life of action, there is this same person, witnessing, recording and then judging what they have witnessed. It is precisely 'the situation of people deprived of human rights', the stateless, however, that they are, as Arendt (OT: 296) observes in her seminal *The Origins of Totalitarianism*, 'deprived, not of the right to freedom, but of the right to action; not of the right to think whatever they please, but of the right to opinion'. The right to freedom does not, in other words, guarantee the presence of persons capable and willing to respond to one's actions; the right to think freely does not ensure the company of listeners, willing to validate one's thoughts and thereby endow them with the status of an opinion. Thus, the stateless are devoid of what Arendt identifies as fundamental: 'a right to have rights', which is the right 'to live in a framework where one is judged by one's actions and opinions' along with 'a right to belong to some kind of organized community' (OT: 296–97). Living outside of a community where persons act and give witness to action, one can formulate words and envision deeds, but one does so knowing that no judgement of any kind awaits them.

In a lecture given at Berkeley in 1955, Arendt observed that uprooted and stateless persons, living without the protection of a community and with no legal status, 'fall into a void' (S: unpaged). 'What is unprecedented', Arendt (OT: 293) later observed of stateless persons living in the twentieth century, 'is not the loss of a home but the impossibility of finding a new one'. This loss, and the accompanying descent into a 'void', equates to something more than the fact that stateless people occupy a non-place, beyond the home they once knew and the home they now long for. This is a void perpetually suspended between a future one can invest hope in and a past where one might remember and, in this act of remembrance, locate one's roots. To be displaced now is to be uprooted with nowhere at all to enroot. This means that the belief, expressed with such confidence at the end of the eighteenth century, 'that rights spring immediately from the "nature" of man' (OT: 298), has been called into question by the new reality of statelessness. In the void the stateless now occupy, there are no spectators and thus no one to guarantee their rights.

Displaced children, deprived of a place to call a home, may also find themselves denied access to the type of education that might prepare them to strike out roots in the world, to actualize their newness through action and speech. To make sense of this claim, let's consider Arendt's account of the responsibility of the educator to the young. Arendt introduces two, subtly but nevertheless crucially, different ways in which adults might attend and respond to the newness of young lives. It is 'the central aim of all modern education efforts', Arendt (BF, 188) writes, to attend to 'the welfare of the child', before she goes on to observe:

> The situation is entirely different in the sphere of educational tasks directed no longer toward the child but toward the young person, the newcomer and stranger, who has been born into an already existing world which he does not know.

This distinction between the child and the young person entails two entirely different educational responsibilities. First, there is the responsibility to attend to the welfare of the new child, to the new *life* of the child. Second, there is the responsibility to educate the new *person*, so they might come to know and then take up a place in the world with others. Arendt's thus understood natality to mean that each human newcomer is both a new life, born onto an old earth, and a young person, newly arrived in an established world. As the child is not the same as the young person, so the world, that is both established and perpetually dependent on the arrival of newcomers for its continued survival, 'is not identical with the earth or with nature' (HC: 52).

Schooling, which aims only at compensating for the actual and assumed difficulties experienced by displaced children, risks so attending to the welfare of young lives that it ignores its responsibility to educate young people. In short, compensatory practices in schools risk ignoring the fact that children seeking refuge are both new lives and young people. What defines the educational experience of a young person 'is not so much responsibility for the vital welfare of a growing thing as for what we generally call the free development of characteristic qualities and talents', that is, for 'the uniqueness that distinguishes every human being from every other, the quality by virtue of which he is not only a stranger in the world but something that has never been here before' (BF: 188–89). To be a stranger and to be a newcomer are not, then, the same and should not be equated to one another. And yet, when we look at a child forced to leave their home, and see only what they have been through and how they continue to suffer, we hold them as strangers and not as newcomers.

To see and to listen to a displaced young person as a newcomer means recognizing that the same child that has experienced the world's brutality also heralds 'the fact of natality', which Arendt (HC: 247) describes as the 'miracle that saves the world, the realm of human affairs, from its normal "natural" ruin'. However, underscoring different forms of individualized and compensatory approaches to the education of displaced children there is the same fundamental error, since they all advance from the same premise that these children are lacking a voice, when they may in fact be deprived, not of a voice with which to speak, but of other persons who will listen to what they have to say and see them for who they are becoming. As Nguyen has written of refugees:

> The problem here is that the people we call voiceless oftentimes are not actually voiceless. Many of the voiceless are actually talking all the time. They are loud, if you get close enough to hear them, if you are capable of listening, if you are aware of what you cannot hear. The problem is that much of the world does not want to hear the voiceless or cannot hear them. (Nguyen, 2018: 20)

What is attended to when displaced children are listened to carefully is their newness and their distinctiveness, that is, their capacity to act and to speak, and in so acting and speaking, to 'show who they are, [to] reveal actively their unique personal identities and thus [to] make their appearance in the human world' (HC: 179). Attentive listening, in other words, allows for the 'disclosure of "who" in contradistinction to "what" somebody is' (HC: 179). Indeed, as Kristeva (2001: 172), commentating on Arendt's distinction, notes: '"What" someone is can be reduced to social appearance and biological attributes.' However, one appears in the world before spectators, 'who receive and interpret the acts of each newcomer by implicitly asking him the question, "*Who* are you?"' (original emphasis, Kristeva, 2001: 173). So, what of the displaced child, living in the absence of such attentive witnesses and listening, the child who is asked not, 'Who are you?', but is rather told what they are and what they are lacking?

By way of answering this question, we now turn to Arendt's (OT: 294) critical observation that the 'new refugees' of the twentieth century 'were persecuted not because of what they had done or thought, but because of what they unchangeably were – born into the wrong kind of race or the wrong kind of class'. To refuse to reduce a displaced young person to 'what' they are in this way requires constant vigilance on the part of the educator against any 'equation of refugee student difference and marginality with deficit and lack' (Keddie, 2012: 1295), and against any 'deficit thinking about the aspirations and capabilities of refugee children' (Sidhu, Taylor and Christie, 2011: 98). This means that it is 'crucial to remember that these refugee students are not simply "victims", although they are often constructed as such', that 'being a refugee is only one aspect of their subjectivity' (Ferfolja and Vickers, 2010: 151). It is a question of learning to respond to *who* the young person seeking refuge is becoming, beyond *what* they have been reduced to. It might then be possible to prepare a stateless young person for their place in the world, not simply as a refugee, but a potential actor and witness of action, a bearer and an observer of what is new. As Pinson and Arnot (2010: 248) observe, the same 'children whose families are often denied access to the social, political and economic rights of a citizen' should, 'from an educational point of view', be 'placed within a school system designed to prepare young people precisely for membership of a society, for citizenship'.

Crucially, this is, Arendt (RJ: 100) reminds us, 'the world into which we all arrive as strangers', and it is only by virtue of the attention of others and our capability to think, to remember and to act, that we do not leave it that way. For a generation to be born, to live and then to die as strangers to the world can only mean that their elders have eschewed their responsibility and thus left this generation bereft of welcoming and attentive guides to the world. This, before all else, amounts to a failure to educate. It is a failure that Arendt (BF: 185) locates in 'a more general crisis and instability in modern society'. Arendt (HC: 6) names this larger crisis 'world alienation'. Alienation from the world occurs when what can be named and claimed as one's own is prized above and beyond what is between us, connecting us together in a world that we hold in common. It is a state of affairs 'which can be seen everywhere but which presents itself in especially radical and desperate form under the conditions of a mass society' (BF: 191).

When these conditions lead to the estrangement of educators, what inexorably follows is alienation from their twofold responsibility to the world and to the young. Here it is important to reflect on Arendt's (BF: 189) distinction between teachers of children, who know the world and are qualified 'to instruct others about it' and the educators of young people, whose 'authority rests on' their 'assumption of responsibility for that world'. It is in the context of this widespread alienation that specialist interventions and individualized teaching programmes offered to children seeking refuge should be understood. Such responses to the situation of displaced children, far from breaking from the regular ebb and flow of teaching – as opposed to educational – activity, are merely extensions to it.

However, the kind of schooling that is marked by the alienation of its teachers from the world is particularly disastrous for children seeking refuge. Like all educators, an educator of displaced children has a responsibility to be a representative of and a guide to world, but in this case the responsibility is particularly acute. To educate a displaced child is to know that for this child, the promise of the world has been all too absent, while its overwhelming hostility has been all too present. Arendt holds that from the perspective of the child, the educator appears as 'a representative of all adult inhabitants, pointing out the details and saying to the child: This is our world' (BF: 189). Nowhere does this responsibility to represent what has occurred and what occurs now in the world matter more than when an educator stands before a displaced newcomer. This newcomer, uprooted from what was once their home, lives in the starkness of newness. No child more than the uprooted child needs to hear an educator say: 'This is our world.' This is *our* world, the educator says: this world awaits you, in all your distinctiveness. How different this is to the situation in which children seeking refuge encounter, not an educator to guide them, but rather a specialist offering remediating welfare. Here, education is reduced to a mere charity model of schooling that creates 'the conditions for the refugee to be categorised as a medicalized subject of trauma, and the welfare subject whose survival is reliant on the benevolence of the state' (Taylor and Sidhu, 2012: 44). Under these circumstances, it is as if both the educational hand that points back to the past and the educational hand that points forward to the future have been hurled into the air, throwing an already displaced child from an educational transition that might enroot them in what has been so they might come to enroot themselves in what has yet to be. In no case is natality more cruelly transgressed, is the promise of both the child and of education itself more carelessly discarded, than when educators fail to represent the world to young people already forcefully uprooted from the country of their birth.

Beyond Assimilation and Loneliness: Enrooting Displaced Children in the World

Reflecting on his own experiences as a child fleeing Nazi Germany and finding refuge in England, Ron Baker, a professor of social work, writes of the ways a displaced person can be 'dramatically stripped' of 'a relationship web' that connects a person to 'his or her own culture by a range of links and relationships to other people, organizations and social structures' (1983: 2–3). Removed from this web, 'alienated from his cultural roots, the refugee is thrown onto his own resources', observes Baker (1990: 64). The consequences of this loss are described with the following, haunting words by Baker (1990: 66):

> Such loneliness contains what I call a 'dead still centre', a feeling which is extremely difficult to describe (especially if you are a child) and even more difficult to understand and empathize with if you are a concerned helping person.

Using similar language to Baker, Arendt speaks of the 'peculiar loneliness' that 'arises in the process of labor', before explaining that 'this loneliness consists in being thrown back upon oneself' (LI: 34–35). This is the loneliness that arises whenever one is uprooted from what Arendt (HC: 184), in a language that once again falls into harmony with Baker's words, calls 'the web of human relationships'.

In her own bitterly incisive analysis of the experience of seeking refuge, Arendt advances an account of the ways German Jews fleeing Nazi Germany sort to answer their upheaval from the relationship webs they were once embedded within, by way of assimilating themselves into their host societies. Arendt (JW: 272) observes the optimism of those prepared to forget the places, customs and cultures of their homelands, but notes that 'under the cover of our "optimism" you can easily detect the hopeless sadness of assimilationists'. In other words, the optimism of the Jewish refugees was not a way of facing the future, but a way of forgetting the past. It might, in fact, be that the high water mark of such optimistic assimilation is the emptying of the memory. Hence Arendt's observation:

> Assimilation did not mean the necessary adjustment to the country where we happened to be born and to the people whose language we happened to speak. We adjust in principle to everything and everybody. (JW: 271–2)

The success of this quest for total assimilation is thus measured by the extent to which one has divorced oneself from the world, cast off one's roots and so become rootless. Learning to become utterly assimilated means, in short, learning to live with constant loneliness. Arendt locates the definitive account of such loneliness in Kafka's *The Castle*, which conveys 'the real drama of assimilation', since:

> Kafka paints a picture true to reality and to the basic human problem which assimilation involves, if taken seriously. For insofar as the Jew seeks to become 'indistinguishable' from his gentile neighbors he has to behave as if he were indeed utterly alone; he has to part company, once and for all, with all who are like him. (JW: 291)

More than separation from others, however, the loneliness of the assimilated is the condition of being isolated, also, from oneself. It is a matter of parting company, not only from those who are like oneself but also from oneself.

A thoroughly assimilated individual, one who never falls out of line with whatever the ruling conventions happen to be in their society, who always says the 'right' word, appeases and charms, does not act, but rather performs what Arendt (HC) describes as mere 'behaviour'. Such an individual, labouring unendingly to successfully reproduce an identity that can be consumed by others in any given personality market, does not and cannot appear in their distinctiveness – either to others or to themselves. Answering loneliness by attempting to assimilate oneself into any given set of customs or social practices, results only in further estrangement from oneself and, thus, in further loneliness.

Arendt carefully distinguishes 'loneliness', where I am deserted not only of human company but also of the possible company of myself, from 'existential state in which I keep myself company' that she names 'solitude' (LM1: 74). If assimilation, and the particularly corrosive form of loneliness it engenders, is to be countered in schools, they shall need to create spaces for the kind solitude that enables young people to keep themselves company. Stern (2014: 177) identifies three kinds of places within schools that allow for 'three kinds of solitudinous dialogue': there should be 'places to read, to daydream, to be "somewhere else" in the midst of school'; natural and beautiful places where children may 'dialogue with nature'; and, finally, 'daydreaming spots, thoughtful places', where children can come into dialogue with themselves (Stern, 2014: 177). However, the mere opportunity to access such spaces will not, by itself, suffice if schooling continues to so obsessively monitor and measure the progress of children that it omits to grant them the time to withdraw from ceaseless schooling activity so they might, wherever they happened to be placed within the geography of their school, spend some time in their own company.

It is a question of whether or not schools can become patience of thinking. An apposite question, given that thinking is an activity that, as Arendt reminds us, manifests itself only as 'absentmindedness, an obvious disregard of the surrounding world, something entirely negative which in no way hints at what is actually happening within us' (LM1: 72). What such patience might abate is our obsession with doing something for children seeking refuge, with acting upon and for them. In might, that is, allow us to desist in devising interventions and plans for these children for long enough to recognize that what they may need most of all is not be involved in or subjected to activity of any kind, but in fact the opportunity for a complete withdrawal from the pulse of human interaction.

Crucially, for Arendt (BF, 188), 'school is by no means the world and must not pretend to be'. And the lives of young people seeking refuge, along with too many other young lives, convey an especial validation of Arendt's (BF) insistence that it is the indispensable function of the school to protect children from the world. Withdrawn from the world in a school that affords them time and space for solitude, young people who already know too much of the world might come to know something entirely new: themselves, their own distinct and emerging abilities and aptitudes. It is precisely because it protects them from the world, that the school can prepare the young to make a contribution to it. However, this safeguarding role should extend to shielding the young from an adult obsession with endless performance, behaviour and production.

In his memoir of fleeing eastern Afghanistan as a child refugee, Gulwali Passarlay (2015) describes how his idealistic rural existence as the son of a doctor came to an abrupt end when his father and grandfather were killed by US troops. After their deaths, Gulwali and his older brother found themselves caught between Taliban representatives, who wanted them to become fighters, and US forces, who wanted them to become informers. Given these circumstances, Gulwali's mother explained to her sons that Afghanistan was no longer safe and so she was sending them both away. Gulwali was twelve years old. Not long into his journey, and already separated from his brother, Gulwali saw a happy family walk down an Iranian street. In response to this ordinary scene, Gulwali recalled:

> I was already learning that in order to keep going I had to stop loving, stop remembering. Thinking about those I had left behind was too painful. (Passarlay, 2015: 52)

Passarlay's words here vividly and painfully illustrate the appeals of assimilation. Once uprooted from one's homeland, one may seek to be uprooted, also, from the memories that bring life, if only a spectral life, to that land. Of course, remembering that other life, the past life, where one made a difference, where one's words counted and one's acts influenced the lives of others, is no act of escapism, because this is the remembrance of a past so past that it has no presence. In such remembrance one does not retreat into the citadel of what once was, rather one mourns. And yet, this mourning itself might enable one to be closer to the life one has loved, to finally open oneself to what most profoundly presses itself onto the memory. Arendt observes that thinking and remembering constitute 'the human way of striking roots, of taking one's place in the world', before going on to point out:

> What we usually call a person or personality, as distinguished from a mere human being or a nobody, actually grows out of this root-striking process of thinking. (RJ: 100)

It is the miracle of thinking that this person I am is the same person with whom I might converse; whatever cruelties I have endured, I am, in so much as I am able to think about them, not alone in the world and thus not entirely a hapless hostage to whatever the world has done to, and has to say about, me at any given time.

Indeed, a school that ensures their children have sufficient time and space to withdraw so they might be with themselves in thinking activity, may gift a child seeking refuge the opportunity to determine for themselves the meaning of the demeaning stereotypes and the degrading images that are too often directed towards displaced people. It is in line with this insight that Dryden-Peterson (2015: 16) observes:

> One way that refugee children can overcome discrimination is by developing positive identities around their origin-country cultures ... a positive ethnic and cultural identity can buffer against the negative effects of teacher and peer discrimination – effects such as poor academic and self-concepts, and depressive symptoms.

However, thinking itself may be an indispensable condition, not only for the resistance of hostile words and deeds but also for the advancement of new speech and actions. Here we address a crucial aspect of Arendt's (HC) characterization of human action, namely, that it is 'revelatory'. Action reveals to both to the actor and to others the distinctive character of the actor. If I am at odds with the world and at odds with myself also, then the risk of venturing forth a word or deed, the consequences of which are entirely unpredictable, subsides, and in its place emerges not revelatory action, but mere behaviour (Arendt HC). I may address myself in many, quite distinct ways. I might, for example, turn to myself in distaste or in admiration, but neither of these two ways of addressing myself constitute a way of being with myself in dialogue, of thinking with myself. In so much as I address myself defensively, in response to what has been said about me, I do not withdraw *from* the world but rather withdraw *into* myself. If I conceive myself either as a vulnerable subject or as one worthy of praise in spite of all external hostility, I seek not to begin a series of actions and words, but rather to refute what is already established. In short, that which has its origins in that condition of loneliness, in which I am positioned not *with* myself but *for* myself and against others, cannot result in a disclosure of individual distinctiveness.

Arendt (original emphasis, LM2: 217) reminds us that the 'very capacity for beginning is rooted in *natality*', but this capacity is hardly likely to manifest itself in the world all the time that the human potential for starting something new is overridden by a prolonged effort to reject and to resist pre-established and negative categorizes and labels. It is precisely for this reason that schools should afford all children, and especially for those seeking refuge, opportunities to be with themselves. Opportunities, that is, to engage in that internal, thinking dialogue that might teach them that they were born, not to perpetually 'keep going' (Passarlay, 2015: 52), nor to constantly struggle to 'overcome discrimination' (Dryden-Peterson, 2015: 16), but rather to begin.

Conclusion

Arendt holds that all education aims at rooting the newcomer in the world. Our current crisis of mass displacement illuminates just why this aim matters. This chapter has sought to illustrate the significance of this aim by way of examining Arendt's (BF) distinction between responsibility in education, that is, the ability of an *educator* to protect and to respond to the becoming of young lives and to guide them to a world, and welfare in schooling, which involves adopting from the very outset the viewpoint that certain children need a *specialist*, capable of naming and remediating deficiencies. What has emerged as Arendt's central contribution to an understanding of the schooling of displaced children is precisely that it must provide an education and not a prolonged exercise in welfare.

What, then, of the situation in which refugees are responded to as a homogeneous group, capable of making no contribution to their host society, but only of dismantling an imagined social order? Immediately, educators within those societies might give pause to ask the rather desperate question of whether or not it would be better to simply ignore the promise that accompanies the birth of a child in the case of displaced children and desist in the attempt to prepare them to make a contribution to a community that is not willing to include them. Such despair is answered by Arendt's (BF: 188–89) insistence that school is 'the institution that we interpose between the private domain of home and the world in order to make the transition from the family to the world possible at all'. In other words, schools do not include children into the world as it is now, but rather protect them from that world so they guide them towards their future inclusion into a future world. It is precisely for this reason that educators might guide young, displaced people to the world that is perpetually made anew by the actions of newcomers, a world that can, through this endless process of renewal, always be healed of some of its hostility.

However paradoxical it might sound, Arendt's insights into an educational response to the crisis of mass displacement suggest that if schools are to prepare the young for their future inclusion into the world, they must provide them with protection not only from the world, but from ceaseless activity, also. Expressed more positively, this means that schools have to provide secure spaces for thinking and remembering. However, such thinking and remembering, wherein young people might enroot themselves in what they have experienced of and what they think about the world, meet their opposition in assimilation, which, as Arendt's analysis demonstrates, aims at the evisceration of all roots to the past and to the world. Indeed, Arendt's account of assimilation illuminates its capacity to destroy the human plurality of the public realm, in which one might be situated in a 'web of relationships' and, along with it, spaces for meeting oneself in the thinking dialogue. Schools can be places where children enroot themselves, and this means that, alongside their role in preparing young people to situate themselves in the world, they might also be protective places. Schools can be sites of protection, in which children to experience the kind of solitude that enables them to be with themselves, as opposed to a sites of assimilation, in which persons tend to forget themselves.

Arendt (BF) concludes her essay 'The Crisis in Education' by saying that education is where our love for the young precludes us from either letting them find their own way to the world or from setting out a narrow pathway for them to follow to it. Equally, education is where young people neither have to be for themselves nor against themselves; where they neither have to take a stand against nor abandon themselves as they internalize the hostility directed towards them by, a needlessly cruel world. Education could be the place where displaced children discover that they are loved enough to be guided to a world they are to share in common with others and where, in the midst of this passage to their future, they are encouraged to converse with themselves, to be with themselves.

Part Three

Education for Love of the World

7

Hannah Arendt and 'Holocaust Education': Rethinking the Political Educationally

Marie Morgan

Introduction

The life and works of Hannah Arendt (1906–1975) are both intellectually intriguing and relevant to a wide range of human, social and political issues, situations and experiences that transcend the particularities of context and time. Although situating herself firmly as a political rather than educational theorist or philosopher (LI; BF), Arendt's first love was philosophy, and the desire and 'need to understand' continued to be the driving force throughout her life and works (LI: 15). Driven by the desire to understand, the young Arendt's inquisitive philosophical mind led her to begin reading the works of Kant, Jaspers and Kierkegaard in her early teens and to pursue her love of philosophy during her university years (see LI: 6; 14). As academic life progressed and her political thought developed, Arendt turned away from the kind of philosophy, including political philosophy, that she considered to be 'burdened by tradition', with its emphasis on 'man as a thinking being … [rather than] … man as an acting being' (LI: 4). From this point, Arendt developed her interest in, and thus her political thought around, the human potential for a political life of public action. That said, her 'preoccupation with mental activities' remained the driving force for her theoretical undertakings throughout her life (LI: 3). The philosophical point of departure for Arendtian thought is important because it offers insights into her understanding of the political and, as will become clearer below, the educational nature of it. While inextricably linked to the ontic dimensions of politics, including the form of 'state, government and institutions', the desire to comprehend the human condition and why and how individuals act as they do led Arendt to a phenomenological comprehension of the political which 'seeks to understand political experience and issues of political alienation, and to promote interest and active participation by citizens' (Topolski, 2008: 263).

Arendtian thought draws increasing attention from educational quarters (see for example: Biesta, 2013, 2016; Gordon, 2001a; Gunter, 2014; Topolski, 2008; Tamboukou, 2016; Veck, 2013; Zakin, 2017). While Arendt's discussions about education in its institutionalized form are limited largely to her short essay 'The Crisis in Education' (BF), the educational significance of her wider political thought is increasingly coming to the fore as worthy of attention. It is perhaps 'The Crisis in Education' in which Arendt calls for the separation of education and politics, that still receives most attention in educational quarters. The emphasis on this particular work has often led educational theorists to call Arendt's apparent contradictory position between the ontic dimensions of education and the ontological nature of the educational dimension of her political thought into question. In the latter, the education*al* significance of human being, action and activity is, as will become clearer below, the essence of political life, and it is this notion of the educational that characterizes the profundity of education in Arendt. It is here that it becomes necessary to turn to the ways in which totalitarianism and the necessity to learn from the Holocaust are central themes in Arendt's political thought.

In contrast to her limited writings on education, the political catastrophes of the twentieth century, and Nazism and the Holocaust in particular, both inform and are central to Arendt's understanding of the political. Arendt made no secret of the impact her experiences of living in and escaping from Nazi Germany, and the irreconcilable devastation of the death camps, had on her life and work (LI: 23). The educational significance of this is profound because education is, for Arendt, 'an integral medium of human temporality ... [which] ... illuminates the past and reveals possibilities for the future' (Zakin, 2017: 122). The necessity to learn from the travesties of totalitarianism and in particular from the events of the Holocaust plays a significant role in contributing to a comprehension of what it means if 'newcomers', who 'are not pre-existing "whos" but rely on a pre-existing world that can welcome and make possible the becoming of new "whos"' (Zakin, 2017: 122), are to comprehend the world they inherit in ways that enable them to contribute meaningfully to the renewal of the world they share with others. To expose, understand and comprehend, and thus develop the capacity to work against totality and totalitarianism in all its forms and manifestations, was a driving force for Arendt (see, for example, CC, OT, RJ). Arendt challenges us to not only comprehend the obligation to truly learn from the political failures and ensuing disasters that have shaped the fractured world we inherit so that we might act anew, but demands that, as political persons and actors, we assume the responsibility for it (BF). This is particularly so for teachers who are charged with representing the world, as it is, to others (BF). It is this understanding of the necessity to assume responsibility for the world that provides the foundations for the arguments that are developed in the paragraphs that follow.

I argue here that, for Arendt, the educational nature of the political not only informs us about the fractured post-Holocaust world we inherit – characterized by totalitarian regimes and their crimes – but also demonstrates the necessity to seek and gain a deeper understanding of the human condition, its vulnerabilities and its potentialities. The educational aim of this is that we might not only work against the dangers of totality in all its guises but also contribute meaningfully to the renewal of the world we share and to an understanding of political life that is rooted in the recognition of plurality and freedom for all (HC). This, I suggest, forms the basis of what we might, for want of a better description, call 'Holocaust education' in Arendt. This claim is not made lightly for, as will become clearer later, the understanding of 'Holocaust education' I argue for in Arendt is somewhat different to the increasingly established and accepted understanding of 'Holocaust education' that has developed recently in the UK, and in England in particular. But rather than stand in opposition to each other, I suggest here that Arendt's understanding of 'Holocaust education' has much to offer the increasingly popular curriculum focused understanding of 'Holocaust education' and is particularly valuable for teachers and intending teachers of 'Holocaust education' in schools and colleges.

The Educational, the Political and the Threat of Totality

That education is an ontological human endeavour and that the political is educational in Arendt's thought is demonstrated most succinctly by her notion of natality (HC, BF). Understanding the political as educational requires us to see the movement of political life as the process of endlessly becoming and comprehending ourselves, others and the world as well as denoting the capacity for mature judgement and action in the public realm. Arendt's notion of 'natality' becomes central here. For Arendt, the political is educational by nature because it is 'ontologically rooted' in the 'fact of natality' (HC: 177). Natality is both 'the central category of political thought' (HC: 9), because it denotes that 'by virtue of birth men take initiative, are prompted into action' (HC: 177), and 'the essence of education' (BF: 171), because it denotes the fact that 'human beings are *born* into the world' (BF: 171). It is thus in both an educational and political sense that Arendt argues 'this world', the precarious world each 'newcomer' has by birth inherited, 'is constantly renewed through birth' (BF: 193). Central to the educational significance of Arendt's political thought is the fact that every human being arrives in a world that pre-exits them, must learn of and from the world as it is and, in the movement to maturity, not only assume responsibility for the world they have inherited for themselves and for its other inhabitants but also enact their potential and capacity to act anew (HC). What is more, each 'newcomer' must participate in and contribute to the renewal of a pre-existing world whose future is unstable, insecure and uncertain. For Arendt, the uncertainty of the world's future is inevitable because as it is 'made by mortals it wears out; and because it continuously changes its inhabitants it runs the risk of becoming as mortal as they' (BF: 189). It is in this light that Arendt calls for education to 'preserve' (BF: 189) and 'love the world' to 'save it from ruin' (BF: 193). There are no guarantees for the future of a world that is always becoming 'out of joint' at the mortal hands of those have who have dwelt in and shaped it (BF: 189). Totalitarianism and its crimes have perhaps posed the greatest threat to the world with the ultimate 'unprecedented' and irreconcilable 'hell in the most literal sense' being realized in the concentration and extermination camps of the Third Reich (CC: 244). Thus, to fail to understand the necessity to learn from the Holocaust and the totalitarian political principles from which it emerged, risks failing to comprehend the educational import of Arendt's political thought. This is particularly important for teachers who are charged with representing the precarious nature of the world they must protect and take responsibility for, to others.

When considered in the context of 'Holocaust education', the understanding of education developed in 'The Crisis in Education', both informs our understanding of the educational nature of the political in Arendt and demonstrates the centrality of totalitarianism and the Holocaust to her works. Not only does the separation of politics and education that underpins the understanding of education Arendt develops in the 'The Crisis' attract attention from educational commentators in relation to a wide range of issues related to practice and schooling, it attracts attention, and often some criticism, from those who retrieve the educational essence of the political in Arendtian thought (see for example, Biesta, 2013). Taken in isolation, the understanding of education Arendt advances in 'The Crisis' appears somewhat out of step with her wider political thought. However, when contextualized in relation to the specific issues Arendt was addressing (see BF; Topolski, 2008) and the ways in which totalitarianism and the Holocaust informed her understandings of all things, including education *and* politics, 'The Crisis' contributes valuable insights into 'Holocaust education' in Arendt. Thus, rather than call the educational import of Arendt's political thought into question, the separation of education from politics argued for in 'The Crisis' in fact contributes significantly to a meaningful understanding of it. Furthermore, in terms of 'Holocaust education' in the school context – most notably for the necessity for teachers to learn from the Holocaust in order to teach it educationally to others – Arendt's discussion of the role and responsibilities of the teacher that is introduced in 'The Crisis' is particularly relevant and insightful.

Having grown up in the midst of mounting anti-Semitism as the Nazi movement gained momentum in Germany, the young Arendt became increasingly engaged in resistance and, after being arrested and interrogated in relation to her research into anti-Semitism, fled Germany in 1933. Fleeing first to France and to the United States in 1941, Arendt, having been stripped of her German citizenship in 1937, experienced a period of statelessness until becoming a US citizen in 1950. Arendt had experienced and seen first-hand the catastrophic results of an education system which, politicized by and for the new world order of National Socialism and consumed within and by the propaganda machines of the Third Reich, purposefully worked to eradicate both the subjective freedom of individuals *and* the condition of freedom that exists between individuals as the possibility of, and for, political action. Here Arendt witnessed how, when the authority and the democratic responsibility to educate the young falls, under dictatorship, into authoritarianism, 'education' is given over to 'propaganda' (see Buber in Hodes, 1972). Arendt's overwhelming concern was that the resulting 'coercion', 'force' and lack of freedom that characterizes totalitarian forms of 'education' denies children their own potential political maturity and freedom – that is, of 'their own future role in the body politic' (BF: 174). In contrast, for Arendt, education happens when we 'prepare [children] in advance for the task of renewing a common world' (BF: 193). That is, when we prepare them for a life of participation in political action in ways which enable them to contribute meaningfully and freely to a world that does not repeat the failures and atrocities of its past. Thus, education demands that 'we decide whether we love our children enough not to expel them from our world and leave them to their own devices, nor to strike from their hands their chance of undertaking something new, something unforeseen by us' (BF: 193). For Arendt, to know in advance what the contribution of the 'newcomer' will be is closer to the characteristics of totalitarianism than to education, which by definition demands the freedom to initiate the potential to act anew. We will come back to the centrality of political freedom in Arendt's educational thought later.

Wherever the possibility of political totality exists – a threat which is always present for Arendt – educational institutions and structures exist as potential tools for oppression and control by governments and political institutions. Thus, while the separation of education from politics that Arendt advocates in the context of schooling and classroom practice in 'The Crisis' is not without its flaws, when contextualized in relation to totalitarianism and the Holocaust, her warnings about the 'dangers of politicizing education' (Topolski, 2008: 267) gain a deeper significance and better demonstrates why she considered the 'divorce … of education … most of all from the realm of public, political life' necessary (BF: 192). In short, Arendt sought to maintain a space between education and politics to protect the vulnerable mind of the child who as 'a new human being and … a becoming human being' is 'new in a world that is strange to him' (BF: 182).

While the potential for political action is inherent in the 'newcomer', education and, thus, teachers, have a responsibility to protect the vulnerability of the child while at the same time representing that world, as it is, to the child. The teacher's role is paramount here. Grounded in the authority of the teacher who assumes responsibility for 'introduc[ing] the young person to the world as a whole', education, for Arendt, must 'teach children what the world is like' without instructing 'them in the art of living' (BF: 192). That is, education must recognize freedom – political and subjective – as the necessary condition for mature, political life and action. Teachers, by virtue of their role, are defined by the responsibility they assume, not only for the education of the child but also for the world they represent:

> Educators … stand in relation to the young as representatives of a world for which they must assume responsibility although they themselves did not make it, and even though they may, secretly or openly, wish it were other than it is. This responsibility is not arbitrarily imposed upon educators; it is implicit in the fact that the young are introduced by adults to a continuously changing world. Anyone who refuses to assume joint responsibility for the world should not have children and must not be allowed to take part in educating them. (BF: 186)

In a post-Holocaust world, teachers have a responsibility not only to represent the realities of that world to the children they teach but also to learn about the world they assume responsibility for in order that they might represent it as truthfully and meaningfully as possible. This is particularly challenging for teachers of 'Holocaust education' who are charged with teaching the 'indecipherable' meaningfully to children and young people (Levi, 1989: 36). This is a dilemma that goes to the very core of 'Holocaust education' and the difficult decisions teachers have no choice but to make about what and how they teach.

'Holocaust Education'

While great strides have been taken to establish and maintain 'Holocaust education' as a mandatory element of the history curriculum 'in state-maintained schools' in England since its inclusion in the National Curriculum of 1991, there is still much work to be done (Pearce, 2017). The establishment of an ever-increasing body of research and set of resources for teachers notwithstanding, the shortcomings of 'Holocaust education' in practice are many, and they continue to 'pose compelling questions about the nature of teaching and learning about the Holocaust' in England (Pearce, 2017: 232). This includes questions about 'its core precepts, its central aims and intended outcomes, and how far the popular understandings of "Holocaust education" are suitably cognizant of what teaching and learning actually entail' (Pearce, 2017: 232). The challenges faced by those who carry the responsibility for teaching others about the Holocaust are many, and teachers are perhaps being short changed when it comes to 'Holocaust education' because, as Foster argues, 'despite ... widespread engagement with events and narratives related to the Holocaust, limited attention has been paid to how teachers understand the Holocaust and how they teach about it in schools' (2018: 133). If teachers have not themselves studied and learned from the Holocaust in ways sufficient to teach it meaningfully to others, serious questions remain about the nature and educative significance of 'Holocaust education' as a curriculum subject (see for example: Cowan and Maitles, 2017; Pearce, 2017; Lawson, 2017). Furthermore, the wider implications of the ways in which 'Holocaust education' has been included and represented in the National Curriculum and taught in schools and colleges has 'played a central role in the formation of a Holocaust culture in the United Kingdom – particularly in England' are not to be taken lightly (Pearce, 2017: 232). If teachers of 'Holocaust education' are, consciously or not, contributing to the development of a 'Holocaust culture', then it is essential that they do so from an informed and critical position. Thus, it seems time to take a 'step back' from the 'lessons' of 'Holocaust education' to not only reconsider some of the challenges and complexities of teaching about the Holocaust but also seek a rethinking of a form of 'Holocaust education' that speaks to the necessity for teachers and intending teachers of the Holocaust to study and comprehend their subject in ways which are not only informative to them but also formative for them in the most profound and meaningful ways. Only then will all teachers who are charged with teaching others about the Holocaust be well placed to make responsible, critical decisions about its educative significance in ways which inform their decisions about how best to teach others about it. Issues such as the inherent complexities of the subject, appropriate limitations to and of content, and the necessity to be mindful of the ways in which their own comprehension and teaching of the Holocaust might contribute to, and critically call into question, a wider public understanding of 'Holocaust culture' (Pearce, 2017) make 'Holocaust education' a particularly challenging curriculum area for teachers.

Although the road to securing 'Holocaust education' as an established and recognized subject has been long fought and hard won, the call for wider recognition of the educative significance of the Holocaust is far from a recent phenomenon. The last few decades have seen a general increase in awareness of the necessity to learn from the Holocaust lead to the establishment of 'Holocaust studies' and 'Holocaust education' as recognized genres and fields of study in their own right (See for example, Dietz in Villa, 2005; Pearce and Chapman, 2017; Pearce, 2017). Since the liberation of the camps (and before), survivors, witnesses and those with a passionate interest in the subject have worked tirelessly for the necessity to study and learn from the Holocaust to be widely recognized. Underpinned by the fundamental desire for studying the Holocaust in ways which ontologically inform our comprehension of human being, actions and activities so as to develop our understandings of, judgements upon, and responses to, issues such as injustice, prejudice, dehumanization and persecution, the educational value of studying the Holocaust is now generally taken as given in England. This, in itself, is indicative of a relatively recent shift in 'Holocaust culture' (Pearce, 2017).

'Holocaust Education' in Arendt

In the aftermath of the liberation of the camps in 1945, and following the initial establishment of information and knowledge about Nazism, its policies and ideologies, and the scale and nature of the atrocities committed, it was then largely left to particular events at later dates to (re)awaken the awareness of the educational significance of the Holocaust (Landau, 1998). One such event was the 1961 trial of Adolf Eichmann, which Ronnie Landau (1998) describes as a 'watershed in our consciousness of the educational importance of the … [Holocaust]' (2). While somewhat controversial at the time, Arendt's contribution to this 'watershed' moment through the development of her thesis on the banality of evil in *Eichmann in Jerusalem, a report on the banality of evil* is not to be underestimated (Landau, 1998: 2). In *Eichmann in Jerusalem*, Arendt develops an understanding of 'evil', and associated forms of 'thinking' and 'non-thinking', which contributes significantly to her understanding of guilt, responsibility and the development of the capacity for moral judgement that she develops in later works (see for example, EJ; RJ; Morgan, 2016).

Contra the outrage *Eichmann in Jerusalem* attracted at the time of publication and the years after, Arendt's argument that the widespread 'evil' that made the death camps a reality was 'banal' does not detract from the guilt of the perpetrators. Rather, in her analysis of Eichmann both as a private, non-thinking individual and as a contributor to the political totalities of Nazism and its atrocities though his direct actions, Arendt demonstrates a threat that lies in the political principles of totalitarianism and the banal form of evil that issues from it – for the whole of humanity. Furthermore, the criticisms Arendt received for raising difficult questions about the complicity of some Jewish councils in the organization of the ghettos and transportations to the camps was misplaced as she certainly did not intend to suggest that the Jews bore any responsibility for the crimes of Nazism (see EJ; LI 26). Rather, Arendt demonstrates that to learn profound lessons about the human condition and the ways in which its capacity for the 'freedom to think' and the freedom to act that is compromised within, and distorted by, the conditions of totalitarianism that threatens us all, we must risk being disrupted by the most troubling questions that evoke (critical) 'thinking' (as opposed to the 'non-thinking' of those such as Eichmann). It is this kind of (critical) 'thinking' that Arendt associates with the development of the capacity for moral judgement (RJ; Morgan, 2016).

The Holocaust challenges understanding in ways that few other subjects of study do. How does thought think and understand the unthinkable? How do teachers represent things that cannot be understood through 'normal' frameworks of judgement in ways which are not reductive and objectifying so that others might learn from them? This is a challenge that all teachers of 'Holocaust education' face, and it is a challenge that has been expressed for over seven decades since the liberation of the camps. In the preface of *If this is a Man* (first published in 1958), Auschwitz survivor Primo Levi said:

> The need to tell our story to 'the rest', to make 'the rest' participate in it, had taken on for us, before our liberation and after, the character of an immediate and violent impulse, to the point of competing with our other elementary needs. (Levi, 2006: 15)

Arendt recognized this necessity and the impossibility of it in her short essay 'The Concentration Camps' (CC) (first published in *Partisan Review* in 1948). Here she warned of the uncompassionate, albeit understandable, resistance to participate with survivors and witnesses following the liberation of the camps. The mismatch between the experience and articulation of the survivor and the capacity of the human mind to 'understand' things with which it cannot reconcile itself led the world, said Arendt, to 'want[ing] to hear no more of these things' (CC: 237). For Arendt, to learn from the Holocaust presents us with many unresolvable challenges not least because 'things that evade human understanding and human experience; things therefore that, when suffered by men, transform them into "uncomplaining animals"' have a tendency to work against, rather than encourage, the kind of educational participation called for by Levi (CC: 237). When the desire for understanding fails, or resistance to it prevails, the potential participant is left as 'cold ... and baffled as the writer himself' which all too often leads to the more troubling (and un-educational) responses of apathy and knowledge resistance (CC: 237; Rose, 1996; Kessel, 2001). The implications of this are both educational and political because the failure to comprehend human suffering and to understand the political principles which provide the conditions of possibility for it, in turn, fails to 'inspire those passions of outrage and sympathy through which men have always been mobilised for justice', and thus one's capacity for political action and potential to contribute to the renewal of the world in ways which work against the threat of totality is compromised (CC: 237).

Arendt remained clear that there can be no reconciliation *with*, forgiveness *for* or understanding *of* what happened in the concentration and extermination camps (LI: 23). But she was equally clear that it would be a perilous failure not to learn from the ways in which, as she says in 'We Refugees', 'contemporary history has created a new kind of human beings – the kind that are put in concentration camps by their foes and in internment camps by their friends' (JW: 265). For Arendt, comprehending and enquiring into the darker potentialities of the human condition is essential if we are to call ourselves into question in ways which enable us to work for the preservation of the world we inherit and to contribute to its renewal in ways which work against the kinds of political principles that seek to destroy it (OT; RJ). More recently, in *Mourning Becomes the Law*, Gillian Rose (1997) articulates this educational necessity in terms of the need to move 'beyond the limits of voyeurism' (54). It is only in this movement, argues Rose, when we find ourselves 'unmanned' at the deepest level, that is, when the safety of our own position is called into question, that we experience 'the unprotected exposure of our singularity, of our otherness to ourselves, [and] we sense the "we", which we otherwise so partially and carelessly assume' (Rose, 1996: 54–5). For Rose too, the movement of education demands that we both disrupt and are disrupted at the deepest level in order that we might gain insights into 'our vulnerable singularity and our hesitant universality' (Rose, 1997: 55), our private and public selves, so that we might ask ourselves the most profoundly educational question in relation to the Holocaust – 'how easily could we have allowed this to be carried out' (Rose, 1993: 36). It is such a position that makes participation with, rather than the understanding of, the suffering of the victims the essence of 'Holocaust education'. It was Arendt's willingness to disrupt and to be disrupted that enabled her, as Rose said, to expose 'the inequality and insufficiency of the universal political community of her day' and to do so 'without retreating to any phantasy of the local or exclusive community' but to stake 'the risks of identity without any security of identity' (Rose, 1997: 39). Importantly here, in terms of 'Holocaust education' at least, Arendt offers us ways to draw meanings which are formative, both privately and politically, from things that we may never be able to fully comprehend and understand.

Totalitarianism and the Vulnerability of the Human Condition

While the 'unprecedented' horrors of the camps 'the number of victims ... the method, the fabrication of corpses and so on ... to which we cannot reconcile ourselves' are incompatible with understanding, the political principles of totalitarianism, other manifestations of Nazi ideology, and the social and political conditions of their possibility can and must, to a certain extent and least, be comprehended (LI: 23; OT: vii–ix). This is an essential political and educational endeavour for Arendt, for wherever the threat of totalitarianism remains, humanity is vulnerable. The fact that totalitarianism arose and thrived in a 'non-totalitarian world' means that the threat of 'the most radical denial of [political and subjective] freedom' remains in a world which is no more or less totalitarian than the one that had housed Nazism and the Holocaust (EU: 328). For Arendt, no one is exempt from the threat of totalitarianism whose 'victory' does not just 'coincide with the destruction of humanity' but seeks to 'destroy the essence of man' (OT: viii). This does not detract from the necessity to recognize the nature and form of the destructive characteristics and crimes of any particular totalitarian regime, but rather demonstrates that the ontological and political principles which provide the conditions of possibility from within which they emerge, in essence and thus in potentiality if not in actuality, transcend the particularities of context and time.

That totalitarianism, in its attempts to eradicate the pluralities, contingencies and freedoms of humanity has arisen and 'succeeded' to the extent that it has, and because its potential to re-emerge remains, Arendt sought 'a new political principle ... whose validity this time must comprehend the whole of humanity' (OT: ix). This new political principle is one that recognizes the pluralities and contingencies of being and action, and thus the condition of freedom that is their possibility. Thus, the 'new political principle' Arendt seeks, works against totality in all its guises. It is a principle that calls for every 'newcomer' to come to assume the responsibility for 'examining and bearing consciously the burden which ... [the twentieth] century has placed on us' so that they may understand the necessity for a comprehension of the political which actively moves against totality (OT: viii). This responsibility is one that accompanies the inheritance of a world – ruptured by the travesties of its past – that we must learn to be at home in. The centrality of freedom to thought and action is a fundamental element of 'Holocaust education' in Arendt and if she offers one warning above all others it is that freedom as the necessary condition for thought and action is not only worth protecting but also essential for the future of a world that is home to all.

Although Arendt moved tirelessly against the dangers of political totalities and the political ideologies and regimes that resulted from them, she remained committed to the idea that, through the renewal of the world, it is in some way always possible that 'amends can be made for just about everything at some point in politics' (LI: 23). It is the capacity for renewal that makes this possible, and the freedom to act that carries the potential for political reconciliation. Thus freedom, for Arendt, is a 'political phenomenon' because it is the *necessary* condition for public action (Biesta, 2013: 105). Freedom, for Arendt, is not an outcome of thinking or of action. While '[a]ction, to be free, must be free from motive on one side [and] from its intended goal as a predictable effect on the other' it is not a 'phenomenon of the will' (BF: 150). Rather, while 'not to say that motives and aims are not important factors in every single act ... action is free to the extent that it is able to transcend them' (BF: 150). It is this transcendence that frees the political actor (including the teacher) from the kinds of 'preformed judgements' and 'prejudices' that move crises to disasters (BF: 171). The political and educational significance of this is profound and demonstrates that, if teachers are to learn from the Holocaust in order to teach it, freedom is vital.

The Freedom to Teach and Concluding Thoughts

Is there a moral obligation to teach children about the Holocaust or is there a moral obligation to protect them, for a time at least, from the political horrors of the world they have inherited? These are questions that all teachers of 'Holocaust education' must ask themselves. If, as Arendt says, the child who is 'not yet acquainted with the world ... must be gradually introduced to it', she would likely be cautious of the extent to which a curriculum-based notion of 'Holocaust education' should form part of a child's schooling (BF p186). But, regardless of whether or not Arendt would be sympathetic to, or sceptical of, this popular understanding of 'Holocaust education', the insights she offers to and for teachers are invaluable. 'Holocaust education', for Arendt, requires teachers to participate in the witnessing of the depravities of Nazism and the irreconcilable suffering of its victims in ways which move us beyond the position of mere observers, or 'voyeurs' (Rose, 1997). To teach is to assume the responsibility to represent the world to others and in 'education ... responsibility for the world takes the form of authority' (BF: 186). This is far from straightforward for Arendt because teaching, learning and education do not necessarily go hand in hand.

> One can educate without at the same time teaching; an education without learning is empty and therefore degenerates with great ease into moral-emotional rhetoric. But one can quite easily teach without educating, and one can go on learning to the end of one's days without for that reason becoming educated. (BF 192)

If the responsibility to teach is defined by the authority of the teacher, then the authority of the teacher is defined by freedom. But the freedom of the teacher is realized in the responsibility that accompanies their role, and it is a responsibility to and for themselves, the world and the vulnerable and impressionable minds and beings of others 'who respond to [their] initiatives and take up [their] beginnings' (Biesta, 2013: 106). The educational movement of the teacher of

'Holocaust education' does not compromise the condition of freedom that is necessary for the child as a unique 'newcomer' to the world to participate and act anew, but works to reveal and protect it.

The separation of education from politics advocated in 'The Crisis' also implies a separation between education and the educational movement of learning which is inextricably entwined with the political, for Arendt. The fact that education without learning (and learning is decidedly education*al*) would be empty and devoid of meaningful responsibility for the world and for others demonstrates the complexity of Arendt's understanding of the educational import of the political. The overwhelming question that emerges here is whether it is the separation of education and politics that protects the young from the dangers of politicization or an education that recognizes the educational significance of the political. This is a question for every teacher who, in taking up the freedom to teach, assumes responsibility not only for the children and young people they hold a position of authority over but also for the world they represent through the subjects they teach. Arendt clarifies this thus:

> The teacher's qualification consists in knowing the world and being able to instruct others about it, but his authority rests on his assumption of responsibility for that world. Vis-a-vis the child it is as though he were a representative of all adult inhabitants, pointing out the details and saying to the child: This is our world. (BF: 186)

Recognizing and understanding this is essential for all teachers but it is particularly poignant for teachers of 'Holocaust education'.

Thus, if teachers are to be free to teach, to take responsibility for the world they have inherited, which 'they may, secretly or openly, wish … were otherwise' (BF: 186), and to represent this world to the vulnerable child in ways which move the child to learn, their own educational development is paramount. In short, one has to work on one's own self before one can work for the selves of others. For only when teachers are at home in the world can they represent that world to children in ways that enables them to no longer be strangers in it.

8

Can you Learn Democracy in a Classroom? John Dewey and Hannah Arendt on the 'Paradox of Size'

Aaron Schutz

Introduction

How can we best teach the skills of citizenship? In education, for a loose group of progressive educators, the answer for more than 100 years has been grounded in the work of John Dewey (see Dewey, 1916; Westbrook, 1991). In his Laboratory School at the turn of the twentieth century, children learned a form of collaborative democracy that has deeply influenced progressive educators. Children learned to bring the unique knowledge and capacities of each to bear on common projects for social improvement (see Mayhew and Edwards, 1936). In his later writings, Dewey drew together what he learned in the School and other experiences (like his work with Jane Addams) into a coherent set of flexible principles for authentic collaborative democracy (see Westbrook, 1991). While other writers and scholars like Paulo Freire and Hannah Arendt[1] have been slowly added to the canon of progressive democratic education, this core conception has remained relatively stable. Progressive democratic educators today, despite differences, largely focus on replicating key aspects of Dewey's basic vision in their classrooms.[2]

---

[1] While Arendt was not a proponent of what she understood as 'progressive' education (see her essay 'The Crisis in Education' in BF), her work has nonetheless been appropriated by progressives like Maxine Greene (1988). For a discussion of some of the tensions involved in this appropriation see Schutz and Sandy (2015) and Schutz (2002).

[2] A Google Scholar search of John Dewey and 'democratic education' found nearly 3,000 hits in just the last five years. And not just in education. As Muldoon (2016) noted, 'since the deliberative turn in the 1990s, deliberative democracy has not only become the dominant approach in democratic theory, but according to John Dryzek, "the most active area of political theory in its entirety"' (184). I say 'largely' because there are other conceptions including essentially anarchistic ones (see Miller, 2002; Schutz, 2011) and caring visions of classrooms built on dyads that never form fully into broad collaborative spaces (see Nel Noddings, 1984; Schutz, 1998).

In this chapter, I focus on one core question: Does Hannah Arendt's vision of the council system solve the challenge Dewey faced in imagining how his conception of collaborative democracy might govern a polity? Or, does Arendt's vision make Dewey's vision a useful one to teach, by itself, to students as a democratic solution to our larger governance challenges?

Dewey and Arendt were driven by extraordinarily similar desires for democracy. While I discuss key differences, the basic structure of their conceptions of democratic collaboration looked quite similar and drew from very similar foundations. In fact, Maxine Greene (1988), who largely introduced Arendt to the education community, generally treated their visions of democracy as equivalent.

Dewey and others in this progressive educational canon developed their strategies largely in classrooms, small groups and small schools. Thus, partly as a result, the form of democracy they developed essentially treats the wider society as if it were a correspondingly kind of enormous democratic classroom. But a large polity is not a classroom, and it is an open question whether tools that work in small intimate spaces can also serve effectively in larger realms of governance. Jane Mansbridge (1992) termed this the political 'paradox of size', an issue grappled with by many other political theorists (see Parkinson and Mansbridge, 2012). And if Laboratory School-like practices cannot be effectively scaled up, familiar progressive democratic classrooms may actually miseducate students, to one extent or another, about what broader democratic participation actually looks like or can look like (see Kahne and Westheimer, 2006). Fundamentally, if we provide students with ineffective tools for democratic citizenship we may degrade their capacity for effective democratic action. We would need to look to other forms of democratic action which, while possibly less appealing, when used in concert with the form progressives prefer, may address reality in more concrete ways.

In his one book of political theory, *The Public and Its Problems*, Dewey (1927) attempted to solve the problem of scale for democratic collaboration and, as I note below, by his own admission, failed to do so. Arendt, however, believed that she had found at least the beginnings of a solution in the examples of the 'council movements' that emerged at different moments in Europe in the first half of the twentieth century. Dewey hoped someone like Arendt would come along after him and solve the 'paradox of size'. Did she? Can principles of democratic action derived from the council movements recover collaborative democracy for Deweyans seeking to use it as a foundation for broad-based conceptions of citizenship and democratic governance? This chapter explores the potential and limitations of her solution to Dewey's challenges.

I ultimately show that, despite similarities, Dewey and Arendt were seeking to solve fundamentally different kinds of challenges with their democratic visions. Dewey sought to develop a society informed at all levels by the experimental collaboration of those affected by it. While both were deeply concerned about the ability of individual voices to make themselves effectively heard, this was Arendt's *core* concern. She explicitly ruled out Dewey's focus on the consequences of action and instead focused solely on a model that allowed individual voices to always reveal themselves at every level of a governmental structure. Thus, despite their similar models of democracy, Arendt simply wasn't interested in solving Dewey's problem.

The Tensions of Collaboration

Arendt spoke in much more detail than Dewey about the tensions involved in creating collaborative spaces that valued both collective action and individual uniqueness. On the one hand, emerging as a fully unique individual in a collaborative public space is impossible. 'The thoughts of the mind, the delights of the senses', Arendt emphasized, 'must be "transformed, deprivatized, deindividualized", as it were, into a shape to fit them for public appearance' (HC: 50). In public, we talk about issues that are of common concern, and only what is relevant from our own perspectives can be brought into the space lest the space break apart into discussions on issues defined so divergently that the common realm disintegrates, destroying 'the in-between which relates us to and separates us from others' (HC: 197). Collaborative spaces like these require some restriction on what comes into that space because contributions must be relevant to what is common to the group.

Conversely, while some uniqueness must be left out of the space for it to become 'common', too much agreement, too much sameness, would also destroy it. We can't really engage in democratic dialogue around things we all agree on, because there wouldn't be anything to talk about. Each individual must be able to arrive at her own interpretation of their common project, yet not interpret it so uniquely that the common nature of the object is lost. These projects 'must be seen in a variety of aspects without changing their identity, so that those who are gathered around them know they see sameness in utter diversity' (HC: 67).

Because we are all unique, we never agree *perfectly* on everything, but some things are simply not worth holding a public discussion about.[3]

Further, both Dewey and Arendt agreed participants needed to know the others in the space well enough to recognize the uniqueness of each person's contribution requiring that the relationships exist over time. People need to get to know 'who' each other is as a unique individual to know 'what' they mean when each participates.

A core tenet of collaborative democracy is that each participant must be able to engage with others while remaining a recognizably unique individual. Only in this way can participants take advantage of, understand and respond to the unique contributions made by others. But both understood that as the numbers in this space get larger, one's capacity to recognize individuals qua individuals declines. The positions of others become vague and then, progressively, one is forced to either put others' positions into categories that combine multiple perspectives together to represent those of groups, or to look to leaders of particular factions. The individual contribution in large spaces becomes quickly degraded. Increasingly, one can recognize the individual uniqueness of only a small number of spokespersons. As Arendt noted, one inexorably enters the realm of statistics where individual 'acts' below the level of identifiable leaders 'can statistically appear only as deviations or fluctuations' (HC: 55).

Democracy and the Problem of Scale

In *The Public and Its Problems,* Dewey (1927) tried to imagine how one could construct a coherent broad-based state governance structure sufficiently respectful to this model of what I think of as 'classroom democracy'.[4] The core challenge of governance in a large polity, Dewey argued, was that large numbers of otherwise unrelated people were constantly affected by the actions and events that they could often neither control nor perceive directly. He called people in this common situation a 'public'. Think of downstream cities being affected by pollution from a power plant forming a kind of 'public', for example. A nation or a world, Dewey argued, would be adequately governed if it could address the challenges of these myriad publics.[5]

---

[3] This gets us into a range of areas of Arendt's thought, including her discussion of what she called the *social* in modern life, which I will not address here.
[4] I make this argument in detail in Chapter 3 of Schutz (2011).
[5] Dewey referred to the 'Public' in the title of the book, but he was really speaking of many different overlapping 'publics'.

Dewey's vision, it is important to stress, was a fundamentally 'scientific' one. He envisioned people working together experimentally to solve problems, and he sought in his schools to create what one might call deliberative scientists. In this vision, people work together in the world, act on it and suffer the consequences, learning as they go and solving problems through their actions. Collaboration made this process more effective because each individual had a fundamentally unique perspective on the world. Together, they know and can do much more than they can do alone. The outcomes of such deliberative spaces are important not simply because they are democratic, then, but because they are, in the ideal, scientific: because they solve real problems in the world and move society forward in some way.

Acting 'intelligently' Dewey (1927) argued, involves tracing, in some limited, imperfect way, the effects of an individual or collective act into the world. It 'demands ... perception of the consequences of a joint activity and of the distinctive share of each element in producing it' (35). And it is this common understanding of what is being accomplished that 'creates a common interest; that is concern on the part of each in the joint action and in the contribution of each of its members to it' (188). The scientific act of understanding what we are doing is central to the democratic nature of the act.

Because one could not imagine effective, large groups constantly making collaborative decisions about broad 'public' problems, Dewey (1927) acknowledged that addressing the problems raised by a 'public' required some kind of administration – leaders, or what he termed 'officials' – to act in some coherent manner. Laws, for example, are unenforceable without judges to establish what they mean. Officials give a public a 'form' in his terms. Officials must act to represent the collective public response to something like the *dangers* of pollution on the one hand, and the power *needs* of industry and householders that produce it on the other. But he opposed any administrative structure that contravened the core commitments of the ideal of collaborative democracy. The closer any administrative structure came to operating independently of the unique perspectives of the democratic public it was representing, the less it approximated collaborative democracy. As a result, Dewey argued that the selection and guidance of officials is a 'primary problem of the public' (77).

If we have a group the size of a classroom, we may be able to talk (and try out experiments) about a problem and come to some tension-filled agreement on an action. While we may commit an action, the multiple perspectives on that action will be maintained, to some extent, and we can keep acting as we discover the results of our actions. But as the spaces get larger, people increasingly lose an understanding of these unique perspectives. One person cannot understand and respond to the unique perspectives of more than a relatively small number of others. What other people 'mean' by what they say and do is dependent upon who they 'are'. To understand their stance, I need to actually know them as persons. But once we get to regions the size of states (and, of course, much sooner than that) we (officials, leaders and participants) can, at best, only interpret or even invent what a collection of individuals as *imaginary* collective might think. Voting doesn't help, because voting only puts people into categories (Yes or No), hiding the unique perspectives that inform the votes. Dewey (1927) noted that '"we" and "our" exist only when the consequences of combined action are perceived ... and "I" and "mine" appear on the scene only when a distinctive share in mutual action is consciously asserted or claimed' (151–2).

When they act, 'officials' essentially create a collective agreement that does not ever, strictly, exist. Individual perspectives on pollution must be collapsed into a law, and then decisions about what this law means must be collapsed into actions that reflect a kind of shared Rousseauean public 'will'. In essence, public officials are accountable to a collective vision that *does not*, strictly, *exist*. To prevent them from taking over and overwhelming the actual multiple perspectives of participants, then, Dewey restricted the power of officials. Their unavoidably creative and subtly dominating aggregation of myriad views into singular laws and policies is only palatable in Dewey's model when the issues involved or the differences likely to emerge between individual interpretations are seen by participants as relatively unimportant. Leaders of publics in Dewey's scheme in *Public* could only make decisions on things that everyone already basically agreed upon and didn't care enough about to bother taking a unique stance on. Think, for example, about the meaning of the colour red as 'stop' America. Whatever disagreements we might have about this are so minimal that it is okay if officials continue to assume we all agree on it. Only this allows public decision-making that does not corrode the core commitments of collaborative democracy.

This is a solution that is no solution at all, however. For it solves the problem only when we are so indifferent and in agreement that we can't be bothered to form a collaborative group around an issue in the first place. In other words, Dewey's solution only applies to problems that have ceased to be problems. It does not allow a public or officials to deal with the core central issues of a time. And, of course, this begs the question: What about all the questions we don't agree on? What about when the perspectives of people who need coal power are pitted against cities that don't want their rivers poisoned?

Ultimately Dewey (1927) was unable to solve this problem, and he understood that he had not solved it. 'To many', he noted at the end of *Public*, 'the conclusions which have been stated' about the possibility of creating structures of democratic governance based on collaborative democracy, 'will seem close to the denial of realizing the idea of a democratic public' (185). Alan Ryan (1995) noted that Dewey's vision of a democratic polity based on his approach to democratic practice seemed not to be 'an intelligible project' (414), while Robert Westbrook (1991) pointed out that that, ironically, the limits of Dewey's account seemed actually to 'reflect the implausibility of the project itself' (316).

Hannah Arendt's Solution: The Council Movements

Arendt thought that she had found a solution to a similar problem of 'representation' in the council movements that sprang up 'spontaneously' at the beginning of a range of different revolutions during the first half of the twentieth century. She believed they provided concrete evidence, in Deweyan terms, that one might be able to coherently solve the problem of scale and thereby allow classroom democracy to serve, by itself, as training for citizenship in at least a particular form of governance. She saw the council movements as at least somewhat successful pragmatic experiments in broad-based collaborative democracy.

As she described them in *On Revolution* and elsewhere, council movements emerged spontaneously at the beginning of different revolutions. Within factories and military camps, small political spaces where individuals knew each other over time came into being where participants made democratic decisions about what would happen there. In the Russian Soviets that were part of the revolutions of 1905 and 1917, the German revolution of 1918 and the Hungarian revolution of 1954, among other examples, configurations of 'councils' formed themselves into quasi governments organized in the structure of a pyramid with people elected out of local councils into higher-level coordinating committees (see Comack, 2012; Lomax, 1990; Smith, 1985). Delegates elected to higher levels could be recalled at any time if the council members felt they were not adequately representing them. This resembled another model she lauded, the 'ward system' discussed by Jefferson, who believed that 'only by breaking up "the many" into [smaller, sub-]assemblies where everyone could count and be counted upon "shall we be as republican as a large society can be"' (OR: 266; see 254).

Delegates elected 'up' to higher levels of councils were in a liminal position with respect to 'representing' the perspectives of their lower-level colleagues.

On the one hand, Muldoon (2016) makes it clear that Arendt meant them to represent their fellows in *some* manner. On the other hand, to maintain the 'public' nature of dialogue in higher-level groups, delegates would necessarily need to act out of their own unique perspectives. Otherwise, one would not have a true public space, but instead a collection of people simply acting at the beck and call of their electors. Delegates, then, hold a complex and tension-filled role in this vision. They must reflect to some extent some imaginary collective opinion of their fellows, but not so much that their actions lose the character of their own individual and unique perspective on the issues at hand. They cannot try to 'categorize' what the body they came from 'believed' in some simple way because they need to come to the coordinating groups as individuals, themselves. Only in this way can the 'public' character be maintained on the higher levels.

Almost counter-intuitively, those elected were trusted to act for a group by being their unique selves, by *not* simply 'representing' some collective opinion. Thus the key characteristic of a delegate is that their electors *trust* them. Delegates' individual perspectives are respected by their peers even if they don't support what some simple majority wished them to do, with the caveat that they can be recalled if their own perspective diverges too far from the sense of the group that sent them.[6] Delegates, Arendt argued, should be chosen 'exclusively by [colleagues'] estimation of a man ... not bound by anything except trust in his personal qualities' (OT: 499).

What you have, then, is a pyramid of councils, each operating as its own kind of public realm. Delegates balance their need to reflect the perspectives of their local groups with the need to be themselves in this space lest the 'public' aspect collapse into a conglomeration of inhuman and relatively simplistic interest group presentations.

Here, Arendt was trying to sustain the possibility for what she termed 'action'. She rejected efforts to treat politics like one was making something, like a chair, as if one was trying to accomplish something one planned ahead of time. This is a complex area of her thought, but in a simple sense, 'politics' for her was a space of constant action where each individual constantly contributes their own unique perspective. Like Dewey, she rejected, for example, the standard approach to representative democracy, in which people elect leaders who can speak for them. Representative democracy collapses the plural nature of the political, the individual and unique agency of each actor, into the sovereignty

---

[6] Muldoon (2016) notes that Arendt 'vacillates', I would say necessarily, 'between two alternative conceptions of representation: mandate and independence, both of which she ultimately rejects' (149).

of the state, creating the illusion that there is some collective will that can be decided upon (Tassin, 2007). It rents out, if you will, decision-making power to a small group that acts as if it were the voice of the people. In this way, it does not extend politics; from her perspective, it destroys politics. It represents a pragmatic solution to the problem of governance by essentially destroying the relevance of everyone's individual voices to the realm, handing off governance to an exclusive group.

For Arendt, 'action' in the political realm is not an effort to control something or establish something permanent or concrete. Instead, one acts as a unique individual by making a contribution into an unpredictable web of human relationships. She emphasizes that 'since action acts upon beings who are capable of their own actions, reaction ... is always a new action' and leads to completely 'boundless' consequences (HC: 190). And 'it is because of this already existing web of human relationships, with its innumerable, conflicting wills and intentions, that action almost never achieves its purpose' (HC: 184). What actually happens as a result, no one can control. Any effort to control its outcome only ensures that its 'utterly fragile meaning is destroyed' (HC: 196). Maintaining this core aspect of action in public is a key aim of the council scheme, as Arendt saw it. It is impossible for any individual participant or group to control the outcome, and at every level the capacity for individual unique contributions is preserved. Each level is linked together loosely by trust, a vague form of 'representation' and only at the extremes by recalling a delegate.

Note that the council system is no perfect solution to the 'paradox of size'. The very existence of a process of recall meant that leaders who were voted 'up' were always potentially under threat if their decisions diverged too far from those held by their fellows. And it is not clear that the participants in the councils generally understood their elections to higher councils in the manner Arendt's theory defined. Nonetheless, the councils provided an actual case study of something that seemed workable in principle, that at least began to address the challenge of the 'paradox of size' but that did not resort to some simple representative democracy approach that eliminated the individual agency of most participants. The fact that the role of a delegate involves a precarious balancing act is not necessarily a critique of Arendt. It simply reflects the realities of the human condition and the limited options for political structure in Arendt's understanding.[7]

---

[7] Muldoon (2016) maps out as best he can a concrete conception of how these councils might have worked, based on vague references in Arendt.

Arendt was not arguing that we should somehow replicate the councils wholesale. They were too diverse, cobbled together spontaneously somewhat differently in different locations. This is a loose tradition, not some concrete model that she refers to. In fact, Arendt never failed to emphasize that historical events and structures could never simply be recreated in new times for new and always uncertain purposes. As Muldoon (2016) emphasizes, in Arendt's view, the council examples provided a set of *principles* and a kind of proof of concept that she believed later democrats could draw upon. There was no certainty that these principles would always inform something workable – something she frequently acknowledged after her extensive treatment of them in *On Revolution*. But she believed they provided concrete historical evidence that a solution to the problem of scale that had eluded Dewey had actually been found at moments in human history.

In fact, Arendt wasn't sanguine about how easily such new structures could be created. When asked whether something like the councils could be recreated, she noted that the possibility was 'very slight, if at all'. This is different from Dewey's conclusion, however, because she presents at least something like a solution. She went on to note 'and yet, perhaps – after all – in the wake of the next revolution', it might be possible (CR: 189).

Note that I tend to agree with Jeffrey Issac (1994) that it is best to see the councils in Arendt's work not as a *replacement* for representative government, but as a mostly parallel structure to put pressure on and guide such a more traditional bureaucratic, representative democratic government using collaborative democratic strategies. Arendt's own perspective on this was not consistent, although Muldoon (2016) concludes that Arendt herself did ultimately put the councils forth as a model for a replacement government.[8] Many of the historical councils she studied, however, refused to throw out the old bureaucracy and, like the 1917 Soviets, often operated in parallel to and provided oversight for existing government structures. Muldoon (2016) acknowledges that 'an analysis of the actual decisions of the council delegates reveals a consistent disinclination towards abolishing other formal institutions of government' (86). Regardless of Arendt's preference, it is difficult to see that a council model would have the durability to act as a government over the long term.

---

[8] In part, this failure to take power resulted from the lack of preparation these spontaneously generated structures had for the complex task of taking over the bureaucracy. Muldoon (2016) notes that 'while Arendt presents the councils as a new form of government, they operated more frequently as oppositional institutions that sought to control and regulate governing bodies' (63).

Conclusion

Dewey's 'officers' could not act on issues perceived as complex problems by a public because then they would be exerting authority not given to them by the collective. They would not be responding to the unique voices of those affected by a particular problem. While Arendt assumed that there was some level of 'representation' involved in her model, she fundamentally solved this problem by envisioning publics as operating in a different fashion. Instead of trying to 'represent' an imaginary collective, those elected to higher level councils were essentially to act as individuals so that each public became its own unique collection of perspectives themselves. In essence, she elevated the principle of individual voice over the principle of collaborative agreement. In doing so, he solved only part of the problem of scale in Dewey's larger conception of experimental democracy.

The public realm, made possible at a broad scale by the council system, would make a certain way of being human possible over time for everyone who wished to participate in governance. To become a 'public' citizen requires a 'public' realm where each can appear before and act with others as unique individuals. Only a space of this kind truly celebrates and makes possible a true democracy, Arendt believed, a space where human beings appear before and work with each other as equals. She even noted that 'to be deprived of it means to be deprived of reality, which, humanly and politically speaking, is the same as appearance' in a public space, where every common object appears from the unique perspectives of all participants (HC: 199). Only such a space, for Arendt, truly celebrated what was most important about human beings, and only such a space could accurately be called political. The structure of the council system was so compelling to her because it provided a potentially (if never actually) permanent structure within which people could work together and make decisions about their world as authentic human beings. For only action in relatively intimate public spaces like those created in the councils allows multiple people to work together while retaining their own unique identity and perspectives.

In contrast, Dewey did not value democratic engagement that wasn't directly connected to practical influence on the world around it. His was a 'pragmatic' commitment to democracy – democracy was important because of what it could accomplish. In Dewey's vision, if an agreement isn't reached in a collaborative, experimental way by those affected by some problem, it is not legitimate. He understood the problem of scale for individual voice, and it is a challenge for his vision, but only active *collaboration* across everyone with a substantive stake in the outcome provides a warrant for adequate decision-making in a public realm. Every person, he believed, should have democratic influence over things that affected them.

Dewey's is fundamentally an outcome-based analysis, which Arendt rejected, because she opposed conceptions of politics based on making particular things and arriving at particular ends. She believed that 'the innermost meaning of the acted deed and the spoken word is independent of victory and defeat and must remain untouched by any eventual outcome, by their consequences, for better or worse' (HC: 205).[9] In fact, she argued that 'the attempt to replace acting with making' something specific 'is manifest in the whole body of argument against "democracy"' (HC: 220). Aspects of Dewey's (1927) vision of experimental science do fit with her vision of public action, since any accomplishment in his understanding was always just one piece of an endless task of engagement with the challenges of the world. As he emphasized, 'since conditions of action and of inquiry and knowledge are always changing, the experiment must always be retried' (34). Nonetheless, however, his vision of democracy was ultimately dependent upon achieving better rather than worse *consequences* in ways that Arendt opposed. 'Consequences', he emphasized in his discussion of public action, always 'have to be taken care of, looked out for' (27).

Arendt's solution is based in the simplest sense on trust. Members of councils at the lower levels trust the judgement of the council members they vote for – they trust that the kind of person they are means that the way they respond to some issue will in some sense reflect a reasonable solution to any problem that comes up, even if, in extreme cases, they reserve the right to recall them. Public action as unique actors is thus possible on every level of the council structure. Because this doesn't give direct influence over outcomes to participants across the pyramid of councils, however, this is not an adequate solution for Dewey. Dewey did not want people in a democracy to 'trust' in the independent decisions of 'delegates' (or 'officials'). In fact, he would likely complain that, despite its focus on democracy at every level of the pyramid, Arendt's vision actually recapitulates some of the problems both saw in standard forms of representative democracy. Ultimately, Arendt's council system doesn't solve Dewey's core problem of collaborative, experimental participation. It does not provide a solution to the specific challenge of scale that most worried Dewey.

---

[9] 'It is from the experience of this full actuality' of public action 'that the paradoxical "end in itself" derives its original meaning; for in these instances of action and speech the end (*telos*) is not pursued but lies in the activity itself ... and the work is not what follows and extinguishes the process but is imbedded in it; the performance is the work .... This specifically human achievement lies altogether outside the category of means and ends' (HC: 206).

Given that Dewey and Arendt are two of the most prominent thinkers to attempt to solve this problem, it raises deep questions about the ability of a space the size of a classroom or a small school, where one can create safety and a sense of community where everyone knows each other, to constitute a realistic model of a polity. In fact, for similar reasons of scale, the larger field of deliberative democracy, which emerges out of work like Dewey's and Arendt's, seems to have given up on the idea that these forms of classroom democracy, *by themselves*, can provide useful models for governance, looking instead to a complex collection of what they call 'deliberative systems' (Parkinson and Mansbridge, 2012). What one can collaborate on in this small envelope seems unlikely to be representative of what could work in the world beyond the schoolhouse doors. And this creates significant challenges for those who would teach Deweyan forms of democracy, exclusively in classrooms as forms of civic education.

Thinking in Dark Times: Learning to Repair and Renew Our Common World

Eduardo Duarte

Introduction

Hannah Arendt described her teaching as inspired by the hope that her students would be ready and able to respond when they were confronted with 'certain extreme things which are the actual consequences of non-thinking' (Hill, 1979: 309). Upon reading this description, most readers of Arendt understand her response to be consistent with her major publications such as *The Human Condition* (HC) and *Life of the Mind* (LM1/2); specifically, it is consistent with her lifelong concern to protect the public realm: the world we share in common with one another, a world that at one and the same time brings us together and distinguishes each of us from the other. This common world, or public realm, is the sine qua non of human existence, and, from a philosophical point of view, the only horizon that guarantees truth and certainty – existentially the common world guarantees human plurality. This world is also the source of our collective responsibility, because despite divisiveness and increasing fragmentation, the fact remains that there is one world, which is *our* world, where we cohabitate, for good or ill. For Arendt, the centrality of the world, the common, the public realm, cannot be overstated:

> It means, first, that everything that appears in public can be seen and heard by everybody and has the widest possible publicity. For us, appearance – something that is being seen and heard by others as well as by ourselves – *constitutes reality*. Compared with the reality which comes from being seen and heard, even the greatest forces of intimate life – the passions of the heart, the thoughts of the mind, the delights of the senses – lead an uncertain, shadowy kind of existence unless and until they are transformed, deprivatized and deindividualized, as it were, into a shape to fit them for public appearance. (HC: 50, emphasis mine)

It is her concern with protecting the always vulnerable public realm that lead Arendt, in her most widely read and cited piece on education, 'The Crisis in Education', to advance the thesis that 'the function of the school is to teach children what the world is like and *not* to instruct them in the art of living' (BF: 195). The aim of this chapter is to unpack the two sides of Arendt's most fundamental thesis on education. Unpacking her thesis about the purpose of the school reveals significant philosophical assumptions that can only be understood when read within the wider context of Arendt's writings, which includes the ancient philosophical inspiration for her philosophy of education. Further, when we unpack that key thesis, which is composed, almost dialectically, of a positive and negative imperative – 'please teach what the world is like', and 'do not teach them the art of living' – we discover why Arendt resonates today as educators find themselves called upon to educate a resistance to any number of threats to our common world.

The body of this chapter has four parts. In Part One, I introduce Arendt's 'conservative' – in the sense of conservation – education by way of emphasizing the kind of thinking that this education imbues, and the particular kind of place it requires. In part two, I focus on Arendt's hypothesis that thinking can 'condition' us against evil-doing. In this second part, I show that when we place 'conditioning' within an educational context this category is a retrieval of the Hellenic *paideia*. Before moving on to explore the implications of that retrieval, parts three and four present the connection between Arendt's educational dictum regarding the preparation for world repairing/renewal and the ontological meaning of this *common* world. This presentation offers an analysis of Arendt's education thesis by revisiting some key figures of ancient philosophy, specifically, Heraclitus and Epictetus. On the one hand, with Heraclitus, we gain insight into her call to teach 'what the world is like', and we understand better the connection between a world that is 'always changing' and the 'initiators' who are making, repairing and renewing this dynamic world. On the other hand, with Epictetus, we understand better Arendt's emphatic rejection of teaching 'the art of living' or the Stoic philosophy of life. The Stoic art of living arises from the realization that the human person is essentially powerless in the face of *Logos*, the universal logic that organizes and determines the order of things. A deep dive into the ontology of the Stoic world view reveals how following *Logos* disempowers students from repair/renewal of the world, and it leaves them vulnerable to the current climate that sows division, discord and conflict. When we contrast the Stoic world/universe (operating independently, with necessity) to the Heraclitean world/universe of flux, we gain a deeper philosophical appreciation for Arendt's description of the world as 'always changing' and/or 'out of joint' and, further, 'the work of human hands'. When the world is understood as dynamic and open-ended, students are likely to be inspired to enact their power to repair and renew the common, shared, public realm and thereby to resist politico-cultural forces (e.g. populism and nationalism) that seek to divide humanity against itself. The chapter concludes by showing how Arendt's philosophy of education is guided by the imperative to cultivate *amor mundi*, love of the world, and that this imperative is taken up when educators take up the challenge of teaching in such a way that they are contributing to the formation of thinkers, that us, thoughtful people committed to the repair and renewal of a common world.

Conserving Natality in the Conservatory of Thinking

Arendt's normative prescription for education, specifically the schooling of children, is quite consistent with her concern for the protection of thinking. For Arendt, the fundamental aim of education, to conserve the natality of the child, is only possible when educators reserve a time and place for thinking. In fact, as I have argued (Duarte, 2010), the two go hand in hand. In this piece, I hope to show why and how the complementary educational goals of conserving the fact of natality and protecting of the activity of thinking are carried forward precisely by teaching 'the world as it is'. But in order to understand that connection, we must first revisit Arendt's description of thinking.

If a primary aim of education is to prepare students to renew a common world, then it is the responsibility of the educator to ensure students have a *place* of thinking where they are able to imagine alternative futures for the world they are inheriting, especially when they are facing a contra-public ideology that threatens the co-flourishing of unity and plurality, which is to say, threatens the very existence of the common world they are called to repair and renew. I call this unique place in education the 'conservatory of thinking' (Duarte, 2010), and thereby build upon Arendt's category of 'conservative education' which describes an education that is focused on conserving student's *natality*, that is, their natural-born capacity to bring something new into the world. A conservatory of thinking is a place where student natality is conserved via the unleashing of their power of imagination.

In *Thinking*, Arendt delineates the 'autonomy of mental activities' (LM1/2). A kind of freedom arises insofar as the activities of the mind are unconditioned by historical and cultural events. Existing in the 'standing now' (*nunc stans*) of eternity, the mind transcends the temporality of labour, work and action. Yet, in a curious relationship, while the activities of the mind are always related to the world, they are not *of* or *in* the world. The transcendence of the thinker moves them into a *utopos*, a 'nowhere' that can be described as a virtual place of speculation and imagination.

The mind's activities are always the result of a withdrawal, a move that is disruptive insofar as it takes the embodied person away from everyday life. And among the three mental activities (thinking, willing and judging), Arendt concludes that it is thinking that distinguishes itself as the most disruptive. Thinking is 'out of order' because it inverts all ordinary relationships: 'What is near and appears directly to our senses is now far away and what is distant is actually present. While thinking I am not where I actually am; I am surrounded not by sense-objects but by images that are invisible to everybody else. *It is as though I had withdrawn into some never-land*' (LM1/2: 85, emphasis mine).

The never-land where the thinker moves, otherwise known as the no-where or *utopos* (utopia), denotes the landscape upon which thinking moves when the thinker has withdrawn from the world. For Arendt, this 'never-land' is a *re*-presentation of the life-world, of lived experienced in the world. What is important is the opportunity this withdrawal offers for students to enact a form of thinking that takes them into an encounter with the power of imagination, a power that is unleashed in response to call of the world. This call arrives to students in the form of an offering: the opportunity to make a mark, a difference and to make the world a better place for all. Thinking via imagination enables students to face with hope what appears to be a dire circumstance to envision what could be otherwise. In this sense, thinking is a re-creative activity that is akin to the work of the artist who takes up and transforms what is given in the matter of a Jasper Johns, who famously said about artistic production: 'Take up an object. Do something to it. Do something else' (Castelman, 1986). Thinking via imagination entails theoretical recreation of the world, and happens through what Arendt calls *re-presentation*: 'Making present what is actually absent, is the mind's unique gift, and since our whole mental terminology is based on metaphors drawn from vision's experience, this gift is called imagination, defined by Kant as "the faculty of intuition even without the presence of the object"' (LM1/2: 76).

The life of the mind that moves through imagination towards reasoning (*vernuft*) is described by Arendt as the process of meaning-making, which she distinguishes from the intellectual process of cognition or knowing. For Arendt, imagination is at the core of a creative interaction with the world, which, as she describes it, is the creative work of human hands. Thinking via imagination disrupts the 'givenness' or everydayness of the world, and with this disruption prepares the way for the creative work that constructs, repairs and renews the world. Thinking's interruption of everydayness encounter with the power of imagination, a power that is always central to initiating an alternative to the given state of affairs, which is to say, a renewal of the world.

Education as Formation of a Thinker

Arendt's declaration that her teaching was inspired by the hope that her students would be ready and able to respond when they were confronted with 'certain extreme things which are the actual consequences of non-thinking' emerges from persistent questions that captivated her from her early writing on totalitarianism (OT) to her last writing on the life of the mind (LM1/2). Her description of the source of these questions was crystalized in the introduction to *Life of the Mind*, where Arendt writes of the pervasive 'absence of thought' that confronted her as she explored the existential roots of systematic evil. In turn, throughout the years of conducting her research a basic question returned again and again, imposing itself upon her: 'Could the activity of thinking as such, the habit of examining whatever happens to come to pass or to attract attention, regardless of results and specific content, could this activity be among the conditions that make [people] abstain from evil-doing and even actually "condition" them against it?' (LM: 5).

The use of the word 'condition' is, for Arendt, a necessary corrective to the rise of social psychology in her time. Further, her distinction between 'action' and 'behaviour', which she worked out in *The Human Condition* (HC), is part of an important conceptual backdrop that sets the scene for her writing on education, specifically, her strongest claim of all: *the fundamental aim of education is to conserve the natality of the student*. Our natural-born capacity to bring something new into the world is enacted against all odds, in large part because the world we are born into is stubbornly, and, for Arendt, necessarily resistant to accommodating the newcomer *qua* beginner. Arendt goes so far as to describe the appearance of the new as occurring under 'the guise of a miracle'. Nevertheless, the durability and dependability of the world, which offers us existential certainty, that is, a collective 'home' for humanity, is contingent upon its makers and caretakers to constantly regenerate it. Hence the need for the student to be educated in such a way that they recognize the imperative to repair and renew the 'old' world, and, further, understand the responsibility that follows from responding to this imperative: introducing something novel is always potentially disruptive to the 'old' world, and care must be taken to conserve the world as a common, hospitable place for humanity in its plurality to flourish. After all, the world is inherently durable, but not indestructible, and of the threats it faces, the gravest may be the degeneration of its caretakers. And this process of degeneration occurs when 'behaviour' becomes the norm. Such is the outcome when education is organized around predetermined outcomes, and schooling becomes a highly mechanized and programmed system. Here we see the manifestation of the banality of evil that captivated Arendt, and that she was convinced could be thwarted by the formation of thinkers.

When hypothesizing that thinking can 'condition' against evil-doing, Arendt is returning to what might be considered a foundational question of philosophy and perhaps an original or inceptual question of philosophy education: Does evil emerge from an absence knowledge? By following Kant's distinction between 'thinking' and 'knowing' Arendt was able to respond to the claim that those who played active roles in systematic evil (slavery and genocide) were knowingly following the established rules and obeying orders. 'Knowledge' does not inoculate from evil-doing, but, paradoxically, will aid and abet its occurring. A thinly disguised quality of 'knowing' is obedience, and submission to rules, or what might be described as a passive acceptance of regulations. But knowing is also an active reproduction and refinement of order. This is why, as Thomas Kuhn (1962) showed, science is so successful in establishing research communities: scientists work within paradigms that relinquish them from questioning basic theoretical assumptions. Hence, Heidegger's (1968) oft-misunderstood, but here aptly applied, assertion: 'Science does not think' (8).

Indeed, in contrast to knowing, thinking emerges from reflection, which Arendt describes as the silent two-in-one dialogue between me and myself (*eme emauto*). Moreover, thinking is marked by spontaneity and open-endedness, and is driven to take up questions that have no definite answers but are pursued nonetheless. It is in the pursuit of these questions that the thinker is formed. In turn, what seems obvious is that the question that imposed itself on Arendt demands a pedagogical response: if we believe thinking can 'condition' people against evil-doing, then we must insure that thinking is part of their 'formation', which is to say, their formal education, or, to put the matter in more specific terms, a central part of their *formative* education. The synonymous relation between 'conditioning' and 'formation' is crucial for understanding how and why education plays a central role in resolving the problem of evil-doing insofar as it 'conditions' or 'forms' a student into a thinking/acting person, that us, a person who is capable of initiating something new, but also perceiving for themselves. It is important to recognize that for Arendt, education remains what it has always been since the Hellenic denotation of *paideia* as the 'proper' formation of the educated citizen. Education as formation (*paideia*) is the central concern of Plato's *Republic*, which is ostensibly organized around the question of justice. It turns out the question is resolved not by way of recognition (knowing, perceiving and recognizing the abstract ideal or form of justice), but by way of formation (making the *polis* just by way of its citizens). And thus the focus of the dialogue that makes up Plato's *Republic* is the educational formation of the just citizen. Some, including Arendt, would argue that the question of formation is not limited to his *Republic*, but is in fact the question that connects most if not all of his writings. And this is because the question of formation (*paideia*) is at the heart of the public project of philosophy that was initiated by Socrates (PAP).

From Thinking to World-Building

At this juncture, it may appear as if I am guilty of the very problem Arendt identifies as generating the crisis in education – namely, the *pathos* of the new. The crisis, which she insists is the turning point when we are confronted by the joint responsibility for both the new (student) and the old (world), has arisen because educators, especially in the era of student-centred, constructivist, progressive education, are suffering (*pathos*) from a desire to insure the singularity and uniqueness, in sum, the freedom of the student is protected. My analysis appears to be emphasizing one side of the twofold responsibility, and my line of interpretation thus far appears to be stacking the deck against the first half of her education thesis that is motivating my analysis. Recall that Arendt states emphatically, 'the function of the school is to teach children what the world is like and *not* to instruct them in the art of living' (BF: 196). My emphasis on natality would appear to be out of synch with the priority Arendt places on the world. This priority seems quite evident when we consider that she concludes 'The Crisis in Education' (BF) by underlining that education is always the result of a decision, or, in her words, 'deciding whether' to welcome the newcomer into this old world, and, in doing so, 'prepare them in advance for the task of renewing a common world' (BF: 196). What is crucial here is that education must teach what the world is like, and for Arendt, that entails forming them into world-builders committed to repairing and renew a common world.

Arendt's well-known dictum asserts that the vocation of the educator is a moral calling to introduce students to the world (the *shared* public realm). Of course, there are a host of questions unfolding from Arendt's directive, the most important of those focusing on the sense and degree of Arendt's apparent 'realism'. When she tells us to teach children what the world is like, she is directing us to introduce them to the worldliness of the world: the world's capacity to both bring us together and distinguish us – its permanence, stability and durability. The successful result of education will be the formation of children into adults who repair and renew this common world. But it also seems reasonable to presume that this goal is only ever met when the worldliness of the world is understood as something that cannot be taken for granted, and, on the contrary, that it's vulnerable 'objectivity' must be protected, that is, the 'world' as a common shared space is never guaranteed. It follows that the introduction to what the world is like will inevitably include teaching about potential and actual threats to the common. And this leads us to the pressing question: what is at stake in taking up Arendt's directive in the current moment of nihilism when denigrating 'name calling' has become normalized and represents a threat to the world. On the 'current moment' as nihilistic, specifically with respect to education and the threat to worldliness, I follow Nietzsche description of nihilism as the ubiquity of the profane and the annihilation of 'reverence', the razing of what could 'elevate us'. In sum, the loss of 'the sacred' or that which *can not be laughed at*. The derisive laughter of the nihilist makes a dark comedy of the common world.

The common world, or what in *The Human Condition* she calls 'the public realm', is the condition for the possibility for each and every human *qua* person to see and be seen, and to hear and be heard: 'In the public world, common to all, persons count, and so does work, that is, the work of our hands that each of us contributes to our common world' (BF: 186). The world is what brings us together, and at the same time offers us the space to distinguish ourselves in relation to one another. Further, the world is what we inherit, repair and renew for the sake of freedom. In this sense, we do not possess freedom, but, rather, freedom appears *in the world*: our 'coming into the world, is equated with the appearance of freedom in the universe' (BF: 167). Indeed, freedom relies on the existence of a single world held in common by many. With the birth of every person, 'something new comes into an already existing world which will continue to exist after each individual's death' (BF: 167). The world is the *unum* for the *pluribus*. In turn, it is the *commonality* that is always at stake for Arendt: the gathering and distinguishing force of the world that allows for natality to emerge in the form of singularity and plurality. And it is precisely this shared or unified character of our world that is under threat when, for the sake of the new, we turn education into a laboratory of behaviourism.

While she consistently maintains the twofold emphasis on child and world, it is a concern for the common world that remains a priority for Arendt. Education is conservative 'in the sense of conservation', and this is 'the essence of the educational activity' (BF: 192). And the primary responsibility, which is where we identify the moral authority of the teacher, emerges from the call of the world that demands to be repaired and renewed. The teacher's moral authority rests on their 'assumption of responsibility for the world ... pointing out the details and saying to the child: This is our world' (BF: 192). And, further, she adds, 'this responsibility is not arbitrarily imposed upon the educator; it is implicit in the fact that the young are introduced by adults into a continuously changing world' (BF: 189). What is quite clear, then, is the priority Arendt places on the conservation of the common world. The destruction or eclipse of the common is the destruction or eclipse of the fundamental spatio-temporal condition for the possibility of human freedom, plurality. Paradoxically, when we lose what is common between us the result is a generic form of human existence, or what Arendt describes as 'behaviour'. The common or public realm is always under the threat of being conquered by 'mass society', which is defined by conformism (a synonym for 'behaviour'): 'Society expects from each of its members a certain kind of behavior, imposing innumerable and various rules, all of which tend to "normalize" its members, to make them behave, to exclude spontaneous action'(HC: 40).

What needs further clarification is the ontological status of the world. When she describes the existential character of the world – how it exists – she identifies it as 'continuously changing' and says 'we are always educating for a world that is or is becoming out of joint'. And she is uncharacteristically imprecise with this descriptor 'out of joint', which is intended to denote the 'mortality' of the world: 'This is the basic human situation, in which the world is created by mortal hands to serve mortals for a limited time as home. Because the world is made by mortals it wears out; and because it continuously changes its inhabitants it runs the risk of becoming as mortal as they' (BF: 192). The descriptive categories 'continuously changing' and 'becoming out of joint' indicate the dynamic freedom of the world's makers: humans. In short, because the world is the work of free people, it is the homeplace of freedom. And this is consistent with the link Arendt makes between the (a priori) essential quality of the human, natality, and the (a posteriori) phenomenal appearance of this quality. Indeed, it is the essence of natality to demand a place for its appearance. The world comes into being because humans need a world. It is, to use anachronistic language, the essence of human nature to build a world, which, for Arendt, is akin to a work of art. The world, in this sense, is the tangible outcome of human freedom: 'It is not the free creative process which finally appears and matters for the world, but the work of art itself, the end product of the process' (BF: 154). She traces this back to the Hellenic concept of *archein*, 'which covers beginning, leading, ruling, that is, the outstanding qualities of the free [person]', and 'bears witness to an experience in which being free and the capacity to begin something new coincided. Freedom ... was experienced in spontaneity' (BF: 166). The upshot of the coincidence between 'being free' and the capacity 'to begin' is the ontological priority of natality, understood as the essence of being human. The world follows from the existence of humanity, but more precisely, humanity and world co-arise, and, as a result, bear the same dynamic character ('continuously changing'). In turn, when Arendt writes that 'coming into the world, is equated with the appearance of freedom in the universe' (BF: 167), she is drawing on Augustine's Roman and Christian rendering of the order of things: 'Because he *is* a beginning, man can begin; to be human and to be free are one and the same. God created man in order to introduce into the world the faculty of beginning: freedom' (BF: 167).

Teaching What the World Is like versus Teaching the Art of Living

With this analysis of the world and world-building in mind, we can now revisit Arendt's principal thesis on education. The sentence where this thesis is articulated is made up of two distinct fragments that must be thought together. In the first fragment, which we might call the positive imperative assertion, Arendt insists *we must* teach students 'what the world is like' (BF). And in the second fragment, which we might call the negative imperative assertion, she insists we must not teach them 'the art of living'. Once identified and understood from a purely analytic perspective, the two fragments must be taken up via a historicist perspective, and thereby guided by Arendt's history of philosophy, which places importance on the late Hellenic Stoic philosophers such as Cato, whose voice figures prominently at the conclusion of Arendt's magnum opus, *The Human Condition*. In sum, Arendt's principal thesis on education can only be fully understood after one has traced the genealogy of fundamental concepts that are put to work therein.

Tracing the origin of the second fragment of the thesis is fairly straight forward, because we know Arendt is referring to the Stoic practice championed by Epictetus when she insists we must not teach 'the art of living'. Arendt's summary of Epictetus reveals the source of her caution against teaching the art of living, especially when we understand the fundamental assumptions of the Stoic's life philosophy, specifically their view of human agency, which delimits what, for Arendt, is the most significant characteristic of the human condition: natality.

For the Stoics, human agency is strictly limited by a universe ordained by a perfect Deity that has made the best possible world. At the core of the Stoic *technē* is an acceptance of a Supreme Maker. Spontaneity, chance and randomness are foreclosed within this well-ordered universe, and acceptance of this order entails strict obedience to it. In turn, the Storic 'art' of living is a technology of the self that attempts to embody the virtue of military service. Epictetus (1972) writes: 'So to it is in the world; each man's life is a campaign, and a long and varied one. It is for you to play the soldier's part – do everything at the General's bidding, divining his wishes, if it be possible' (3.24: 31–5).

Accepting the existence of the Deity's good work, and then obeying this General's orders is at the core of the Stoic 'art' of living, which is better translated as 'technique' or even, to borrow from Foucault (2005), a 'technology' of the self. As Arendt describes it, with Epictetus thinking has lost its theoretical quality because it is now always linked directly to everyday life: 'What counts is not "theory" in the abstract but its use and application .... In other words, thinking has become a *technē*, a particular kind of craftsmanship' (LM1/2: 154). Anticipating the later educational movement of *Bildung*, with its emphasis on autonomy, the Stoic 'art' emphasizes singularity, but at the expense of the political/public realm, which is anathema to Arendt's educational project that is ultimately focused on preparing students to the repair and renew a *common* world. Education must lead students to the *technē* of world-building, which is to say a commitment to the principle of *koinon*, the common (public realm), which gives rise to *koinonia*, to the communal world that is held in common because it gathers us together and also allows us to distinguish ourselves through action. The *koinon* of humanity, what we all hold in common, is our singularity, our uniqueness that enables plurality to flourish. The *pluribus* is gathered together into an *unum* by the communal spirit of a many simultaneously joined together and distinguished in a common world. The many that are a one form the human community or 'humanity' in the juridical sense of universal human rights, and for this reason Arendt consistently places emphasis on the political and legal implications of the world. And it is precisely the juridical that the Stoics as philosophers turned away from with their *tekhnē tou biou*, art of living practices that were exercises in meditation, reflection that required freedom *from* the political, public arena. For Arendt, 'what Epictetus called "action" – [is] an action in which you acted in unison with no one, which was supposed to change nothing but your self' (LM1/2: 154). One needs to read this description of the Stoic *tekhnē* ('art') against Arendt's description of action in *The Human Condition*: 'Action, as distinguished from fabrication, is never possible in isolation; to be isolated is to be deprived of the capacity to act' (HC: 188). Here is where we can begin to understand the warning against teaching the art of living.

If Arendt's primary concern for educators is that they prepare students to respond to the persistence of 'extreme things' (evil) in the world, then the Stoic formation of the *prokoptôn* (student) into a *sophos* (philosopher) fails to achieve that end. This is because the outcomes of Stoic education are *apatheia* (aloofness, indifference and dispassion) and *ataraxia* (tranquillity, serenity and peace of mind), characteristics of excellence or virtue that come from following the life that the divine architect has arranged. It turns out, however, that in learning 'art of living', which is a form of disciplined obedience to the 'good order' of the world, the student's natality, or power to initiate something new, is eclipsed. Rather than becoming prepared to repair and renew the common, the Stoic art of living counsels one to remain aloof and indifferent to varieties human affairs that, anyway, one has no power to effect. Passivity is a virtue. As Arendt describes it: 'According to [Epictetus], what must be learned [is] to make life bearable' (LM1/2: 154). What Stoic 'philosophy teaches man is an "art of living", how to deal with life'. She goes on, quoting Epictetus, 'Ask not that events should happen as you will, but let your will be that events should happen as they do, and you shall have peace' is the quintessence of this 'wisdom'; for 'it is impossible that what happens should be other than it is' (LM1/2: 155). Such passivity and fatalism is antithetical to Arendt's educational project, and it is not difficult to recognize in the Stoic *sophos* the prototype of the banality of evil, that is, the thoughtlessness of one who is obedient to the 'order' of things, and, as a result, is morally bankrupt and incapable of rendering a judgement, nor of intervening if and when the so-called order is made up of 'extreme things'. Epictetus' art of living, she writes, manifests 'in the *apatheia* and *ataraxia* of the "wise man", that is, in his refusal to react to whatever good or evil might befall him' (LM1/2: 154).

The compelling reason why we should not teach the art of living is obvious for Arendt, who wrote, 'The sad truth is that most evil is done by people who never make up their minds to be good or evil' (RJ: 180). This statement must be read within the larger context that includes her reporting from the trial of the Nazi Adolf Eichmann in Jerusalem, an experience that leads her to identify the banality of evil stemming from obedience. As she famously reported in her book on Eichmann, from listening to the Nazi's testimony, 'the longer one listened to him, the more obvious it became that his inability to speak was closely connected with an inability to think, namely, to think from the standpoint of somebody else' (EJ: 49). As Amos Elon (2006) describes it, Arendt's report from the Eichmann trial revealed how the Nazis normalized 'evil': 'In the Third Reich evil lost its distinctive characteristic by which most people had until then recognized it. The Nazis redefined it as a civil norm' (xiii). Fascists and the totalitarian state they orchestrate, she concluded, succeeded by conditioning adults to behave like 'good' children: passive and unaware of their power to act freely, nor to think with conscience. And what they achieved was the formation of an apolitical persona who represents the most corrupted of the Stoic *sophos*. While the *sophos* retained the will to refuse to react, the 'citizen' of totalitarian state has relinquished their capacity to respond. But this does not absolve them from responsibility. It merely changes how we understand the emergence of 'extreme things' in our world. For regardless of the circumstances, 'politics is not like the nursery; in politics obedience and support are the same .... Evil comes from a failure to think' (EJ: 279).

In turn, for Arendt, to teach students what the world is like is at one and the same time to conserve their natality, for human natality, our capacity to initiate something new, is a manifestation of that dynamic flux of the universe. Repair and renewal of the world is thus a *mimetic* undertaking: our making, unmaking and remaking of the world is an imitation of universal flux. Arendt's thesis is thus grounded in an ontological description of the world, which emerges from a discourse that stretches all the way back to Heraclitus' universe of flux and spontaneity. For Heraclitus (1991), the universe ('cosmos') is organized by the unifying force of *Logos*, which gathers and disperses all things and everything. In his most well-known fragment, Heraclitus describes universe as like a river that is constantly flowing, and declares: 'You cannot step twice into the same rivers' (Heraclitus, 1991: frag. 12). And in fragment 124 he writes: 'The most beautiful universe is a pouring out of sweepings at random.' He reiterates this in fragment forty-two, where he insists the conditions for the possibility of human experience follow from the dynamic flux that is directed by *Logos*: 'We step and do not step into the same rivers; we are and are not.'

We might also recognize a Heraclitean source for Arendt's lifelong concern to protect the commons (public realm), which is to say, to protect the world as that which is held in common because it holds us in common, bringing us together and distinguishing us. For Heraclitus, wisdom (*sophia*) arises from receiving (listening-to) and following the way of *Logos*. Wisdom is common (*koinon*) because all things are held together by a common gathering force (*koinonia*): 'So we must follow the common, yet the many live as if they had a wisdom of their own' (Heraclitus, 1991: frag 2). Here we might understand why the affirmative side of the important fragment is able to maintain the important dual responsibility of the teacher who must protect both the student (new) and the world (old), which coexist in a Heraclitean harmony of opposites: 'It is an attunement of opposite tension, like that of the bow and the lyre' (Heraclitus, 1991: frag 51). The affirmative imperative insists we must teach what the world is like, and if we place Arendt's thinking within the Heraclitean discourse, it turns out that when students learn what the world is like they are learning that it is 'continuously changing'. And, further, when they learn what the world is like they will gain a deeper understanding of and appreciation for their natality, that is, their natural-born capacity to initiate something new. They are beginners because they can begin something, which is precisely what students are doing all the time when they put a new idea into motion by asking an inquisitive question, share a new perspective by writing an essay or poem, produce a new computer code, document a new sociological trend or perform a unique arrangement of an old piece of music. It turns out that learning that the world is continuously changing and inserting oneself into this dynamic flux are two sides of the same *koinon*!

Cultivating *amor mundi*: The Original Educational Imperative

The twin educational imperatives to teach what the world is like and to not teach the art of living both follow from the assumption that the faculty of thought is connected to our human capacity for telling right from wrong, as Arendt puts it in the introduction to *The Life of the Mind*. The activity of thinking, she insists, is in fact principal among the human activities that form us into people who 'abstain from evil-doing' (LM1/2: 5). But to be clear, thinking is not conditioning us to merely 'abstain' from evil, but, rather, forming us into people who are capable raising questions, making critique, rendering judgements and, more importantly, intervening on behalf of the public realm that always vulnerable. The implication for education in the contemporary moment is clear, although it may seem at odds with our increasingly complex technological innovations, and the emergence of the 'knowledge society'. While 'smart' classrooms are presumed to produce 'smart' students, what the contemporary world is calling for is the formation thoughtful students: 'If, as I suggested before, the ability to tell right from wrong should turn out to have anything to do with the ability to think, then we must be able to "demand" its exercise from every sane person, no matter how erudite or ignorant, intelligent or stupid' (LM1/2: 13). Knowledge and thinking are distinct, and as Arendt insisted, 'absence of thought is not stupidity; it can be found in highly intelligent people ... wickedness may be caused by the absence of thought' (LM1/2: 13). And while she followed Heidegger and consistently maintained that 'thinking does not bring knowledge as do the sciences ... does not produce usable practical wisdom ... [and] does not endow us directly with the power to act' (LM1/2: 3), this quintessential human activity, one where we feel most alive, is utterly dependent and immediately related to the existence of the world, the public realm. Thinking, which happens when we take up a silent dialogue with ourselves, happens when we *retreat* from the light of the public. Further, we are propelled by the power of imagination to explore the phantasmagorical realm of thought because we confidently assume we will return to the world. Thought, emerging from our capacity to initiate, depends on the continued existence of the world, and, as such, the thinker is always intimately connected to the world that is the original source for their thought.

As Arendt put it, 'our feeling for reality depends utterly upon appearance the existence of a public realm into which things can appear out of the darkness of sheltered existence' (HC: 51). Ultimately, then, education must always strive to cultivate *amor mundi*. Thinking and the formation of thoughtful people will always emerge from an unmitigated love of the world. And here, at the conclusion, it is worth noting with some irony that one of the most compelling sources for advancing Arendt's educational thesis on the necessity of cultivating *amor mundi* is the very Epictetus whose 'art of living' Arendt cautioned educator's against. Epictetus, for whom philosophy, that is, the practice of thinking, must be learned *precisely* because it leads us to repair and renewal of the world, or, as he writes:

> True philosophy doesn't involve exotic rituals, mystical liturgy, or quaint beliefs. Nor is it just abstract theorizing and analysis. It is, of course, the love of wisdom. It is the art of living a good life. As such, it must be rescued from religious gurus and from professional philosophers lest it be exploited as an esoteric cult or as a set of detached intellectual techniques or brain teasers to show how clever you are. Philosophy is intended for everyone, and it is authentically practiced only by those who wed it with action in the world toward a better life for all. (Epictetus, 1995: 84)

Conclusion: The Promise of Education Revisited

Helen M. Gunter and Wayne Veck

Introduction

Education is important – for children, families and communities. Functional and licensed skills are important for the economy, but education is more than this – having a job provides a person with a living but education gives a person and others a reason to live and to live a good life. For Arendt, education has some especial features related to plurality and natality, and this is espoused by Young-Bruehl and Kohn (2001) who state that for children: 'Being educated is being protected by responsible adults who have the authority to shape the child's transitional growth into the world' (226). When adults enter and present the self in the public realm, the educative opportunities abound: 'In the modern world, adults do not conservatively give one another a shared tradition, they have to make a common world' (Young-Bruehl and Kohn, 2001: 226). While Arendt wrote intensively and sometimes controversially about education in two short essays (BF; RJ), it is her broader insights into the public realm that help educators and researchers to think about the purposes of education. To paraphrase Arendt – we need to think about what we are doing when we take action within and for education, and when we take action that impacts on and even threatens education.

In this concluding chapter, we therefore return to the broad themes that have shaped the essays in this book, where we recognize that public services education is being devastated because it is located within an unfolding crisis in how the human condition is being defined and enacted. Arendt can help us to think about this and to engage with ways of approaching the naming, confronting and dealing with our predicaments and confusions. Education can be framed as a promise and located in a process of promise-making because, in Arendt's terms, the actions involved are about 'the power of stabilization' (HC: 243). According to Arendt, humanity can only be understood through two facts: plurality or the inherent distinctiveness of the person, and natality or how birth means that a human can do new things. Both generate the reality of difference, potential volatility and unreliable exchange relationships, and so in Arendtian thinking, there is a need to engage with the Western tradition of thought that elevates mutuality in the public realm in order to counteract the problems of human frailty combined with the lack of predictability in human affairs, or 'the impossibility of foretelling the consequences of an act within a community of equals where everybody has the same capacity to act' (HC: 244). As we established in the Introduction, education is an important site for promises or the stability in the provision of services and authoritative professionals, and promise-making is evidence in the public common school to which all children have access. Our co-authors have engaged with the reality, potential and challenges to the promise of education, where they and we have recognized the threats generated by living in the current exposition of times that are worthy of Arendt's characterization of 'dark times' (MD). We intend in this final chapter to provide a summary of the ideas and debates, and consider how our research agenda in education can be revitalized through thinking with Arendt.

The promise of Education – Endangered

The media is replete with stories of how children are in danger. Headlines include:

Teenage suicides in England and Wales rise 67% since 2010. (Khan and Bulman, 2018)

It's not just school shootings; children across the US are dying from gun violence.' (Lockhart, 2018)

Three years on from Alan Kurdi's death and life is no better for child refugees in Europe. (Fallon, 2018)

FGM 'increasingly performed on UK babies'. (Collinson and Furst, 2019)

Still separated: nearly 500 migrant children taken from their parents remain in US custody. (Sacchetti, 2018)

The children of ISIS foreign fighters: are protection and national security in opposition? (Athie, 2018)

Number of children in poverty surges by 100,000 a year, figures show. (Bulman, 2018)

This is just a fraction of the reports about the global abuses of children, where opportunity is limited and lives are endangered. However, the drama of such headlines veils the everyday issues of children who go to school in nation states that are affluent and peaceful, but where education is in danger. So, we can witness another set of headlines, with a focus on public services education in England:

> This £14m school ending in shocking failure – and it is STILL costing taxpayers months after it closed. (Williams, 2017)

> 'Every lesson is a battle': why teachers are lining up to leave. (Tickle, 2018).

> Cash strapped schools are asking parents for money. (Turner, 2018)

> It's worse than Carillion: our outsourced schools are leaving parents frozen out. (Chakrabortty, 2018)

> Excluded pupils 'abandoned by schools'. (Coughlan, 2018)

> St Olave's is not alone. Schools with dodgy practices are everywhere. (Millar, 2018)

A range of work on public education services across nation states is demonstrating that children are objects to be impacted on by segregated provision, corporate colonization and the deprofessionalization of teachers (e.g. Adamson et al., 2016; Gunter, 2018). It seems that the promise of public services education is broken.

In securing certainty through promising, Arendt recognizes what she calls 'guideposts of predictability' (HC: 244) where there is a tension between knowing a situation through the promises made and the need to generate strangeness about a situation in order to facilitate action. For Arendt, promises are obligatory because they have been generated by and for the benefit of the public realm, where individuals present the self in relation to others. Domination by others in sovereign positions thwarts and puts the public realm in danger because the 'in-between' space in which politics is located is squeezed and may disappear (PP). Politics denial is obstructing our capacity for promise-making, where Geiselberger (2017) identifies the anti-politics of populism as 'the great regression' where issues raised in earlier decades are now real: 'international terrorism, climate change, financial and currency crises, and lastly, great movements of migrants – while politically no one was prepared for them'. He goes on to say

> subjectively, there is evidently an utter failure to establish a robust sense of a cosmopolitan collective identity. On the contrary, we are at present witnessing a resurgence of ethnic, national and religious us/them distinctions. (xiii)

This is the new dark times. Austerity is a political project that is taking place at a time of intensification in the deep cleavages in the social fabric. The great regression is evident in the provision of public services education, whereby public services education has been too successful and is threatening elite domination and so is being discredited and dismantled (Gunter, 2018; Gunter et al., 2017).

How public education is secured and enacted in localities as well as nation states is the focus of critical education policy research, and in thinking with Arendt about such matters, we are not alone in considering what this all means for children and educational purposes (e.g. Norris, 2011). Like Gordon (2001a,b), we recognize the importance of 'civic issues' in our research and discussions, and nearly twenty years later, and following Arendt's (HC) view of political exchange in the public realm, we and our co-authors are on the same territory dealing with the same issues, or what Gordon (2001b) identifies as 'the present apathetic states of public affairs in the United States is intolerable and that education has a crucial role to play in transforming this state of affairs' (3–4). What is distinctive about our contribution at this moment in time is that our co-authors are working in a public realm within and across nation states where the darkness has intensified and extended in ways that actually threaten the actual notion of education based on public ownership and access. Chapters by Berkowitz, Gunter and Nixon illuminate the growing importance of the private where a person can think and imagine, but also recognize the objectification of the private in ways that elevate a freedom as personal property rather than a relational exchange process. It seems that what is a public matter has been removed from the public realm. As Nixon identifies the growth in populism is an erosion of trust, where the presentation of the self in relation to others in order to understand denies judgement and action.

Our chapters engage with this matter in a range of ways. For example, Veck confronts children as refugees, where he concludes that 'education could be the place where displaced children discover that they are loved enough to be guided to a world they are to share in common with others and where, in the midst of this passage to their future, they are encouraged to converse with themselves, to be with themselves' (Chapter 6). Such an analysis is important for children who are stateless, where at their arrival (at an airport, at a border crossing or on a beach) they demonstrate plurality and natality in ways that can be read as challenging the world that they are seeking to enter into. How do we handle the demand for assimilation with the need to remember? This is also important for children who are rendered 'stateless-within-a-state' or how children are ordinarily denied plurality and natality through living in poverty or who are shot by adults with guns.

A number of our authors scrutinize teacher authority. What our collection identifies is how there are trends that are actively limiting teachers to undertake teaching due to the conceptualization of authority as technical data collection rather than education, where teacher judgement has been reduced to performative calculation. Such trends are evident in what Arendt recognizes as the crystallization of totalitarianism (OT), and while she argued that this is not inevitable it, is the case that conformity through fear is now prevalent (Gunter, 2014). How this is visible in the everydayness of schools needs to be confronted where, for example, Morgan reminds us about how teachers can and do prepare children for the world, but in doing this they have to prepare them for a world that demonstrates cruelty to children like them (Chapter 7). So, there is a need for teachers to enable children to understand the Holocaust: 'Teachers, by virtue of their role are defined by the responsibility they assume, not only for the education of the child but for the world they represent.' Such a responsibility requires teacher education and not just training according to competency templates. As Biesta (2013) argues both with and against Arendt, the separation of politics and education needs to be rethought, as children as well as adults need 'to be at home in the world and to bear with strangers' (118). We now turn to how our co-authors have recognized the illumination that this brings in dark times.

The Promise of Education – Researched

The media is replete with positive stories about children and education:

Should we give children the vote? We ask nine kids what they think. (Moorhead, 2018)

Malala returns to home town in Pakistan for first time since shooting. (BBC, 2018)

Young people across the UK called to make their mark. (Youth Parliament, 2019)

March for our lives: hundreds of thousands demand end to gun violence – as it happened. (Holpuch and Owen, 2018)

Brave four-year-old's 999 call that saved mum's life after she collapsed on stairs. (Middleton, 2018)

I'm a child carer. (Hilpern, 2015)

There is much in these stories that speak to the exceptionalism of events where children rise to the challenge. It seems that the everyday achievements of children often go on without this type of recognition or remark. However, as these stories demonstrate, children can and do respect plurality and are realizing natality. Our argument is that even in dark times it is the case that children with adults can provide illumination, and that adults have duties in this regard. To repeat: 'Education is the point at which we decide whether we love the world enough to assume responsibility for it' (BF: 193). Integral to adult obligations is promise-making and keeping, because they enable 'islands of certainty in an ocean of uncertainty' (HC: 244), where children have the security in which to learn to know the world, and by virtue of being born are enabled to change it. The educative position of teachers along with parents and the wider public realm is vital to the glimmers of light that are generated by plurality and natality, and this is what Nixon means when he says:

> That was why the conceptual trinity of thinking, willing and judging was of paramount importance to her: thinking is rooted in the inwardness of our being in the world; willing asserts our selfhood within and to the world; and judgement reaches out to engage with the world as it presents itself to us externally and objectively. It is within the world – and only within the world – that we are capable of 'the enlargement of mind' that makes us fully and complicatedly human. (Chapter 3)

Arendtian studies continue to demonstrate the vitality, but challenges involved in the inter-relationship of the private world of thinking, willing and judging with the presentation of the self in the public realm. This is demonstrated by Berkowitz who identifies the 'double aspect' of entering a world that exists with pressures to assimilate and having the capacity to do new things or be progressive in that world by the fact of being born (Chapter 1). Our co-authors are concerned like other writers to challenge Arendt's notion of time and development, or how she characterizes children as children and then they are adults (see Biesta, 2010). Baluch troubles the Arendtian claim that politics and education should be separate, not least because children are actively involved in politics both with and against adults. Indeed, Veck reminds us that stateless children 'must receive an education and not a prolonged exercise in welfare' (Chapter 6), and must be treated as children rather than having to handle the problems that adults have responded to with abdicated thought. Politics is actively involved in education. In examining how children are given access to the fact of the Holocaust, Morgan argues that 'the overwhelming question that emerges here is whether it is the separation of education and politics that protects the young from the dangers of politicisation or an education that recognizes the educational significance of the political' (Chapter 7).

Our co-authors have helped us by using Arendtian scholarship to think about the bigger issues involved in education. Duarte shows that education is not about training in order for children to fit the world, but is about enabling the relationship between thinking and action to be examined: 'Forming us into people who are capable of raising questions, making critique, and rendering judgements, and, more importantly, into intervening on behalf of the public realm that are always vulnerable' (Chapter 9). Education means we are 'thoughtful':

> In dark times thoughtfulness becomes an indispensable resource of resistance and hope. Without it there can be no considered judgement and no concerted action based on deliberation and the weighing of alternatives. Education, argued Arendt, is a space devoted to thoughtfulness: a protected space for the young, a more robust forum for those moving into adulthood. She would have warned against any suggestion that we are born thoughtful. Rather, we are thoughtful through our initiation into, and participation in, a supportive environment of learning that withstands the thoughtlessness of routinized behaviour and the blandishments of thinking divorced from 'the world as it "really" is'. To be thoughtful is to be grown up, and to be grown up is to learn how to understand – and engage with – the world 'as something that is shared by many people'. (Chapter 3)

Thoughtfulness means that we do not just deliver technical solutions to discipline the human condition. The factory system that we know about through to the artificial intelligence that we think we know about is generating notions of the 'smart' ways of working. However, there remain enduring issues of ethics, wisdom and discretion, and in Arendtian terms, we need to form and understand standpoints relationally in the public realm. Dillabough in Chapter 4 examines the challenges involved in how we set out to present the self and to understand others, particularly how we categorize others through our identity and as an exercise in identity confirmation. We may author the self and others in ways that are unfair, where the dark times of performative education actually create isolation rather than opportunities to exchange meanings. This is why Schutz's analysis of democracy in classrooms is helpful in Chapter 8, where he considers the long-standing goal of progressive education regarding how children can be prepared for the public realm in ways that are tangible and realistic, but also doable and manageable. The scaling up of the classroom to the polity through Arendt's work on councils is helpful, because it enables us to provoke the fact that we are all unique but we share things in common. The legitimacy and actuality of teacher authority are located in how children live in real homes and communities with illness, death, unemployment, drugs and criminality, but they must be enabled to experience and understand the realism of this world and the possibilities of a different world within the classroom. As Schutz argues, we cannot scale up classroom democracy as there is more to this process than the role of the school, but such experiences enable children to learn about the conserved world and the spontaneity that their arrival in it generates. In sum, the current dark times are premised on the autonomy of the individual where freedom is a personal property, whereby thinking with Arendt generates illuminations of freedom as relational. If education is anything it all, as Nixon shows, it is about how 'I', 'we' and 'they' locate in the public realm.

The Promise of Education – Questioned

If education is in dark times, but with flickers of illumination from the real world, and from our co-author's thinking about the real world, then the question we want to address is this: What are the implications for educational research in the social sciences? This is a challenging but important question, and one that we raise even though we cannot fully address it here. However, what we can do is to recognize that educational research is in dark times, but again where the purposes, achievements and potential of such research within, for and about change is in the public domain (e.g. Apple, 2013). Our concern here is to consider how thinking with Arendt is taking place (e.g. Biesta, 2010; Gordon, 2001a; Gunter, 2014, 2018; Norris, 2011; Veck and Jessop, 2016), and what is gained by such thinking.

Importantly, Arendt is a great teacher, and she enables great teaching and learning in others. As Young-Bruehl and Kohn (2011) state: 'There is plenty of evidence that the perplexities that obsessed the twentieth century have not disappeared and that men and women from virtually every corner of the earth who are turning to Arendt are still striving for release from oppression' (255). There are two important matters here. The first notes how leading edge thinking is taking place about totalitarian trends in communications that is informed by Arendt's thinking (e.g. Susskind, 2018; Zuboff, 2019). And the second is about taking action because: 'There is a dangerous tendency today to refuse to listen to others who disagree with us. We don't really want to consider different viewpoints, except to condemn or ridicule them' (Bernstein, 2018: 72). Certainly, the UK journalist and broadcaster James O'Brien (2018) has deployed his reading of Arendt (and other writers) to take action differently, where he has used the questioning of and debate with callers to his radio show in order to seek understandings of what people are saying about religion, immigration, sexuality and rights. This has both exposed the ordinariness of dark times in everyday lives, but also how entering the public realm through talking about 'beliefs', 'opinions', 'myths' and 'lies' enables some people to be persuaded otherwise. This is just one example of why we should read and think using Arendt within wider civil society.

Bernstein (2018) makes the point that we read Arendt not only due to the enveloping dark times, but also because 'Arendt claims that even in the darkest of times we can hope to find some illumination' and importantly such 'illumination … comes not so much from theories and concepts but from the lives and work of individuals' (2). Those individuals may be people like journalists who work in public, but they can be citizens who think and do things differently in private. Bernstein (2018) goes on to say that Arendt 'helps us to gain critical perspective on our current political problems and perplexities. She is an astute critic of dangerous tendencies in modern life and she illuminates the potentialities for restoring the dignity of politics. This is why she is worth reading and rereading today' (3). So we ask: Why is she worth reading and rereading for researchers? There are a number of issues that we want to raise based on the potential generated by our co-authors.

The first thing that we want to say is that Arendt provokes researchers to think about the limitations of research in the social sciences. Notably Arendt identified how researchers can be methodologically 'trapped by their own ideas' (EU: 11), can make claims based on canonical categories that miss the realities of lived lives, and can politically be entrapped in totalitarian conditions where to her horror intellectuals in Germany went along with the Nazis. As Arendt says: 'friends "coordinated" or got in line. The problem, the personal problem, was not what our enemies did but what our friends did' (LI: 18). Hence as researchers we have to expose the proactive and unreflexive collaboration of researchers with non-educational reforms that profit elite interests, and so we might ask: Why is school improvement and effectiveness so popularized when the advocacy for change and the knowledge claims are about improving and making effective a system that unjustifiably segregates and disposes of children on the basis of their bodies, parental faith and income? Such a question can be legitimately generated because in a post-Holocaust world, all methodological designs and processes have been rendered redundant, and so the social sciences have to be uncompromisingly rebuilt.

Research reconstruction has a number of features that Arendt can help us with. There is a need for researchers to focus on what is taking place: 'She believed that serious thinking should be grounded in one's lived experience' (Bernstein, 2018: 9). Hence the currently globalized reforms of education is about elite dismantling of public education in plain sight, where public investment in all children as educable is being removed through the denial of juridical rights to an education combined with the interplay of tax cuts and profit. So as McCarthy (2012) states, we need Arendt's 'courage and wisdom' if we are 'to create economic justice, political solidarity and civic participation in a global society marked by scandalous inequities and new forms of ideology and terror' (294). Audaciously researching what is taking place in education seems to be the focus of a small but globalized network of critical education policy researchers, who work both within and beyond the sanctity of method, and take inspiration from what Canovan (1995) describes about Arendt where she 'sets off, then, to think "without a banister" to hold on to, reflecting freely upon events' (6). Events may look to be the same as the recent past, but unhistorical analysis can be used in ways that obscure. In Arendtian terms, the attacks on the United States on September 11, 2001, is not the same as the bombing of Pearl Harbour in 1941; and so a school seeking Grant Maintained Status from 1988 in England may look similar to a school becoming an academy from 2000, but the former was based on a parental ballot for the school to remain or leave the local education authority, and the latter was informed by a parental questionnaire administered by a private business (Gunter, 2011). Using Arendtian 'pearl diving' enables the past to be respected and related to the present, and 'one treats the past by acting either as a collector or as a pearl diver, digging down for those treasures that lie now disjointed and disconnected' (Benhabib, 2003: 173). Consequently, history is not one event after another, but an analysis of how what is current is distinctive from, but also located in, its antecedence.

In taking this approach, there will be ontological and epistemological criticisms, ones that are not new and are ongoing, particularly how critical researchers who have sought to expose and replace raced, classed and gendered knowledge production have faced attacks. So, in Arendtian terms, if we did more writing to understand, rather than to be graded, then we may be able to engage with meanings and explanations that get us thinking differently, and certainly beyond binaries. We will continue to face criticism from those who have a stake in existing categories or even in organized lying (particularly in regard to TINA claims or 'there is no alternative'). Like Arendt, we may write in ways that invite controversy, and like Arendt, there may be readings of our work that we have not actually written.

Therefore, a second matter we want to raise for researchers is to do with knowledge. As Apple (2013) argues, elite knowledges belong to us all, and so they should not be rejected, but actively engaged with. In doing so, we may recognize that Arendt could be regarded as a 'conservative', and certainly Mary O'Brien (1981) regards her as an illustration of 'female male-supremacists' (9). In confronting critical contentions about Arendt's analysis, that are also evident in educational research, Gordon (2001b) argues that

> tradition should be conceived as a series of innovations, itself full of breaks and fissures and the kinds of reinventions that the young can make. In her view, the task is not to revitalise our ties with tradition and the past. It is rather to discover those ideas and values that, though they have undergone change, have survived in a different form and can be used to interrupt, critique, and transform the present. (3)

Arendt allows us to relentlessly think otherwise by using our intellectual resources, whereby Honig (1995) challenges the 'feminist' attack on Arendt by arguing that her work demands a different type of question to be asked about knowledge production: 'The question is no longer simply, How does feminist theory change the way we think about Arendt? but also always, How does reading Arendt change the way we think about feminist theory?' (3). Nixon helps us to generate such questioning in order to overcome self-imposed fossilized categories and identities, by reminding us about education:

> Institutions of education are among the few remaining places within which that resource can be valued unconditionally. They are also – crucially – places in which we learn to think in such a way as to distinguish well-founded beliefs from wishful thinking; to distinguish less well-founded beliefs from more firmly founded beliefs; and to understand why such distinctions matter. In our current context – no less than that in which Arendt insisted upon the ethical and political significance of thoughtfulness – thinking matters. For Arendt, thinking was always critical. The notion of critical thinking was, for her, a tautology. Because thinking is always critical; always dialogical; always progressing through distinctions, exploring the intricacies of disagreements, sailing to its goal of consensus through the various side winds of *dissensus*. Only through the long, hard slog of thinking together in and through difference can truth be attained and preserved. (Chapter 3)

The endemic calls to education researchers to be 'relevant' and 'on the same page' with funders, policymakers, and the media is the route to disposability, and so as Nixon implies, we need to recapture criticality (along with 'expertise' and 'evidence') as a legitimate requirement for action.

A third matter that needs to be surfaced here is how we recognize that we are not 'disciples' who follow or 'apologists' who unreflexively defend or 'decorators' who adorn writing with fashionable words. As our authors have shown, how we think critically with and about Arendt needs to be examined because: 'She was often insightful, but at times she could also be obtuse and guilty of what she took to be the worst sin of intellectuals – imposing her own categories on the world instead of being sensitive to the complexities of reality' (Bernstein, 2018: 48). Hence, researchers continue to struggle over her meanings and language, and so we adopt what Benhabib's (1988) identifies as the need to 'think with Arendt and against Arendt' (31). As Schutz shows in Chapter 8, we can engage with Arendt through how her work brings new insights into Dewey's progressive thinking for education, but we can also think against where Berkowitz (Chapter 1) disagrees with the contention that education is a private matter and Nixon (Chapter 3) demonstrates a failure of understanding in her essay 'Reflections on Little Rock' (DM). Not giving up on critical thinking is important, because even though we may identify errors of fact and prudence, the intellectual work we do means that we can 'discover resources in her writings for confronting the perniciousness of racism today' (Bernstein, 2018: 52).

The Promise of Education – Action

So how do we move on? We are all sat at the education table:

> To live together in the world means essentially that a world of things is between those who have it in common, as a table is located between those who sit around it; the world, like every in-between, relates and separates men at the same time. (HC: 52)

Education researchers need to be sat at this table. We can take action at this table:

> Action, as distinguished from fabrication, is never possible in isolation; to be isolated is to be deprived of the capacity to act. Action and speech need the surrounding presence of others no less than fabrication needs the surrounding presence of nature for its material, and of a world in which to place the finished

product. Fabrication is surrounded by and in constant contact with the world: action and speech are surrounded by and in constant contact with the web of the acts and words of other men. (HC: 188)

Education researchers in taking action need to move beyond the survival mode of labour and the technology of work production, and engage in the public realm.

In focusing on research as action, we note that we are not the first or the last people to use Arendtian scholarship to think with about education, and we are thankful for that. What is particular to our research is that the impact of reform on the purposes and conduct of research, and on the university puts our action in peril. It seems that we actively labour and work to deliver measurable 'research impact' rather than take action. Indeed, Ward (2012) not only provides an account of the technology of knowledge production through the marketization of funding for preferred ideas and data, but also how teaching 'is designed to be "teacher proof"' (113) through the use of scripts and data-determined evaluations. Researcher action is premised on not only thinking with Arendt but also examining how researchers have used Arendt to provoke new questions at a time when such questions may not be fundable or measurable or contractable. For example, Judt (2009) asks why so many liberals in the United States silenced themselves in regard to the 'war on terror' under the G.W. Bush presidency:

> Liberal intellectuals used to be distinguished precisely by their efforts to think for themselves, rather than in the service of others. Intellectuals should not be smugly theorizing endless war, much less confidently promoting and excusing it. They should be engaged in disturbing the peace – their own above all. (392)

This is vintage Arendt. Hence researchers need to take action in the public realm in order to confront knowledge production that is complicit with the crystallization of totalitarian conditions. Judt contends that 'Hannah Arendt was not afraid to judge, and be counted' where she got things right and wrong, and on balance 'she got the big things right' (89–90). The enduring challenge for us as thinking and acting researchers in the public realm is the importance of education as a site where research is allowed and continues to bring new insights into ideas, purpose and practices.

Following Benhabib (2003), we want to acknowledge that ourselves as researchers are located in the possibilities of plurality and the opportunities afforded by natality:

> To be sure, it is well-known that every interpretation is necessarily selective. Reading is a dialogue between the author, the reader, and the community of past

and present interpreters with whom one is in dialogue. All reading is polyphonic; it is perhaps less like an ordered conversation than a symphony of voices. (198)

We are members of this symphony, where the potential for productive research music is evident in our chapters. To stretch this metaphor, our 'libretto' of chapters has identified a range of contributions to thinking and doing differently in dark times, where we want to note the enduring challenge of how we deal with 'here-and-now-ness' in regard to research. The predicaments in which educational researchers find themselves are concerned with how to be 'relevant' with 'what works problem-solving' and at the same time make conceptual and methodological contributions in outputs that can be graded as world-leading social science. This is an ongoing issue, where the types of questions that our co-authors have generated are the ones that have led to educational researchers been characterized as self-serving in ways that have exasperated policymakers (see Rudduck and McIntyre, 1998), and to educational research being required to produce data that demonstrates causal relationships between professional practice and outcomes (see Ribbins et al., 2003). Our location in these often hostile and derogatory discursive claims and reform interventions is to engage with the Arendtian provocation to take responsibility for the renewal of the world, where we want to support educational professionals in how they restore and develop their authority as teachers. To do otherwise would be to accept the ruin of the world, and certainly the world of education.

Our co-authors have called for and demonstrated what it means to be thoughtful as a researcher. Respect for thoughtfulness is an important thread through our chapters, where any form of 'here-and-now-ness' requires researchers to support the intellectual work and professional practices of teachers in how they engage with the facts of plurality and natality in the design of the curriculum, pedagogy and assessment. What does that mean? Our chapter writers have provided important insights about how we think and take action as thoughtful researchers:

- Morgan focuses on how children have entered a world that has a cruel past (and present!), and where adults and children could co-construct a cruel here-and-now unless action is focused on doing things differently. Education within and about the Holocaust is about enabling understanding and not about regularizing cruelty, and this requires thoughtful reflexivity both privately and with others.
- Dillabough focuses on identity, and particularly how in the here-and-now a person or group may claim an identity but also have identities imposed

upon them. Education within and about identity needs to 'privilege action over the actor' (Chapter 4), where thoughtful reflexivity has to confront the privileging of the actor as the measurable and evaluated child and teacher.
- Veck focuses on stateless children, and how in the here-and-now our categories are invalid in regard to the action needed to prevent cruelty to children. Education within and about refugee children requires different thinking, where thoughtful reflexivity recognizes that taking one category of stateless children out of the category of stateful children does not create a homogenous group of children.

Our writers have also provided important insights into the potential of thoughtful research:

- Berkowitz presents analysis about how we position ourselves at a time when authority has been lost. Integral to research is to reveal what is happening, and we may normatively consider what educating otherwise might mean, but what Arendtian scholarship does is to consider the actions we take in the world as it is now. Hence here-and-now-ness is not about teacher delivery of predetermined categories, but about the exercise of judgement in ways that are informed by research and knowledge exchanges with researchers.
- Baluch presents analysis about how all, including researchers, are located within the past and future, where any futuring is rooted in the past, and where Arendtian scholarship demonstrates how both have to be part of any analysis or strategy. Hence here-and-now-ness is not about seductive narratives that emotionally manufacture solution-compliance but is about exposing imagined pasts and fantasies about the future, through understanding.
- Gunter presents analysis about the politics of action in how educational researchers can help to renew the world, where Arendtian scholarship demonstrates the distinctiveness of but connections between thinking and action. Hence here-and-now-ness is not about delivery check lists as empowered doing, but is about the knowledge exchanges that support understanding.
- Schutz presents analysis about institutions and so provokes us to think about how the university as an institution, where Arendtian scholarship enables us to think about a public space where human beings with unique identities are located, but how that space can be shared and be a site for political exchanges. Hence here-and-now-ness is not about being ever-ready

to provide solutions but is about – to follow the Arendt table metaphor – to change seats at the table and exchanging ideas and evidence in ways that cross borders and inform new projects.
- Duarte presents an analysis about how we think and act in the common world, where Arendtian scholarship enables us to think about thinking, and how to relate that thinking to the purposes and practices of standpoint production and understanding in the public realm. Hence here-and-now-ness is about the productivity of criticality, where to be critical is not to be in opposition, but to seek to understand and take thoughtful action.

Primary educational research is not perfect and never will be, but this is not a reason to denounce or even try to kill it off. Educational research is enabled and enriched by Arendtian scholarship through the focus on understanding standpoints and taking action in the public realm. That spark of illumination in current dark times comes from educational researchers who individually and in shared contexts provoke understandings.

References

Adamson, F., Åstrand, B. and Darling-Hammond, L. (eds) (2016), *Global Education Reform*, New York, NY: Routledge.
Alexander, H. (2015), *Reimagining Liberal Education: Affiliation and Inquiry in Democratic Schooling*, London: Bloomsbury.
Allen, D. S. (2004), *Talking to Strangers*, Chicago: University of Chicago Press.
Apple, M. W. (2013), *Can Education Change Society?* New York, NY: Routledge.
Athie, A. (2018), The Children of ISIS Foreign Fighters: Are Protection and National Security in Opposition? https://theglobalobservatory.org/2018/12/children-isis-foreign-fighters-protection-national-security-opposition/. Accessed 7 February 2019.
Au, W. and Ferrare, J. J. (eds) (2015), *Mapping Corporate Education Reform*, New York, NY: Routledge.
Avery, H. (2017), 'At the Bridging Point: Tutoring Newly Arrived Students in Sweden', *International Journal of Inclusive Education*, 21 (4): 404–15.
Bajaj, M. and Suresh, S. (2018), 'The "Warm Embrace" of a Newcomer School for Immigrant and Refugee Youth', *Theory Into Practice*, 57 (2): 91–98.
Baker, R. (1983), 'Refugees: An Overview of an International Problem', in R. Baker (ed.), *The Psychosocial Problems of Refugees*, 1–10, London: British Refugee Council and European Consultation on Refugees and Exiles.
Baker, R. (1990), 'The Refugee Experience: Communication and Stress, Recollections of a Refugee Survivor', *Journal of Refugee Studies*, 1 (3): 64–71.
Ball, P. (2017), 'The School of Mum and Dad', *Prospect*, September (258): 58–61.
Batty, D. (2018), 'Some Families are too Shady to Work with: Meet the Tutors of the Ultra-rich'. https://www.theguardian.com/education/2018/mar/13/some-families-too-shady-tutors-of-ultra-rich?CMP=share_btn_link. Accessed 16 March 2018.
BBC (2018), 'Malala Returns to Home Town in Pakistan for First Time Since Shooting'. https://www.bbc.co.uk/news/world-asia-43603844. Accessed 11 February 2019.
Benhabib, S. (1988), 'Judgment and the Moral Foundations of Politics in Arendt's thought', *Political Theory*, 16 (1): 29–51.
Benhabib, S. (2001), 'Judgment and the Moral Foundations of Politics in Hannah Arendt's Thought', in R. Beiner and J. Nedelsky (eds), *Judgment, Imagination and Politics: Themes from Kant and Arendt*, 183–204, New York and Oxford: Rowman & Littlefield Publishers.
Benhabib, S. (2003), *The Reluctant Modernism of Hannah Arendt*, Lahnam, MD: Rowman & Littlefield Publishers, Inc.
Benhabib, S. (2010), 'Hannah Arendt's Political Engagements', in Roger Berkowitz, Jeffrey Katz and Thomas Keenan (eds), *Thinking in Dark Times: Hannah Arendt on Ethics and Politics*, 55–61, New York, NY: Fordham University Press.

Benn, C. and Chitty, C. (1997), *Thirty Years On*, London: Penguin Books.

Berkowitz, R. (2010), 'Introduction: Thinking in Dark Times', in R. Berkowitz, J. Katz and T. Keenan (eds), *Thinking in Dark Times: Hannah Arendt on Ethics and Politics*, 3–14, New York, NY: Fordham University Press.

Berkowitz, R. (2016), 'Reconciling Oneself to the Impossibility of Reconciliation: Judgment and Worldliness in Hannah Arendt's Politics', in Roger Berkowitz and Ian Storey (eds), *Artifacts of Thinking: Reading Hannah Arendt's Denktagebuch*, 9–36, New York: Fordham University Press.

Bernstein, R. J. (2018), *Why Read Hannah Arendt Now*, Cambridge and Medford, MA: Polity Press.

Biesta, G. (2010), 'How to Exist Politically and Learn from It: Hannah Arendt and the Problem of Democratic Education', *Teachers College Record*, 112 (2): 556–75.

Biesta, G. (2013), *The Beautiful Risk of Education*, Boulder: Paradigm Publishers.

Biesta, G. (2016), 'Reconciling Ourselves to Reality: Arendt, Education and the Challenge of Being at Home in the World', *Journal of Educational Administration and History*, 48 (2): 183–92.

Block, K., Cross, S., Riggs, E. and Gibbs, L. (2014), 'Supporting Schools to Create an Inclusive Environment for Refugee Students', *International Journal of Inclusive Education*, 18 (12): 1337–55.

Bohman, J. (1996), 'The Moral Costs of Political Pluralism: The Dilemmas of Difference and Equality in Hannah Arendt's "Reflections on Little Rock"', in L. May and J. Kohn (eds), *Hannah Arendt: Twenty Years Later*, 53–80, Cambridge, MA: MIT Press.

Bowring, F. (2011), *Hannah Arendt, A Critical Introduction*, London: Pluto Press.

Browning, C. (2003), *Collected Memories: Holocaust History and Postwar Memories*, Madison: University of Wisconsin Press.

Bulman, M. (2018), 'Number of Children in Poverty Surges by 100,000 a Year, Figures Show'. https://www.independent.co.uk/news/uk/home-news/child-poverty-increase-children-family-benefit-households-a8268191.html. Accessed 7 February 2018.

Burnham, P. (2001), 'New Labour and the Politics of Depoliticisation', *British Journal of Politics and International Relations*, 3 (2): 127–49.

Busby, E. (2018), 'Grammar Schools Look to Open "Annexes" that Campaigners Claim to be "Back-door" Selection'. http://www.independent.co.uk/news/education/education-news/grammar-schools-annexes-selective-school-selection-damian-hinds-a8220026.html. Accessed 19 March 2018.

Calhoun, C. (2001), *Critical Social Theory*, Blackwell: Oxford University Press.

Canovan, M. (1995), *Hannah Arendt, A Reinterpretation of her Political Thought*, Cambridge: Cambridge University Press.

Carrington, D. (2018), 'Our Leaders are like Children', School Strike Founder Tells Climate Summit', *The Guardian*, Tuesday. https://www.theguardian.com/environment/2018/dec/04/leaders-like-children-school-strike-founder-greta-thunberg-tells-un-climate-summit. Accessed 4 December 2018.

Castelman, R. (1986), *Jasper Johns, A Print Retrospective*, New York: MoMa.

Caverero, A. (2000), *Relating Narratives*, New York: Routledge.
Chakrabortty, A. (2018), 'It's Worse than Carillion: Our Outsourced Schools are Leaving Parents Frozen Out'. https://www.theguardian.com/commentisfree/2018/jul/30/outsourced-schools-parents-primary-academy-trusts. Accessed 7 February 2019.
Chandler, D. and Reid, J. (2016), *The Neoliberal Subject*, London: Rowman & Littlefield International.
Chanter, T. (2001), *Time, Death and the Feminine. Levinas with Heidigger*, Stanford and California: Stanford University Press.
Chitty, C. (2007), *Eugenics, Race and Intelligence in Education*, London: Continuum.
Collinson, A. and Furst, J. (2019), 'FGM "Increasingly Performed on UK Babies"'. https://www.bbc.co.uk/news/uk-47076043. Accessed 7 February 2019.
Comack, M. (2012), *Wild Socialism: Workers Councils in Revolutionary Berlin*, 1918–1921, New York: University Press of America.
Coughlan, S. (2018), 'Excluded Pupils "Abandoned by Schools"'. https://www.bbc.co.uk/news/education-44941691. Accessed 7 February 2018.
Courtney, S. J. (2015), 'Mapping School Types in England', *Oxford Review of Education*, 41 (6): 799–818.
Courtney, S. J. and Gunter, H. M. (2015), '"Get Off My Bus!" School Leaders, Vision Work and the Elimination of Teachers', *International Journal of Leadership in Education*, 18 (4): 395–417.
Cowan, P. and Maitles, H. (2017), *Understanding and Teaching Holocaust Education*, London: Sage.
Dewey, J. (1916), *Democracy and Education*, New York: Macmillan.
Dewey, J. (1927), *The Public and Its Problems*, Columbus, OH: Swallow Press.
Dietz, M. G. (2000), 'Arendt and the Holocaust', in D. Villa (ed.), *The Cambridge Companion to Hannah Arendt*, 86–100, Cambridge: Cambridge University Press.
Dillabough, J. (2016), 'Rethinking Gender, Social Justice and Citizenship in Education: A Turn Toward Relationality', in A. Peterson, R. Hattam, Zembylas, M. and J. Arthur (eds), *The Palgrave International Handbook of Education for Citizenship*, 49–71, London: Routledge.
Dillabough, J. and Dillabough-Lefebvre, D. (2018), 'The Long-distance Ethnographer in the New Academy of Global Fetishes: A Reflection on the Lost Gifts of Ethnographic Exchange in the Young Lives of MK Freedom Fighters in South Africa', in K. Gallagher's (ed.), *The Methodological Dilemma Revisited*, 51–75, New York: Routledge.
Dillabough, J. and Kennelly, J. (2010), *Lost Youth in the Global City*, London: Routledge.
Dillabough, J., Rochez, C. and Balfour, B. (2019), 'Young People Heating Up in the London Kettle: Reading between the Fault Lines of Race and Class Wars of the British Urban Riot Scene (1958–2011)', in P. Trifonas and S. Jagger (eds), *Handbook of Cultural Studies and Education*, 124–51, New York: Routledge.
Dillabough, J. and Yoon, E. (2018), 'Youth Geographies of Urban Estrangement in the Canadian City: Risk Management, Race Relations, and the "Sacrificial Stranger"', *Children's Geographies*, 6: 1–15.

Dorling, D. (2011), *Injustice*, Bristol: Policy Press.
Drury, C. (2019), 'Climate Strike: Thousands of UK School of Classes to Protest Ecological Crisis', *Independent*, Friday. https://www.independent.co.uk/news/uk/politics/theresa-may-climate-change-school-pupils-protest-lesson-time-teachers-a8781046.html. Accessed 15 February 2019.
Dryden-Peterson, S. (2015), *The Educational Experiences of Refugee Children in Countries of First Asylum*, Washington DC: Migration Policy Institute. http://www.migrationpolicy.org/research/educational-experiences-refugee-children-countries-first-asylum.
Duarte, E. (2010), 'Educational Thinking and the Time of the Revolutionary', *Teachers College Record*, 112 (2): 489–510.
Due, C., Riggs, D. W. and Augoustinos, M (2016), 'Diversity in Intensive English Language Centres in South Australia: Sociocultural Approaches to Education for Students with Migrant or Refugee Backgrounds', *International Journal of Inclusive Education*, 20 (12): 1286–96.
Elon, A. (2006), 'Introduction: The Excommunication of Hannah Arendt', in Hannah Arendt Eichmann (ed.), *Jerusalem*, vii–xxiii, New York: Penguin.
Epictetus (1972), *Discourses*, Rosalyn: The Classics Book Club.
Epictetus (1995), *The Art of Living*, trans. Sharon Lebell, New York: Harper.
Euben, P. (2001), 'Hannah Arendt on Politicizing the University and Other Clichés', in M. Gordon (ed.), *Hannah Arendt and Education*, 175–99, Boulder, CO: Westview Press.
Fallon, K. (2018), 'Three Years on from Alan Kurdi's Death and Life is No Better for Child Refugees in Europe'. https://www.independent.co.uk/voices/aylan-kurdi-death-three-year-anniversary-child-refugee-home-office-a8518276.html. Accessed 7 February 2019.
Fearon, J. D. (1999), *What is Identity (As We Now Use the Word)*, Unpublished manuscript, Stanford, CA: Stanford University Press.
Feinstein, L. (2017), *On Genetics and Social Mobility: Why Toby Young's Structural Inequality Argument Is Not Science*, Blogs.lse.ac/politicsandpolicy/on-genetics-and-social-mobility. Accessed 11 January 2018.
Feintuck, M. and Stevens, R. (2013), *School Admissions and Accountability*, Bristol: The Policy Press.
Felman, S. (2001), 'Theaters of Justice: Arendt in Jerusalem, the Eichmann Trial, and the Redefinition of Legal Meaning in the Wake of the Holocaust', *Critical Inquiry*, 27 (2): 201–38.
Ferfolja, T. and Vickers, M. (2010), 'Supporting Refugee Students in School Education in Greater Western Sydney', *Critical Studies in Education*, 51 (2): 149–62.
Fielding, M. and Moss, P. (2011), *Radical Education and the Common School*, Abingdon: Routledge.
Foster, Stuart (2013), 'Teaching about the holocaust in English Schools: Challenges and Possibilities', *Intercultural Education*, 24 (1–2): 133–48.

Foucault, M. (2002), *The Birth of the Clinic*, London: Routledge.
Foucault, M. (2005), *The Hermeneutics of the Self: Lectures at the Collège Du France 1981–1982*, ed. Frédéric Gros, trans. Graham Burchell. New York: Palgrave.
Friedman, M. (2002), *Capitalism and Freedom*, Chicago: University of Chicago Press.
Galston, A. W. (2018), *Anti-Pluralism: The Populist Threat to Liberal Democracy*, New Haven: Yale University Press.
Gardner, P. (2010), *Hermeneutics, History and Memory*, London: Routledge.
Geiselberger, H. (ed.) (2017), *The Great Regression*, Cambridge: Polity.
Gewirtz, S. (2002), *The Managerial School*, London: Routledge.
Gillborn, D., Demack, S., Rollock, N. and Warmington, P. (2017), 'Moving the Goalposts: Education Policy and 25 Years of the Black/White Achievement Gap', *British Educational Research Journal*, 43 (5): 848–74.
Gines, K. T. (2014), *Hannah Arendt and the Negro Question*, Bloomington: Indiana University Press.
Gorard, S. (2018), *Education Policy, Evidence of Equity and Effectiveness*, Bristol: Policy Press.
Gordon, M. (ed.) (2001a), *Hannah Arendt and Education*, Boulder, CO: Westview Press.
Gordon, M. (2001b), 'Introduction', in M. Gordon (ed.), *Hannah Arendt and Education*, 1–9, Boulder, CO: Westview Press.
Gormez, V., Kılıç, H. N., Orengul, A. C., Demir, M. N., Mert, E. B., Makhlouta, B., Kınık, K. and Semerci, B. (2017), 'Evaluation of a School-based, Teacher-delivered Psychological Intervention Group Program for Trauma-affected Syrian Refugee Children in Istanbul, Turkey', *Psychiatry and Clinical Psychopharmacology*, 27 (2): 125–31.
Gove, M. (2017), 'Michael Gove on the Trouble With Experts: *Interview Conducted at the 2017 European Think Tank Summit, Hosted by Chatham House*'. https://www.chathamhouse.org/expert/comment/michael-gove-trouble-experts. Accessed 25 March 2019.
Gov.uk (2017), *Ethnicity Facts and Figures*. https://www.ethnicity-facts-figures.service.gov.uk. Accessed 12 October 2017.
Greene, M. (1988), *The Dialectic of Freedom*, New York: Teachers College Press.
Griswold, A. (2017), '"The Origins of Totalitarianism," Hannah Arendt's Definitive Guide to How Tyranny Begins, has Sold Out on Amazon, January 29, 2017', *Quartz*. https://qz.com/897517/the-origins-of-totalitarianism-hannah-arendts-defining-work-on-tyranny-is-out-of-stock-on-amazon/. Accessed 6 February 2019.
Grunenberg, A. (2002), 'Totalitarian Lies and Post-Totalitarian Guilt: The Question of Ethics in Democratic Politics', *Social Research*, 69 (2): 359–79.
Gunter, H. M. (ed.) (2011), *The State and Education Policy: The Academies Programme*, London: Continuum.
Gunter, H. M. (2012), *Leadership and Education Reform*, Bristol: The Policy Press.
Gunter, H. M. (2014), *Educational Leadership and Hannah Arendt*, Abingdon: Routledge.

Gunter, H. M. (2016), *An Intellectual History of School Leadership Practice and Research*, London: Bloomsbury Press.
Gunter, H. M. (2017), *The Ultimate Privatization: The Case of Grammar Schools.* http://hmgeducationmatters.tumblr.com. Accessed 20 March 2019.
Gunter, H. M. (2018), *The Politics of Public Education: Reform Ideas and Issues*, Bristol: Policy Press.
Gunter, H. M., Hall, D. and Apple, M. (eds) (2017), *Corporate Elites and the Reform of Public Education*, Bristol: Policy Press.
Gunter, H. M. and Mills, C. (2017), *Consultants and Consultancy: The Case of Education*, Cham, Switzerland: Springer.
Hall, S. (1996), 'Introduction: Who Needs Identity?' in S. Hall and P. du Gay (eds), *Questions of Cultural Identity*, 1–17, London: Sage.
Heidegger, M. (1968), *What Is Called Thinking?* trans. J. Glenn Gray and F. Wieck, New York: Harper and Row.
Heidegger, M. (1993), *Sein und Zeit*, Tübingen: Max Niemeyer Verlag.
Heraclitus (1991), *Fragments*, A Text and Translation With a Commentary by T. M. Robinson. Toronto: University of Toronto.
Herzog, A. (2001), 'The Poetic Nature of Political Disclosure: Hannah Arendt's Storytelling', *Clio*, 30 (2): 169–95.
Herzog, A. (2004), 'Arendt's Concepts of Responsibility', *Studies in Social and Political Thought*, 10: 39–51.
Hill, M. A. (ed.) (1979), *Hannah Arendt: The Recovery of the Public World*, New York: St. Martin's Press.
Hilpern, K. (2015), 'I'm a Child Carer'. https://www.theguardian.com/lifeandstyle/2015/jan/03/im-a-child-carer. Accessed 11 February 2019.
Hodes, A. (1972), *Encounter with Martin Buber*, London: Allen Lane.
Holpuch, A. and Owen, P. (2018), 'March for Our Lives: Hundreds of Thousands Demand End to Gun Violence – As It Happened'. https://www.theguardian.com/us-news/live/2018/mar/24/march-for-our-lives-protest-gun-violence-washington. Accessed 11 February 2019.
Honig, B. (1995a), 'Introduction', in B. Honig (ed.), *Feminist Interpretations of Hannah Arendt*, 1–16, University Park: Pennsylvania State University Press.
Honig, B. (1995b), *Feminist Interpretations of Hannah Arendt*, Pennsylvania State University Press.
Honig, B. (1988), 'Arendt: Identity and Difference', *Political Theory*, 16 (1): 77–98.
Honig, B. (1993), *Political Theory and the Displacement of Politics*, Ithaca: Cornell University Press.
Honig, B. (2003), *Democracy and the Foreigner*, Princeton: Princeton University Press.
Issac, J. (1994), 'Oases in the Desert: Hannah Arendt on Democratic Politics', *American Political Science Review*, 88 (1): 156–68.
Jackson, B. and Marsden, D. (1962), *Education and the Working Class*, London: Routledge and Keegen Paul Ltd.

Judt, T. (2009), *Reappraisals*, London: Vintage Books.
Kahne, J. and Westheimer, J. (2006), 'The Limits of Political Efficacy: Educating Citizens for a Democratic Society', *PS: Political Science and Politics*, 39: 289–96.
Kakutani, M. (2018), *The Death of Truth*, London: William Collins.
Katz, I. (2017), 'Have we Fallen Out of Love with Experts?' *BBC News*, 27 February 2017. https://www.bbc.co.uk/news/uk-39102840. Accessed 25 March 2019.
Kearney, R. (1995), 'Narrative Imagination: Between Ethics and Poetics', *Philosophy and Social Criticism*, 21 (5), 173–90.
Kearney, R. (1996), 'Poetics of Modernity. Toward a Hermeneutic Imagination', *Tijdschrift Voor Filosofie*, 58 (4): 785–86.
Kearney, R. (2003), *Narrative Imagination and Catharsis*, Princeton: Princeton University Press.
Kearney, R. (2014), 'The Inescapable Choice: Welcoming or Refusing the Stranger?' ABC *Religion and Ethics*, 25 July. http://www.abc.net.au/religion/articles/2014/07/25/4053636.htm. Accessed 14 January 2019.
Kearney, R. (2017), *On Paul Ricoeur: The Owl of Minerva*, London: Routledge.
Kearney, R. and Taylor, V. E. (2005), 'A Conversation with Richard Kearney', *Journal for Cultural and Religious Theory*, 6 (2): 17–26.
Keddie, A. (2012), 'Pursuing Justice for Refugee Students: Addressing Issues of Cultural (mis)recognition', *International Journal of Inclusive Education*, 12(16): 1295–310.
Kessel, S. (2001), *Hanged at Auschwitz: An Extraordinary Memoir of Survival*, New York: Cooper Square Publishers.
Khan, S. and Bulman, M. (2018), 'Teenage Suicides in England and Wales Rise 67% Since 2010'. https://www.independent.co.uk/news/uk/home-news/teenage-suicides-england-and-wales-2010-ons-a8522331.html. Accessed 7 February 2019.
Kristeva, J. (1991), *Strangers to Ourselves*, New York: Columbia University Press.
Kristava, J. (2001), *Hannah Arendt: Life as a Narrative*, Toronto: University of Toronto Press.
Kuhn, T. (1962), *The Structure of Scientific Revolutions*, Chicago: University of Chicago.
Landau, R. (1998), *Studying the Holocaust*, London: Routledge.
Lawson, T. (2017), 'Britain's Promise to Forget: Some Historical Reflections on What Do Students Know and Understand about the Holocaust?' *Holocaust Studies*, 23 (3): 345–63.
Laybourn-Langton, L., Rankin, L. and Baxter, D. (2019), *This Is a Crisis: Facing Up to the Age of Environmental Breakdown – Initial Report*, Institute for Public Policy Research. https://www.ippr.org/files/2019-02/this-is-a-crisis-feb19.pdf. Accessed 16 July 2019.
Levi, P. (1989), *The Drowned and the Saved*, London: Abacus.
Levi, P. (2006), *If this Is a Man*, London: Abacus.
Lockhart, P. R. (2018), 'It's not Just School Shootings; Children across the US are Dying from Gun Violence'. https://www.vox.com/identities/2018/5/19/17369916/gun-violence-school-shootings-race-santa-fe-high school. Accessed 7 February 2019.

Lomax, B. (1990), *The Hungarian Workers Councils in 1956*, Boulder, CO: East European Monographs.

Long, R. and Bolton, P. (2017), *Faith Schools in England: FAQs*, Briefing Paper Number 06972, 13 March 2017. London: House of Commons Library.

Ludz, U. (2004), *Arendt and Heidegger; Letters 1925–1975*, trans. A. Shields. Orlando, FL: Harcourt, Inc.

MacDonald, F. (2017), 'Positioning Young Refugees in Australia: Media Discourse and Social Exclusion', *International Journal of Inclusive Education*, 11 (21): 1182–95.

MacLean, N. (2017), *Democracy in Chains*, Melbourne: Scribe.

Macpherson, C. B. (2011), *The Political Theory of Possessive Individualism*, Oxford: Oxford University Press.

Mansbridge, J. (1992), 'A Paradox of Size', in G. Bonello (ed.), *From the Ground Up*, 159–76, Boston: South End Press.

Marsh, S., Weale, S. and Adams, R. (2017), *Schools Abandon Exclusion of Sixth-formers After Parents Complain.* https://www.theguardian.com/education/2017/sep/10/schools-exclusion-sixth-formers-parents-complain?utm_source=esp&utm_medium=Email&utm_campaign=GU+Today+main+NEW+H+categories&utm_term=243115&subid=365947&CMP=EMCNEWEML6619I2. Accessed 11 September 2017.

Mattingly, D. J. (2011), *Imperialism, Power and Identity: Experiencing the Roman Empire*, Princeton: Princeton University Press.

May, T. (2016), *Prime Minister's Question Time*, 14 September 2016. https://hansard.parliament.uk/commons/2016-09-14/debates/16091429000002/PrimeMinister. Accessed 9 February 2017.

Mayhew, K. C. and Edwards, A. C. (1936), *The Dewey School: The Laboratory School of the University of Chicago* 1896–1903, New York: D. Appleton-Century.

Mazzei, P. (2018), 'For Parkland Students, a Surreal Journey From "Normal" to a Worldwide March', *The New York Times*. https://www.nytimes.com/2018/03/24/us/parkland-students-gun-violence.html. Accessed 17 January 2019.

McCarthy, M. H. (2012), *The Political Humanism of Hannah Arendt*, Lanham, MA: Lexington Books.

Middleton, L. (2018), 'Brave Four-year-old's 999 Call that Saved Mum's Life After she Collapsed on Stairs'. https://metro.co.uk/2018/08/10/brave-four-year-olds-999-call-that-saved-mums-life-after-she-collapsed-on-stairs-7823646/. Accessed 11 February 2019.

Millar, F. (2018), 'St Olave's is not Alone. Schools with Dodgy Practices are Everywhere'. https://www.theguardian.com/commentisfree/2018/jul/12/st-olaves-schools-marketisation-perfomance-table-pupils. Accessed 7 February 2019.

Miller, R. (2002), *Free Schools, Free People: Education and Democracy after the 1960s*, Albany: SUNY Press.

Moorhead, J. (2018), 'Should we give Children the Vote? We Ask Nine Kids What They Think'. https://www.theguardian.com/global/2018/dec/23/should-we-give-children-the-vote-voting-at-age-6-politics-interviews. Accessed 11 February 2019.

Morgan, M. (2016), 'Hannah Arendt and the Freedom to Think', *Journal of Educational Administration and History*, 48 (2): 173–82.

Muldoon, J. (2016), *Hannah Arendt and Council Democracy*, Unpublished PhD Thesis, Monash University, Melbourne, Australia.

Müller, J.-W. (2017), *What Is Populism?* London: Penguin Books.

Nguyen, V. T. (2018), 'Introduction', in V. T. Nguyen (ed.), *The Displaced: Refugee Writers on Refugee Lives*, 11–20, New York: Abrams.

Nichols, T. (2017), *The Death of Expertise*, Oxford: Oxford University Press.

Nixon, J. (2012), *Interpretive Pedagogies for Higher Education*, London: Bloomsbury Press.

Noddings, N. (1984), *Caring: A Feminine Approach to Ethics and Moral Education*, New York: Teachers College Press.

Norris, T. (2011), *Consuming Schools*, Toronto: Toronto University Press.

O'Brien, J. (2018), *How to be Right*, London: WH Allen.

O'Brien, M. (1981), *The Politics of Reproduction*, London: Routledge and Keegan Paul.

Parkinson, J. and Mansbridge, J. (eds) (2012), *Deliberative Systems: Deliberative Democracy at the Large Scale*, Cambridge: Cambridge University Press.

Passarlay, G. with Ghouri, N. (2016), *The Lightless Sky: My Journey to Safety as a Child Refugee*, London: Atlantic.

Pearce, A. (2017), 'The Holocaust in the National Curriculum after 25 Years', *Holocaust Studies*, 23 (3): 231–62.

Peters, M. A. (2017), 'From State Responsibility for Education and Welfare to Self-responsibilisation in the Market', *Discourse: Studies in the Cultural Politics of Education*, 38 (1): 138–45.

Pinson, H. and Arnot, M. (2010), 'Local Conceptualisations of the Education of Asylum-seeking and Refugee Students: From Hostile to Holistic Models', *International Journal of Inclusive Education*, 14 (3): 247–67.

Ravitch, D. (2010), *The Death and Life of the Great American School System*, New York: Basic Books.

Ravitch, D. (2014), *Reign of Error*, New York, NY: Vintage Books.

Reading: Education Development Trust. https://www.educationdevelopmenttrust.com/~/media/EDT/Reports/Research/2018/r-teachers-of-refugees-2018.pdf. Accessed 20 June 2019.

Ribbins, P., Bates, R. and Gunter, H. M. (2003), 'Reviewing Research in Education in Australia and the UK: Evaluating the Evaluations', *Journal of Educational Administration*, 41 (4): 423–44.

Richardson, E. with MacEwen, L. and Naylor, R. (2018), *Teachers of Refugees: A Review of the Literature*, Reading: I Education Development Trust and IEP/UNESCO.

Richardson, H. (2017), *Drop in Teacher Training Recruits Revealed*. http://www.bbc.co.uk/news/education-39355165. Accessed 16 March 2018.

Ricœur, P. (1975), *La Métaphore vive*, Seuil, Paris; English Translation *The Rule of Metaphor. Multidisciplinary Studies of the Creation of Meaning in Language*, Toronto: University of Toronto Press.

Ricoeur, P. (1995), *Figuring the Sacred: Religion, Narrative, and Imagination*, Minneapolis: Fortress Press.

Ricœur, P. (2004), *History, Memory, Forgetting*, Chicago, IL: Chicago University Press.

Rivers, C. and Barnett, R. C. (2011), *The Truth about Girls and Boys: Challenging Toxic Stereotypes about Our Children*, New York, NY: Colombia University Press.

Rodriguez, R. (1983), *The Hunger of Memory*, New York: Mass Market Paperback.

Rodriguez, R. (2013), 'Do We Need a Common Public Language?' *Failing Fast: The Educated Citizen in Crisis*, Sixth Annual Fall Conference, The Hannah Arendt Center for Politics and Humanities at Bard College, October 3, 2013. https://www.youtube.com/watch?v=UZnGZVt-KR8. Accessed 20 March 2018.

Rose, G. (1993), *Judaism and Modernity*, London: Blackwell.

Rose, G. (1996), *Mourning Becomes the Law*, Cambridge: Cambridge University Press.

Rose, N. (1999), *Governing the Soul*, London: Free Association Books.

Rose, N. and Abi-Rached, J. M. (2013), *Neuro*, Princeton, NJ: Princeton University Press.

Rose, S., Lewontin, R. C. and Kamin, L. J. (1984), *Not in Our Genes*, London: Penguin Books.

Rudduck, J. and McIntyre, D. (1998), *Challenges for Educational Research*, London: Paul Chapman Publishing.

Rumsey, A. D., Golubovic, N., Elston, N., Chang, C. Y., Dixon, A. and Guvensel, K. (2018), 'Addressing the Social and Emotional Needs of Refugee Adolescents in Schools: Learning From the Experiences of School Counselors', *Journal of Child and Adolescent Counseling*, 4 (1): 81–100.

Ryan, A. (1995), *John Dewey and the High Tide of American Liberalism*, New York: W. W. Norton.

Sacchetti, M. (2018), 'Still Separated: Nearly 500 Migrant Children taken from their Parents Remain in US Custody'. https://www.washingtonpost.com/local/immigration/still-separated-nearly-500-separated-migrant-children-remain-in-us-custody/2018/08/30/6dbd8278-aa09-11e8-8a0c-70b618c98d3c_story.html?noredirect=on&utm_term=.109236a15a6c. Accessed 7 February 2019.

Sacks, A. J. (2013), 'Hannah Arendt's Eichmann Controversy as Destabilizing Transatlantic', *AJS Review*, 37 (1): 115–34.

Sahlberg, P. (2015), *Finish Lessons 2.0*, New York, NY: Teachers College Press.

Samuel, R. (1996), *Theatres of Memory: Past and Present in Contemporary Culture*, London: Verso.

Sassen, S. (2014), *Expulsions*, Boston, MA: Harvard University Press.

Saul, S. (2018), 'Arizona Republicans Inject Schools of Conservative Thought Into State Universities', *The New York Times*. https://www.nytimes.com/2018/02/26/us/arizona-state-conservatives.html.

Savage, M. (2017), *Call to Fine Schools that Illegally Exclude Poorly Performing Pupils*. https://www.theguardian.com/education/2017/dec/17/call-to-fine-schools-that-illegally-exclude-poorly-performing-pupils?CMP=share_btn_link. Accessed 20 December 2017.

Save the Children (2016a), *Half of all Refugee Children are out of School Leaving them Exposed to Exploitation and Abuse*. http://www.savethechildren.org.uk/2016-05/half-all-refugee-children-are-out-school-leaving-them-exposed-exploitation-and-abuse. Accessed 9 March 2017.

Save the Children (2016b), 'Out of School Refugee Children - Risk of Exploitation and Abuse', Monday 16 May. https://www.savethechildren.org.uk/news/media-centre/press-releases/refugee-children-abuse-risk. Accessed 4 January 2017.

Schutz, A. (1998), 'Caring in Schools is not Enough: Community, Narrative, and the Limits of Alterity', *Educational Theory*, 48 (3): 373–93.

Schutz, A. (2002), 'Is Political Education an Oxymoron? Hannah Arendt's Resistance to Public Spaces in Schools', *Philosophy of Education 2001*, Urbana: Philosophy of Education Society.

Schutz, A. (2011), *Social Class, Social Action and Education*, New York: Palgrave Macmillan.

Schutz, A. and Sandy, M. (2015), 'Friendship and the "Public Stage": Revisiting Hannah Arendt's Resistance to "Public" Education', *Educational Theory*, 65 (1): 21–38.

Seppänen, P., Carrasco, A., Kalalahti, M., Rinne, R. and Simola, H. (eds) (2015), *Contrasting Dynamics in Education Politics of Extremes*, Rotterdam: Sense Publishers.

Sibieta, L. (2016), 'Grammar Lessons', *Society Now*, Autumn (26): 18–19.

Sidhu, R., Taylor, S. and Christie, P. (2011), 'Schooling and Refugees: Engaging with the Complex Trajectories of Globalisation', *Global Studies of Childhood*, 1 (2): 92–103.

Simmel, G. (2003), 'The Philosophy of Fashion', in D. Clarke, M. Doel and K. Housiaux (eds), *The Consumption Reader*, 238–45, London: Routledge.

Simon, R. (2000), 'The Touch of the Past: The Pedagogical Significance of a Transactional Sphere of Public Memory', in P. Trifonis (ed.), *Revolutionary Pedagogies: Cultural Politics, Instituting Education, and the Discourse of Theory*, 61–80, New York: Routledge.

Skinner, Q. (1969), 'Meaning and Understanding in the History of Ideas', *History and Theory*, 1: 3–53.

Smith, S. A. (1985), *Red Petrograd: Revolution in the Factories*, 1917–1918, New York: Cambridge University Press.

Starr, P. (1988), 'The Meaning of Privatisation', *Yale Law and Policy Review*, 6 (1): 6–41.

Stern, J. (2014), 'Teaching Solitude: Sustainability and the Self, Community and Nature While Alone', *Educational Research Journal*, 28 (1&2): 163–81.

Stoker, G. (2017), 'Embracing the Mixed Nature of Politics', in P. Fawcett, M. Flinders, C. Hay and M. Wood (eds), *Anti-Politics, Depoliticization, and Governance*, 266–82, Oxford: Oxford University Press.

Stonebridge, L. (2019), 'Why Hannah Arendt is the Philosopher for Now, March 20, 2019', *NewStatesman*. https://www.newstatesman.com/culture/books/2019/03/hannah-arendt-resurgence-philosophy-relevance. Accessed 20 August 2019.

Streeck, W. and Schafer, A. (eds) (2013), *Politics in the Age of Austerity*, Cambridge: Polity.

Susskind, J. (2018), *Future Politics*, Oxford: Oxford University Press.
Sutoris, P. (2019), *Educating for the Anthropocene*, Thesis in Progress, Cambridge: Cambridge University Press.
Tamboukou, M. (2016), 'Education as Action/the Adventure of Education: Thinking with Arendt and Whitehead', *Journal of Educational Administration and History*, 48 (2): 136–147.
Tassin, E. (2007), 'The People do not Want', *Journal for Political Thinking*, 3 (1). http://www.hannaharendt.net/index.php/han/article/view/108/182. Accessed 4 March 2016.
Taylor, S. and Sidhu, R. K. (2012), 'Supporting Refugee Students in Schools: What Constitutes Inclusive Education?', *International Journal of Inclusive Education*, 16 (1): 39–56.
Taylor, W. (1963), *The Secondary Modern School*, London: Faber and Faber.
Tickle, L. (2018), 'Every Lesson is a Battle: Why Teachers are Lining Up to Leave'. https://www.theguardian.com/education/2018/apr/10/lesson-battle-why-teachers-lining-up-leave. Accessed 7 February 2019.
Topolski, A. (2008), 'Creating Citizens in the Classroom: Hannah Arendt's Political Critique of Education', *Ethical Perspectives: Journal of European Ethics Network*, 15 (2): 259–82.
Tovey, J. (2019), 'Belongs in a Museum: Greta Thunberg Condemns Politician Against School Strike', *The Guardian*, Wednesday 20 February. https://www.theguardian.com/environment/2019/feb/21/belongs-in-a-museum-greta-thunberg-condemns-politician-against-school-strike. Accessed 20 August 2019.
Turner, C. (2018), 'Cash Strapped Schools are Asking Parents for Money'. https://www.telegraph.co.uk/news/2018/03/30/cash-strapped-schools-asking-parents-money/. Accessed 7 February 2018.
UNHCR (2018), *Figures at a Glance*. http://www.unhcr.org/figures-at-a-glance.html. Accessed 21 September 2018.
Veck, Wayne (2013), 'Participation in Education as an Invitation to Become Towards the World: Hannah Arendt on the Authority, Thoughtfulness and Imagination of the Educator', *Educational Philosophy and Theory*, 45 (1): 36–48.
Veck, W. and Jessop, S. (2016), 'Special Issue: Hannah Arendt 40 Years on: Thinking about Educational Administration', *Journal of Educational Administration and History*, 48 (2): 129–92.
Verger, A., Fontdevila, C. and Zancajo, A. (2016), *The Privatisation of Education*, New York, NY: Teachers' College Press.
Villa, D. (1995), *Arendt and Heidegger*, Princeton, NJ: Princeton University Press.
Villa, D. (1999), *Politics, Philosophy, Terror: Essays on the Thought of Hannah Arendt*, Princeton, NJ: Princeton University Press.
Villa, D. (2001), *Socratic Citizenship*, Princeton, NJ: Princeton University Press.
Villa, D. (2009), *The Cambridge Companion to Hannah Arendt*, Cambridge: Cambridge University Press.

Ward, S. C. (2012), *Neoliberalism and the Global Restructuring of Knowledge and Education*, New York, NY: Routledge.

Weale, S. (2017), *Grammar School 'Unlawfully Threw Out' Student Who Failed to Get Top Grades*. https://www.theguardian.com/education/2017/aug/29/grammar-school-unlawfully-threw-out-students-who-failed-to-get-top-grades. Accessed 30 August 2017.

Weir, A. (1997), *Sacrificial Logic and the Critique of Identity*, New York: Routledge.

Westbrook, R. B. (1991), *John Dewey and American Democracy*, Ithaca, NY: Cornell University Press.

Wild, T. (2018), 'For the Sake of What is New, Hannah Arendt Center Quote of the Week'. https://medium.com/quote-of-the-week/for-the-sake-of-what-is-new-ee3ba174c207.

Williams, J. (2017), 'This £14m School Ending in Shocking Failure – and It Is STILL Costing Taxpayers Months After It Closed'. https://www.manchestereveningnews.co.uk/news/greater-manchester-news/14m-school-ended-shocking-failure-13907978. Accessed 7 February 2017.

Wolin, S. S. (2010), *Democracy Incorporated: Managed Democracy and the Specter of Inverted Totalitarianism*, Princeton and Oxford: Princeton University Press.

Wood, M. and Flinders, M. (2014), 'Rethinking Depoliticisation: Beyond the Governmental', *Policy & Politics*, 42 (2): 151–70.

Yeung, A. (2019), *'British Values'? 'Chinese Values'? The Governance and Re-imagination of Nation Through 'National Values' Education Policies in Britain and Hong Kong*, Doctoral Dissertation, Cambridge: University of Cambridge.

Young, T. (2015), 'The Fall of Meritocracy', *Quadrant*, September 7: 1–21.

Young-Bruehl, E. (1982), *For Love of the World*, New Haven and London: Yale University Press.

Young-Bruehl, E. (2004), *Arendt: For the Love of the World*, New Haven: Yale University Press.

Young-Bruehl, E. and Kohn, J. (2001), 'What and How We Learned from Hannah Arendt: An Exchange of Letters', in M. Gordon (ed.), *Hannah Arendt and Education: Renewing Our Common World*, 225–56, Boulder, CO: Westview Press.

Youth Parliament (2019), 'Young People Across the UK called to make their Mark'. http://www.ukyouthparliament.org.uk. Accessed 11 February 2019.

Zakin, E. (2017), 'Between Two Betweens: Hannah Arendt and the Politics of Education', *The Journal of Speculative Philosophy*, 31 (1): 119–34.

Zuboff, S. (2019), *The Age of Surveillance Capitalism: The Fight for a Human Future at the New Frontier of Power*, London: Profile Books.

Indices

Arendt, key terms

action   4, 8–9, 11, 46–7, 54, 56, 58, 60, 63, 67–8, 72, 74, 77, 78, 80, 81, 84, 89, 92, 96, 98, 104, 105, 109, 111, 113, 114, 118, 120–1, 125, 130–1, 131, 134, 139, 140, 144, 147, 151, 153, 157, 162–6
authority   2, 9, 18–20, 22–7, 31, 34, 37, 38, 43, 47, 80, 81, 85, 99, 113, 114, 121, 122, 144, 151, 155, 158, 164

democracy   3, 12, 13, 30, 47, 48, 89, 91, 123–5, 126, 127, 128, 129, 130, 131, 133–5, 157–8

freedom   12, 19, 22, 23, 28, 31, 46, 49, 51, 53, 59, 79, 90–1, 95–6, 97, 111, 113–14, 117, 119–22, 138, 143, 144–5, 148, 158

imagination   4, 5, 55, 65, 68, 69, 72, 73, 74, 75, 77, 78, 138, 139–40, 150

judgement   2, 5, 39, 47, 53, 54, 55, 56, 60, 96, 111, 116, 117, 121, 154, 155, 165

love of the world   6, 14, 22, 112, 138, 150, 156

natality   2, 4, 18, 32, 36–7, 80–1, 84–5, 89, 95, 97, 100, 104, 111–12, 138, 140, 142, 143–4, 144–5, 146, 148, 149, 152, 155, 156

parvenu/Pariah   83
pearl diving   33–4, 87, 160
plurality   19, 25, 29, 30–1, 46, 47, 49, 50, 53, 55, 74, 75, 76, 77, 80–1, 84, 89, 105, 111, 120, 136, 138, 141, 143–4, 146, 151, 152, 154–5, 156, 163, 164

polis   20–1, 49–50, 56, 78, 142
politics   4, 7, 19, 20–1, 23, 24, 25–6, 27, 28, 29, 31, 32–3, 35–6, 37–3, 46–9, 50, 52, 53, 54, 55, 59, 63–4, 65, 67–9, 70, 71–2, 74–6, 77–8, 80, 85–6, 88–9, 90–1, 92, 109–14, 117, 118, 119–21, 122, 124, 129, 130–1, 133, 134, 146–7, 148, 153–4, 155, 159
promising   2, 3, 8–9, 51, 151–3
Public Realm   3, 4, 7, 9, 10, 13–14, 20, 25, 29, 37, 38–9, 41–2, 43, 63, 80, 89, 92, 97, 105, 111, 114, 125, 131, 133–4, 136–7, 138, 143, 144, 146, 148, 149, 150, 151, 152, 153–4, 156, 157, 158, 159, 163, 166

refugees   48, 69, 71, 93, 94–5, 97–8, 99–102, 103, 104, 105
responsibility   1–2, 9, 11, 12, 13, 14, 18–19, 20, 21, 25, 26–7, 41, 47, 57, 66, 67–8, 69, 71, 73, 74, 77, 81, 95, 96–7, 99, 104–5, 110–11, 112, 113, 114–15, 117, 120, 121–2, 136, 138, 140–1, 142, 144, 148, 149, 155, 156, 164

thinking   5, 11–12, 13–14, 22, 24, 31, 36, 39, 42, 43–4, 50–5, 56, 58–60, 74–5, 85, 87, 91, 94, 102, 103–4, 105, 109, 117, 120, 137, 138–40, 141–2, 146, 149–50, 156, 160, 162
totalitarianism   14, 24, 39, 49, 50, 52, 53, 69–70, 71, 79, 91, 92, 110, 111, 112–14, 117, 119–20, 140, 148, 155, 158, 159
truth   6, 21, 25, 48–50, 53, 55–6, 59, 71, 114–15, 136

understanding   4, 27, 47, 60, 110, 111, 116, 117–18, 119, 127–8, 149, 166

Arendt, named publications

Between Past and Future   2, 5, 14, 18, 19, 20, 21, 22, 23, 24, 25, 26. 27, 28, 29, 33, 36, 37, 39, 41, 42, 43, 50, 55, 57, 63, 64, 73, 80, 81, 84, 93, 95, 96, 97, 99, 102, 104, 105, 106, 109, 110, 111, 112, 113, 114, 120, 121, 122, 123, 137, 142, 143, 144, 145, 151, 156

The Crisis in Culture   20
The Crisis in Education   2, 7, 18, 27, 30, 35, 36, 39, 42, 57, 80, 106, 110, 112, 123, 137, 142

Eichmann in Jerusalem   32, 52, 63, 64, 71, 72, 92, 117, 148

The Human Condition   6, 7, 8, 31, 37, 49, 64, 65, 67, 70, 71, 73, 74, 80, 89, 95, 97, 98, 99, 100, 101, 104, 111, 112, 125, 126, 131, 133, 134, 140, 143, 144, 145, 147, 150, 151, 152, 153, 154, 156, 162, 163

The Life of the Mind   5, 11, 13, 14, 34, 38, 43, 44, 50, 51, 52, 53, 54, 55, 63, 71, 94, 102, 136, 138, 139, 140, 146, 147, 149, 150

On Revolution   30, 49, 130
Origins of Totalitarianism   2, 5, 38, 52, 63, 64, 71, 91, 92, 94, 95, 96, 98, 119, 120, 130, 140, 155

Reflections on Little Rock   7, 29, 30, 35, 36, 39, 57, 162

Truth and Politics   55, 58

We Refugees   93, 118
What is Authority? 23, 24

General index

Adamson, F.   3, 153
Alexander, H.   78
Apple, M. W.   158, 161
Aristotle   37, 38, 76
Arnot, M.   98
Athie, A.   152
Au, W.   81
Auden, W. H.   43, 70
Augoustinos, M.   94
Avery, H.   94

Bajaj, M.   94
Baker, R.   100
Balfour, B.   68
Ball, P.   82
Baluch, F.   9, 32–45, 156, 165
Bard College   18
Barnett, R. C.   82
Batty, D.   82
Baxter, D.   1
Benhabib, S.   7, 32, 34, 36, 38, 65, 78, 160, 162, 163

Benn, C.   88
Berkowitz, R.   9, 14, 17–31, 25, 154, 156, 162, 165
Bernstein, R. J.   2, 4, 5, 7, 57, 159, 160, 162
Biesta, G.   2, 91, 110, 112, 121, 155, 156, 158
Block, K.   94
Bohman, J.   35
Bolton, P.   82
British Broadcasting Corporation   155
Browning, C.   52
Brown v Board of Education   7, 36
Bulman, M.   152
Burnham, P.   85

Calhoun, C.   77
Canovan, M.   79, 160
Carrington, D.   1
Castelman, R.   139
Chandler, D.   87, 91
Chanter, T.   69
Chitty, C.   87, 88, 90

Christie, P. 98
Collinson, A. 152
Comack, M. 129
Coughlan, S. 153
Courtney, S. J. 82, 84
Cowan, P. 115

Dewey, J. 123–5, 126–7, 128, 129, 130, 132, 133–5
Dietz, M. G. 116
Dillabough, J. 10, 63–78, 65, 68, 76, 157, 164–5
Dillabough-Lefebvre, D. 76
Drury, C. 1
Dryden-Peterson, S. 103, 104
Duarte, E. 12, 136–50, 138, 157, 166
Due, C. 94

Edwards, A. C. 123
Elon, A. 148
Epictetus 137, 146, 147, 150
Euben, P. 40

Fallon, K. 152
Fearon, J. D. 64
Feinstein, L. 90
Feintuck, M. 82
Felman, S. 68, 78
Ferfolja, T. 98
Ferrare, J. J. 81
Fielding, M. 90
Flinders, M 86
Foster, S. 115
Foucault, M. 64, 146
Friedman, M. 81, 90
Furst, J. 152

Galston, A. W. 48
Gardner, P. 63, 68, 72, 73, 76
Gewirtz, S. 81
Gillborn, D. 82
Gines, K. T. 57
Gorard, S. 88
Gordon, M. 2, 3, 110, 154, 158, 161
Gormez, V. 94
Gove, M. 12, 13
Greene, M. 123, 124
Griswold, A. 2
Grunenberg, A. 64, 68

Gunter, H. M. 1–16, 3, 10–11, 79–92, 110, 151–66, 153, 154, 155, 158, 160, 165

Hall, S. 64, 70
Heidegger, M. 19, 51–2, 53, 141, 150
Herzog, A. 63, 71, 74
Hill, M. A. 42, 136
Hilpern, K. 155
Hitler 53, 71
Hodes, A. 113
Holocaust 12, 49, 71, 76, 79, 110–22, 155, 156, 159, 164
Honig, B. 32, 42, 63, 64, 65, 66, 72, 78, 161

Issac, J. 132

Jackson, B. 87
Jaspers, K. 109
Judt, T. 163

Kafka, F. 44, 55–6, 101
Kahne, J. 124
Kakutani, M. 48
Kant, I. 47, 54, 55, 109, 139, 141
Katz, I. 13
Kearney, R. 65, 67, 70, 71, 72–3
Keddie, A. 98
Kennelly, J. 68
Kessel, S. 118
Khan, S. 152
Kierkegaard, S. 6, 109
Kohn, J. 57–8, 151, 158
Kristeva, J. 70, 75, 77, 98
Kuhn, T. 141

Landau, R. 117
Lawson, T. 115
Laybourn-Langton, L. 1
Levi, P. 115, 118
Lockhart, P. R. 152
Lomax, B. 129
Long, R. 82
Ludz, U. 27, 52
lying 8, 50, 53, 89, 90, 160

McCarthy, M. H. 160
MacDonald, F. 94
McIntyre, D. 164

MacLean, N.   13
Macpherson, C. B.   90
Mansbridge, J.   124, 135
Marsden, D.   87
Marsh, S.   86
Mattingly, D. J.   65
May, T.   88
Mayhew, K. C.   123
Mazzei, P.   40
Middleton, L.   155
Millar, F.   153
Miller, R.   123
Moorhead, J.   155
Morgan, M.   12, 109–22, 117, 155, 156, 164
Moss, P.   90
Muldoon, J.   123, 130, 131, 132
Müller, J.-W.   47, 48

Nazis/Nazism   6, 52, 53, 94, 110, 116, 117, 120, 121, 148, 159
Nguyen, V. T.   97
Nichols, T.   13
Nixon, J.   2, 10, 46–60, 154, 156, 158, 161, 162
Noddings, N.   123
Norris, T.   2, 154, 158

O'Brien, J.   159
O'Brien, M.   161

Parkinson, J.   124, 135
Passarlay, G.   102, 103, 104
Pearce, A.   115, 116
Pentagon Papers   50
Peters, M. A.   87
Pinson, H.   98
Plato   5, 37, 38, 142
populism   10, 46, 47, 48, 53, 59, 64, 65, 69, 87, 138, 154

Ravitch, D.   81
Reid, J.   87, 91, 92
The Republic   142
Ribbins, P.   164
Richardson, E.   94
Richardson, H.   84
Ricœur, P.   65, 66, 67, 73, 74, 75, 77
Riggs, D. W.   94
Rivers, C.   82

Rochez, C.   68
Rodriguez, R.   17–18
Rose, G.   118, 119, 121
Rose, S.   87, 90
Rudduck, J.   164
Rumsey, A. D.   94
Ryan, A.   129

Sacchetti, M.   152
Sacks, A. J.   6
Sahlberg, P.   90
Sandy, M.   123
Sassen, S.   70, 75
Saul, S.   39
Savage, M.   86
Save the Children   94
Schafer, A   1
Schutz, A.   12, 123–35, 126, 157, 158, 162, 165–6
Sibieta, L.   88
Sidhu, R.   98, 99–100
Simmel, G.   63
Simon, R.   78
Skinner, Q.   64
Smith, S. A.   129
Socrates   5, 11, 54, 142
Stalin/Stalinism   52, 53, 76
St Augustine   22, 145
Stern, J.   101, 102
Stevens, R.   82
Stoics   137, 145, 146–7, 148
Stoker, G.   91
Stonebridge, L.   2, 8
Streeck, W.   1
Suresh, S.   94
Sutoris, P.   76

Tamboukou, M.   110
Tassin, E.   131
Taylor, S.   98, 100
Taylor, V. E.   65, 73
Taylor, W.   87
Thunberg, G.   1
Tickle, L.   153
Topolski, A.   110, 113, 114
Tovey, J.   1
Turner, C.   153

United Nations High Commissioner for Refugees   93

Veck, W. 1–14, 3, 11, 93–106, 110, 151–66, 154, 156, 158, 165
Verger, A. 81
Vickers, M. 98
Villa, D. 37, 55, 56, 116

Ward, S. C. 163
Weale, S. 86
Weir, A. 75
Westheimer, J. 124
Wild, T. 27
Williams, J. 153

Wolin, S. S. 46
Wood, M. 86

Yeung, A. 75
Yoon, E. 65
Young, T. 90
Young-Bruehl, E. 7, 58, 70, 151, 158
Youth Parliament 155

Zakin, E. 110
Zuboff, S. 1, 158

www.ingramcontent.com/pod-product-compliance
Lightning Source LLC
Chambersburg PA
CBHW061834300426
44115CB00013B/2371